D1244721

CARTOON NETWORK

STEVEN UNIVERSE

OUR FEARFUL TRIP

kaboom!

STEVEN UNIVERSE ONGOING Volume Seven, June 2020.
Published by KaBOOM!, a division of Boom Entertainment,
Inc. STEVEN UNIVERSE, CARTOON NETWORK, the logos, and
all related characters and elements are trademarks of and
© Cartoon Network. A WarnerMedia Company. All rights
reserved. (S20) Originally published in single magazine
form as STEVEN UNIVERSE ONGOING No. 25-28 © Cartoon
Network. A WarnerMedia Company. All rights reserved.
(S19) KaBOOM!™ and the KaBOOM! logo are trademarks of
Boom Entertainment, Inc., registered in various countries
and categories. All characters, events, and institutions
depicted herein are fictional. Any similarity between any of
the names, characters, persons, events, and/or institutions
in this publication to actual names, characters, and persons,
whether living or dead, events, and/or institutions is
unintended and purely coincidental. KaBOOM! does not read
or accept unsolicited submissions of ideas, stories, or artwork.

BOOM! Studios, 5670 Wilshire Boulevard, Suite 400, Los
Angeles, CA 90036-5679. Printed in China. First Printing.

ISBN: 978-1-68415-560-6, eISBN: 978-1-64144-726-3

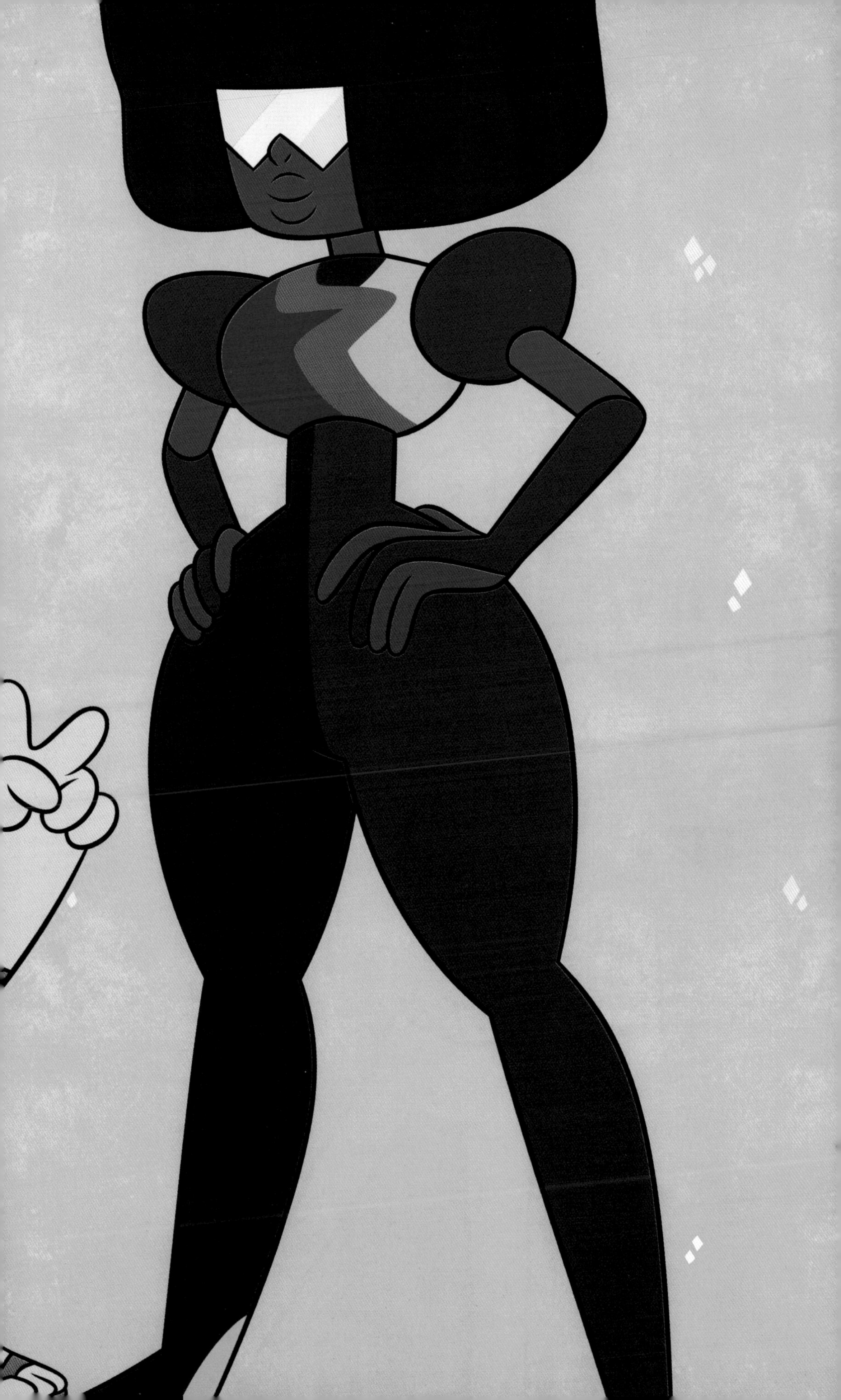

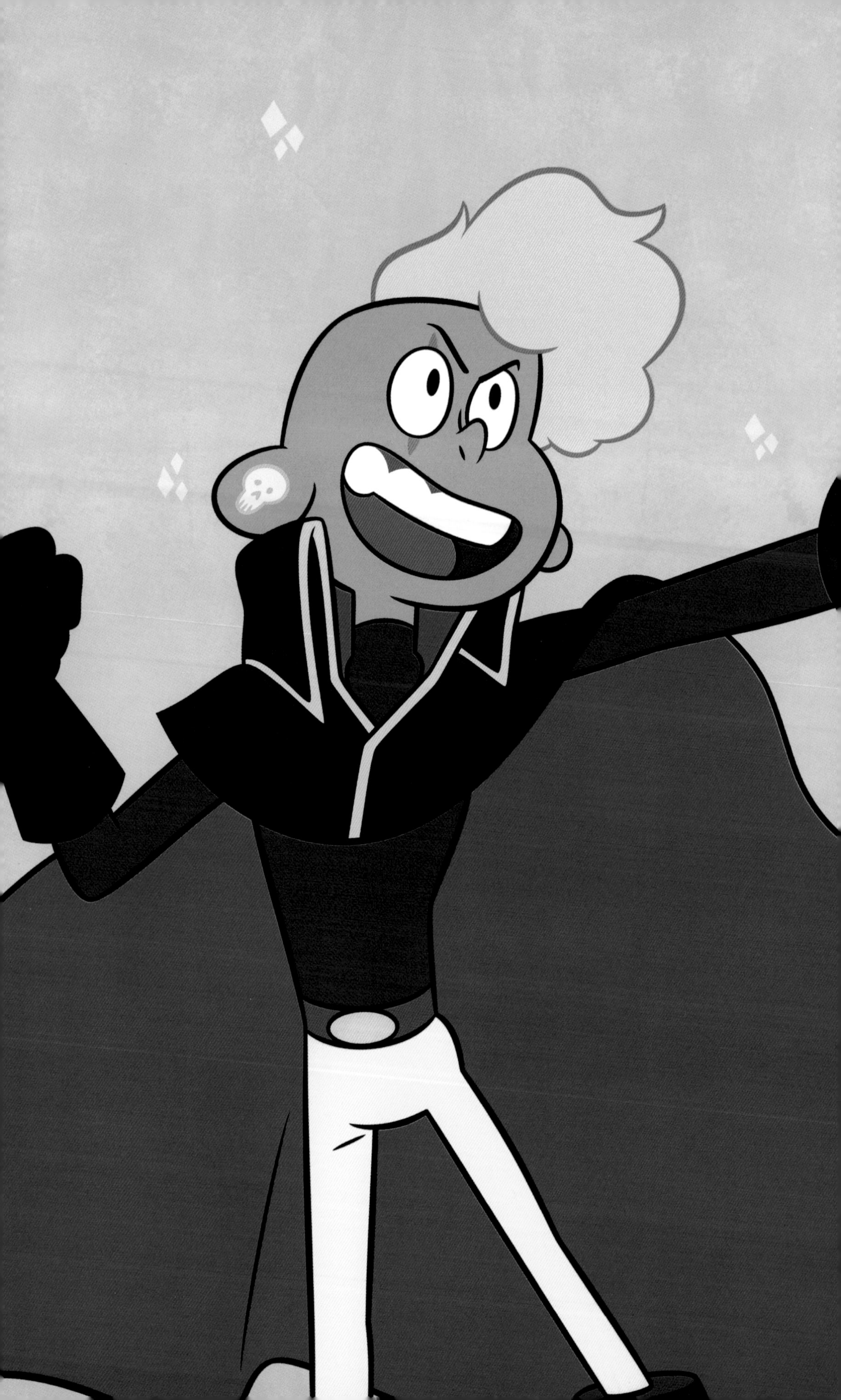

CARTOON NETWORK

STEVEN UNIVERSE

OUR FEARFUL TRIP

created by
REBECCA SUGAR

written by
TERRY BLAS

illustrated by
GABRIELE BAGNOLI

colors by
JOANA LAFUENTE

letters by
MIKE FIORENTINO

cover by
MISSY PEÑA

series designer
GRACE PARK

collection designer
JILLIAN CRAB

editor
MATTHEW LEVINE

Special thanks to
Marisa Marionakis, Janet No, Austin Page,
Conrad Montgomery, Jackie Buscarino and the
wonderful folks at Cartoon Network.

Issue Twenty-Five Main Cover
MISSY PEÑA

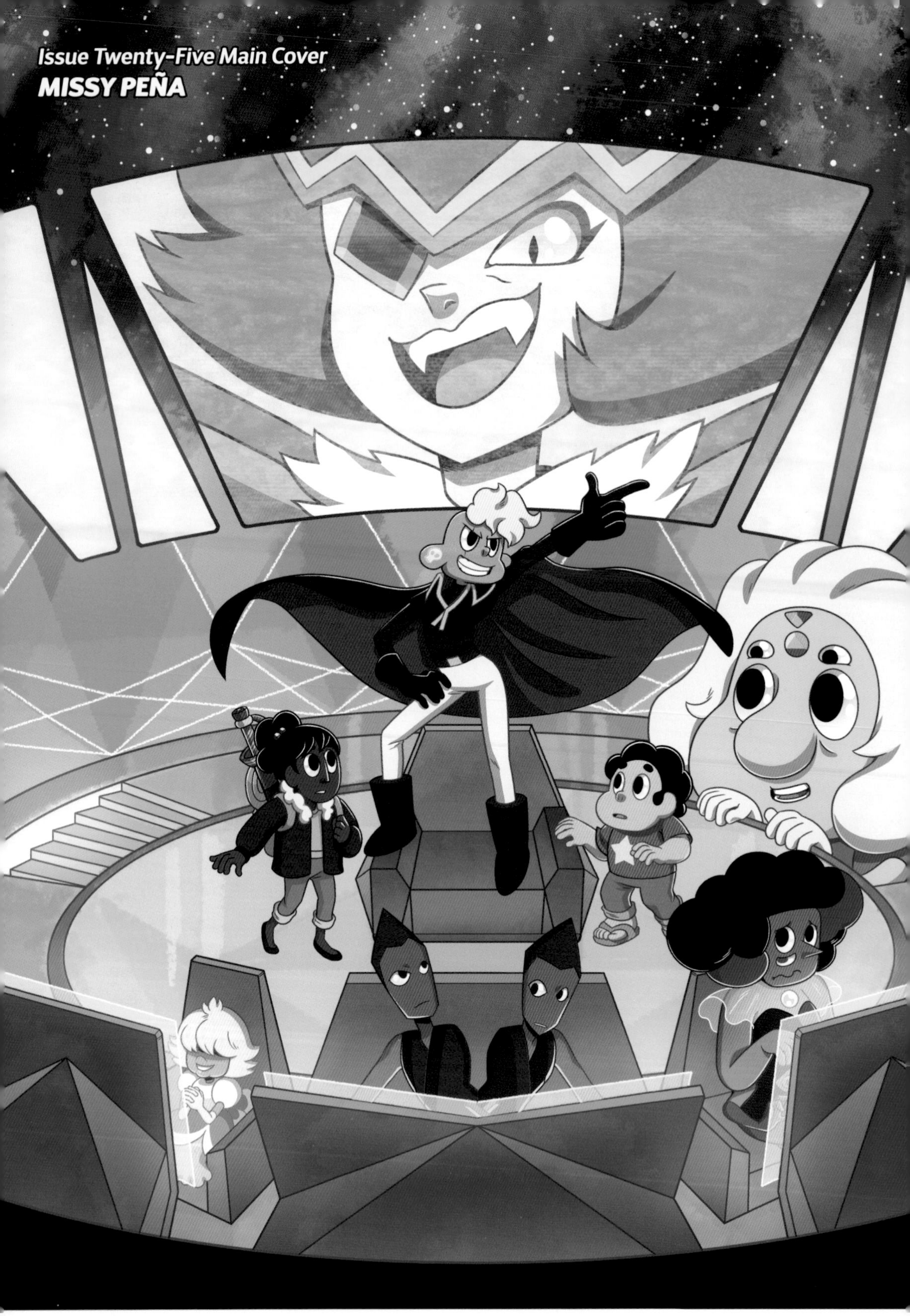

CHAPTER TWENTY-FIVE

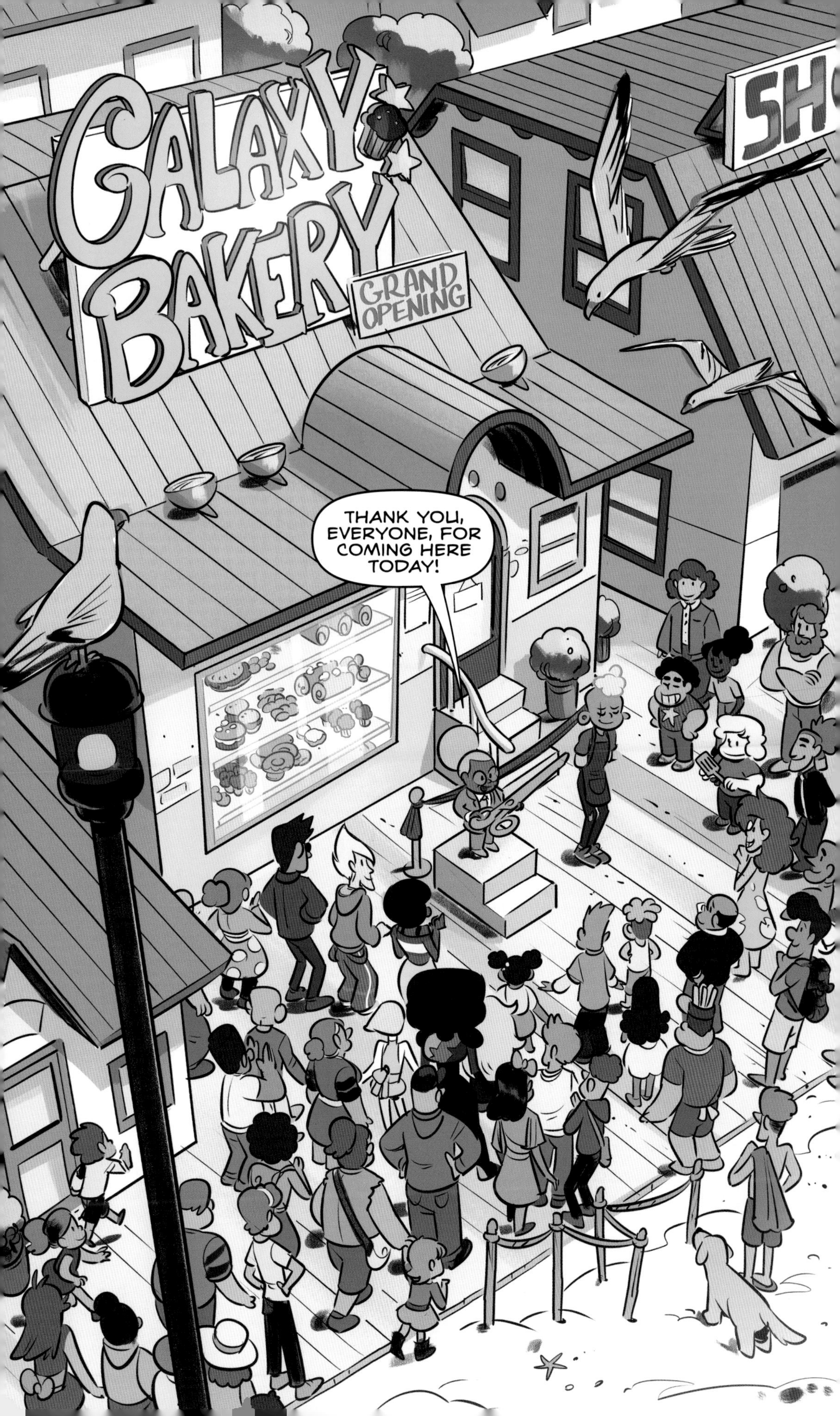
GALAXY BAKERY
GRAND OPENING
THANK YOU, EVERYONE, FOR COMING HERE TODAY!

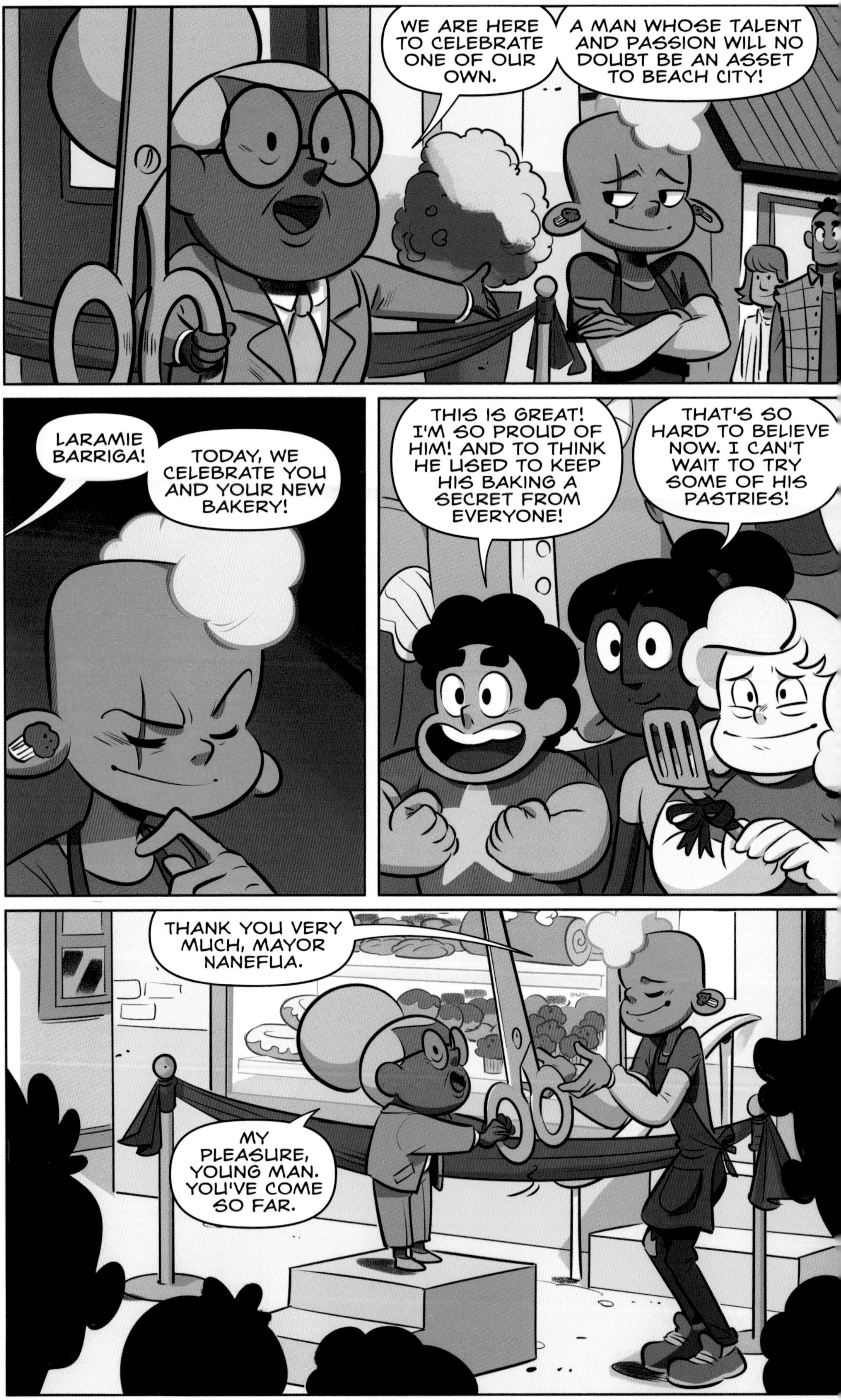
WE ARE HERE TO CELEBRATE ONE OF OUR OWN.
A MAN WHOSE TALENT AND PASSION WILL NO DOUBT BE AN ASSET TO BEACH CITY!
LARAMIE BARRIGA!
TODAY, WE CELEBRATE YOU AND YOUR NEW BAKERY!
THIS IS GREAT! I'M SO PROUD OF HIM! AND TO THINK HE USED TO KEEP HIS BAKING A SECRET FROM EVERYONE!
THAT'S SO HARD TO BELIEVE NOW. I CAN'T WAIT TO TRY SOME OF HIS PASTRIES!
THANK YOU VERY MUCH, MAYOR NANEFUA.
MY PLEASURE, YOUNG MAN. YOU'VE COME SO FAR.

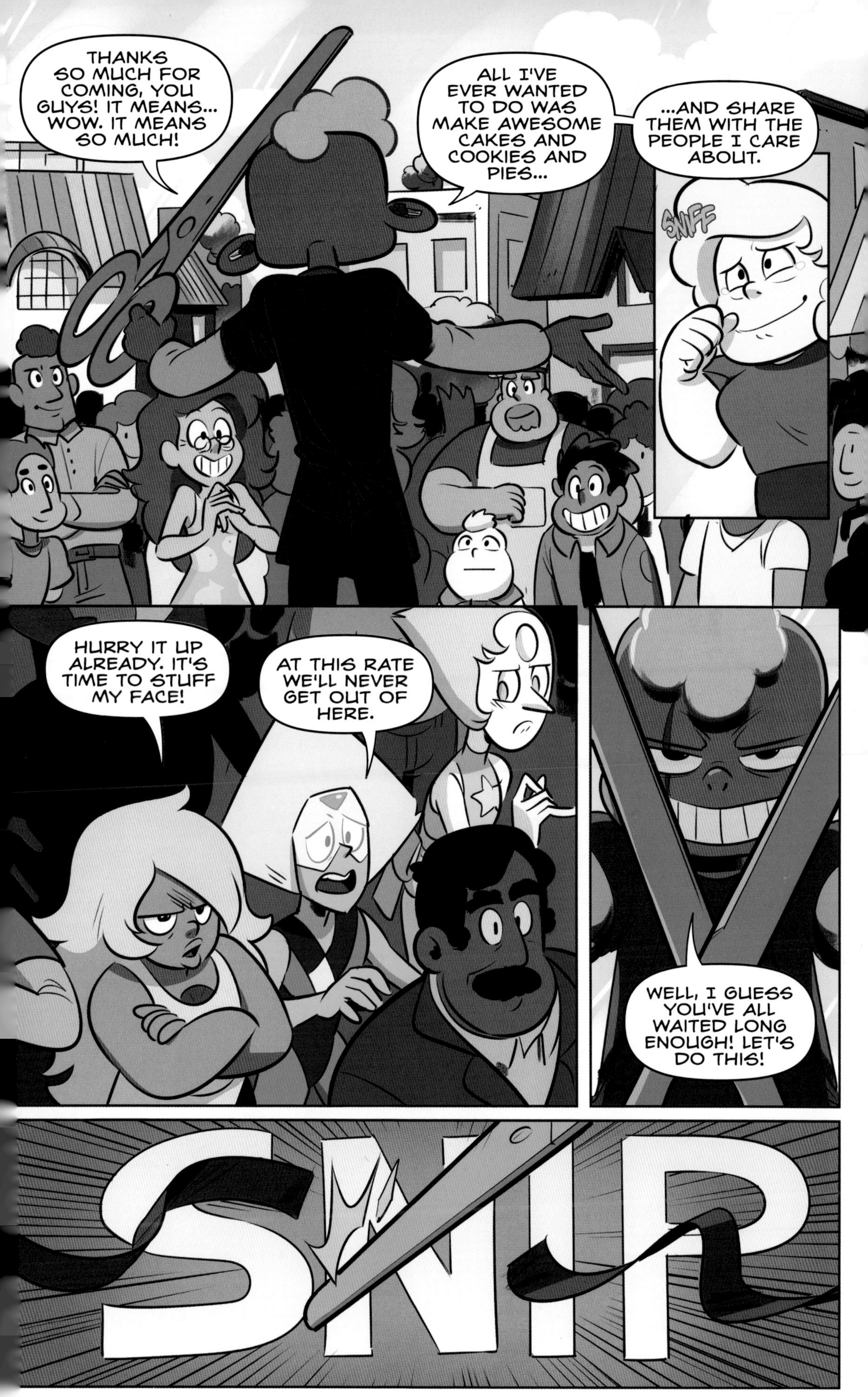
THANKS SO MUCH FOR COMING, YOU GUYS! IT MEANS... WOW. IT MEANS SO MUCH!
ALL I'VE EVER WANTED TO DO WAS MAKE AWESOME CAKES AND COOKIES AND PIES...
...AND SHARE THEM WITH THE PEOPLE I CARE ABOUT.
SNIFF
HURRY IT UP ALREADY. IT'S TIME TO STUFF MY FACE!
AT THIS RATE WE'LL NEVER GET OUT OF HERE.
WELL, I GUESS YOU'VE ALL WAITED LONG ENOUGH! LET'S DO THIS!
SNIP

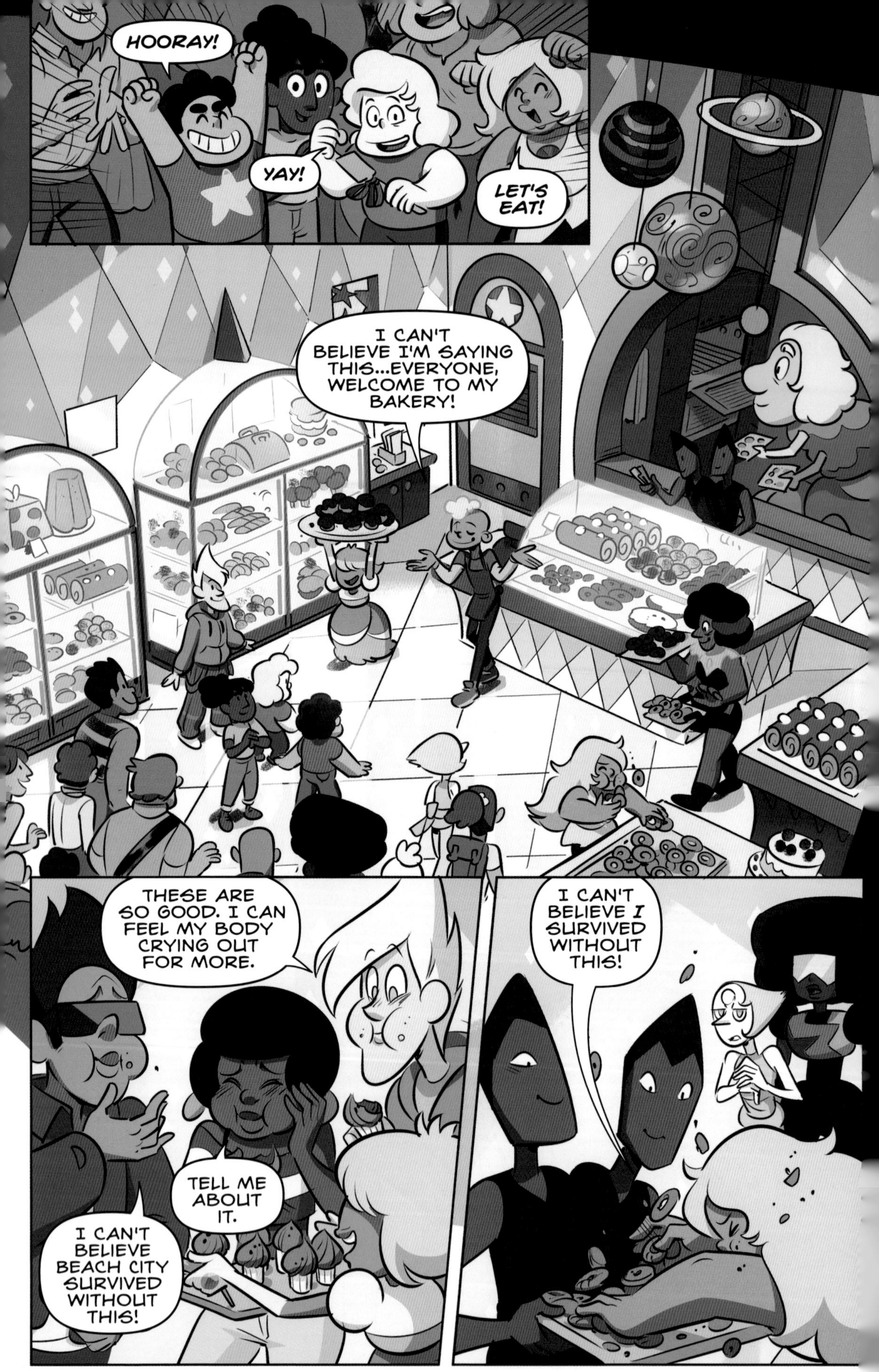
HOORAY!
YAY!
LET'S EAT!
I CAN'T BELIEVE I'M SAYING THIS...EVERYONE, WELCOME TO MY BAKERY!
THESE ARE SO GOOD. I CAN FEEL MY BODY CRYING OUT FOR MORE.
TELL ME ABOUT IT.
I CAN'T BELIEVE BEACH CITY SURVIVED WITHOUT THIS!
I CAN'T BELIEVE *I* SURVIVED WITHOUT THIS!

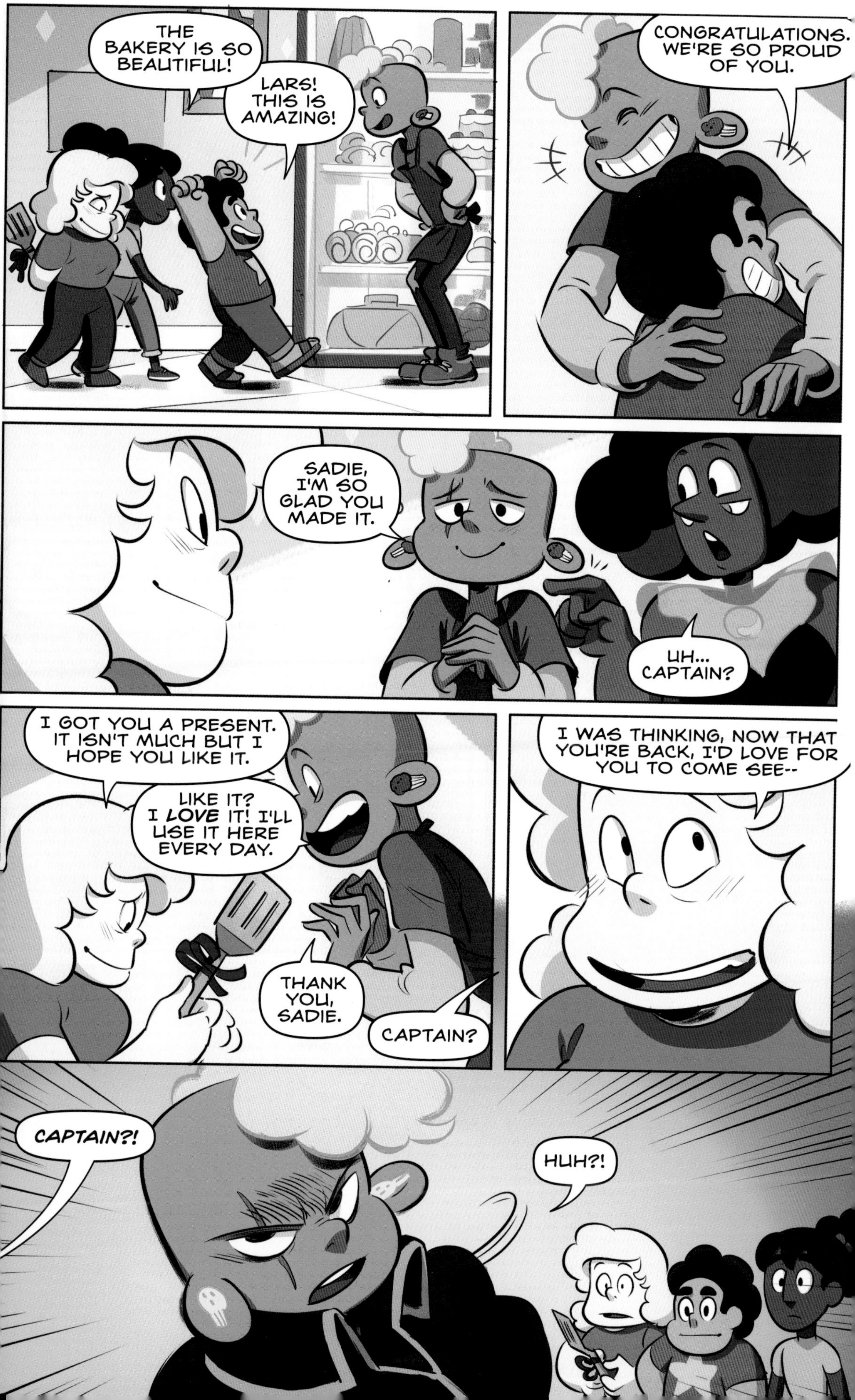
THE BAKERY IS SO BEAUTIFUL!
LARS! THIS IS AMAZING!
CONGRATULATIONS. WE'RE SO PROUD OF YOU.
SADIE, I'M SO GLAD YOU MADE IT.
UH... CAPTAIN?
I GOT YOU A PRESENT. IT ISN'T MUCH BUT I HOPE YOU LIKE IT.
LIKE IT? I LOVE IT! I'LL USE IT HERE EVERY DAY.
THANK YOU, SADIE.
CAPTAIN?
I WAS THINKING, NOW THAT YOU'RE BACK, I'D LOVE FOR YOU TO COME SEE--
CAPTAIN?!
HUH?!

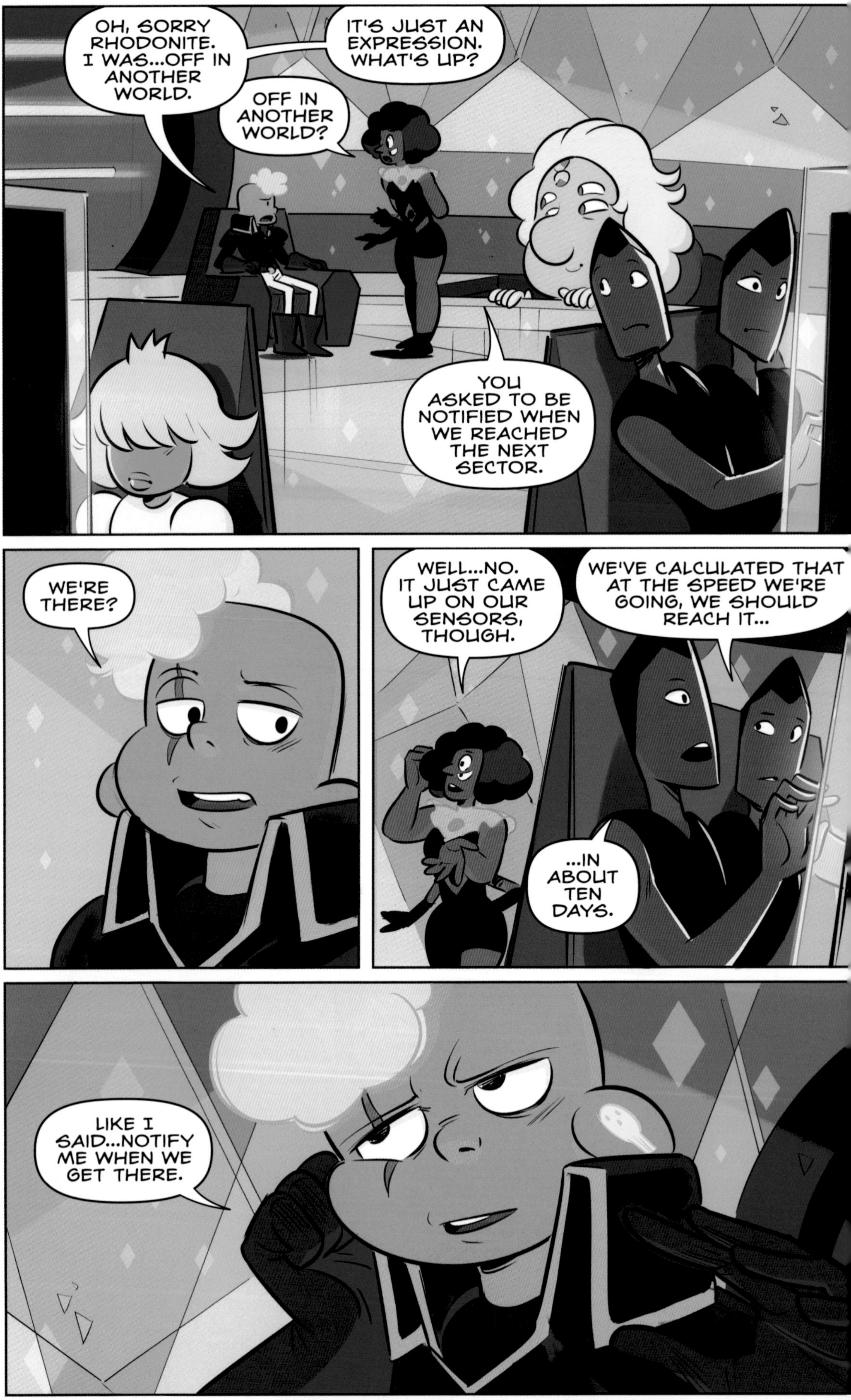
OH, SORRY RHODONITE. I WAS...OFF IN ANOTHER WORLD.
OFF IN ANOTHER WORLD?
IT'S JUST AN EXPRESSION. WHAT'S UP?
YOU ASKED TO BE NOTIFIED WHEN WE REACHED THE NEXT SECTOR.
WE'RE THERE?
WELL...NO. IT JUST CAME UP ON OUR SENSORS, THOUGH.
WE'VE CALCULATED THAT AT THE SPEED WE'RE GOING, WE SHOULD REACH IT...
...IN ABOUT TEN DAYS.
LIKE I SAID...NOTIFY ME WHEN WE GET THERE.

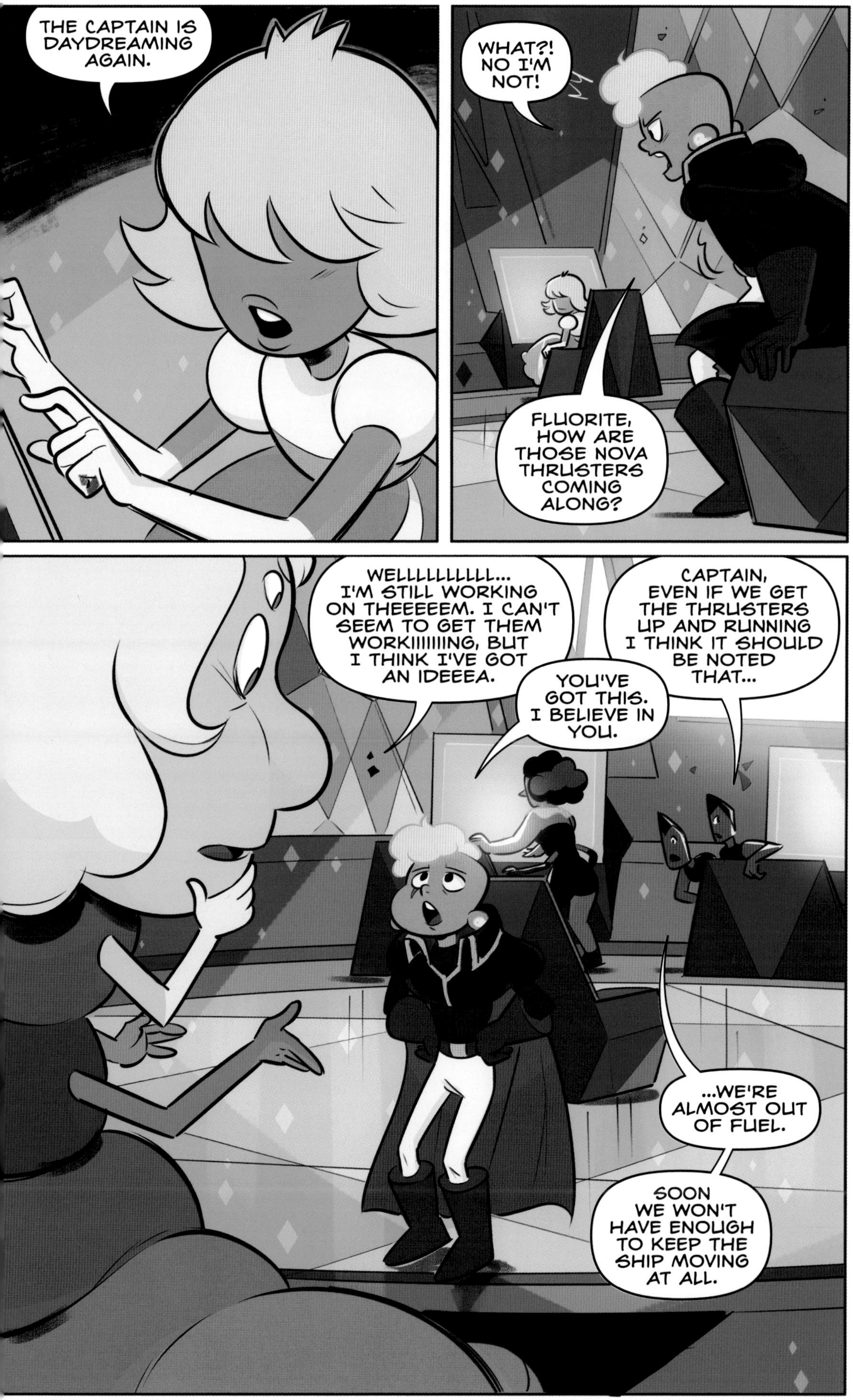
THE CAPTAIN IS DAYDREAMING AGAIN.
WHAT?! NO I'M NOT!
FLUORITE, HOW ARE THOSE NOVA THRUSTERS COMING ALONG?
WELLLLLLLLLL... I'M STILL WORKING ON THEEEEEM. I CAN'T SEEM TO GET THEM WORKIIIIIIING, BUT I THINK I'VE GOT AN IDEEEA.
YOU'VE GOT THIS. I BELIEVE IN YOU.
CAPTAIN, EVEN IF WE GET THE THRUSTERS UP AND RUNNING I THINK IT SHOULD BE NOTED THAT...
...WE'RE ALMOST OUT OF FUEL.
SOON WE WON'T HAVE ENOUGH TO KEEP THE SHIP MOVING AT ALL.

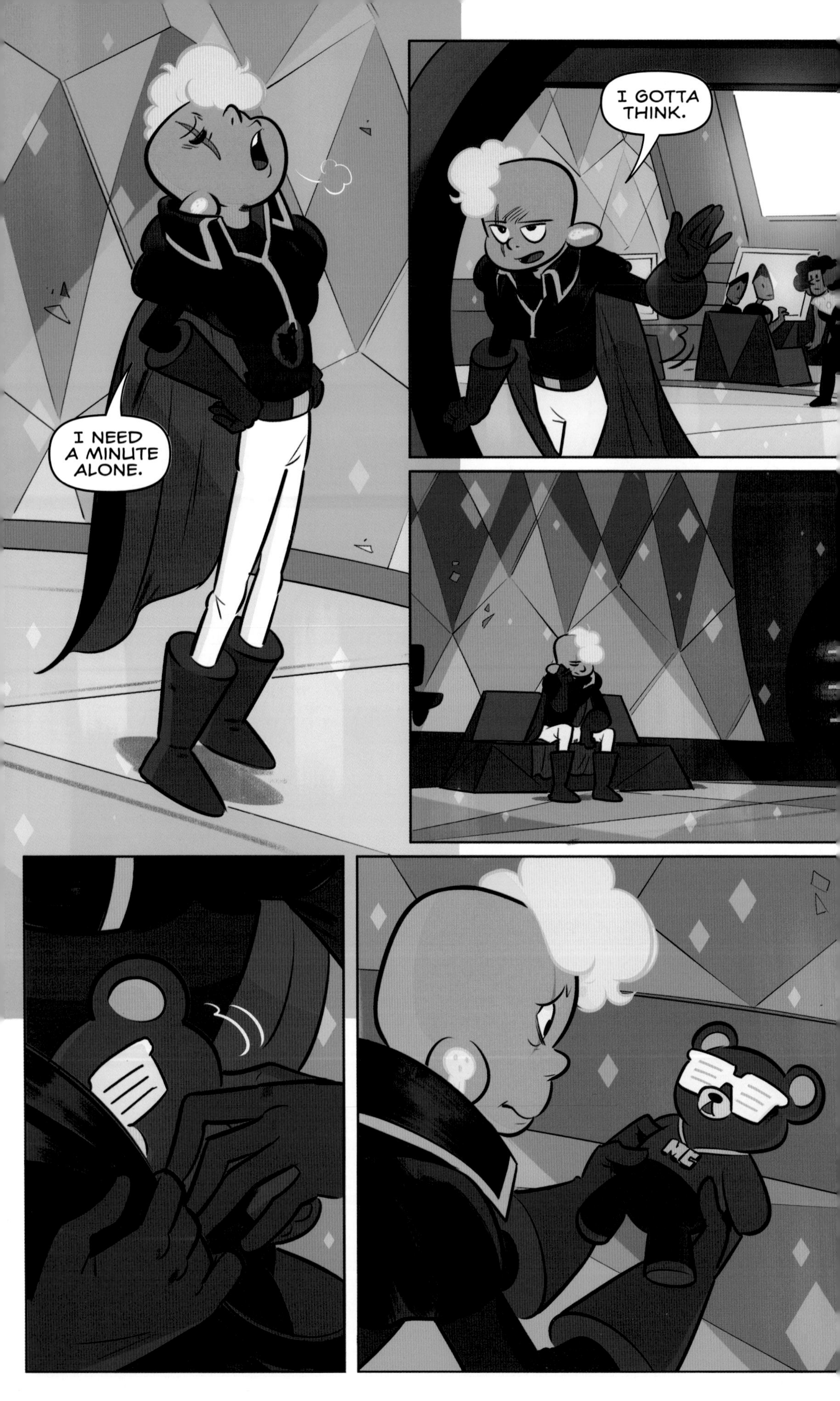
I NEED A MINUTE ALONE.
I GOTTA THINK.
MC

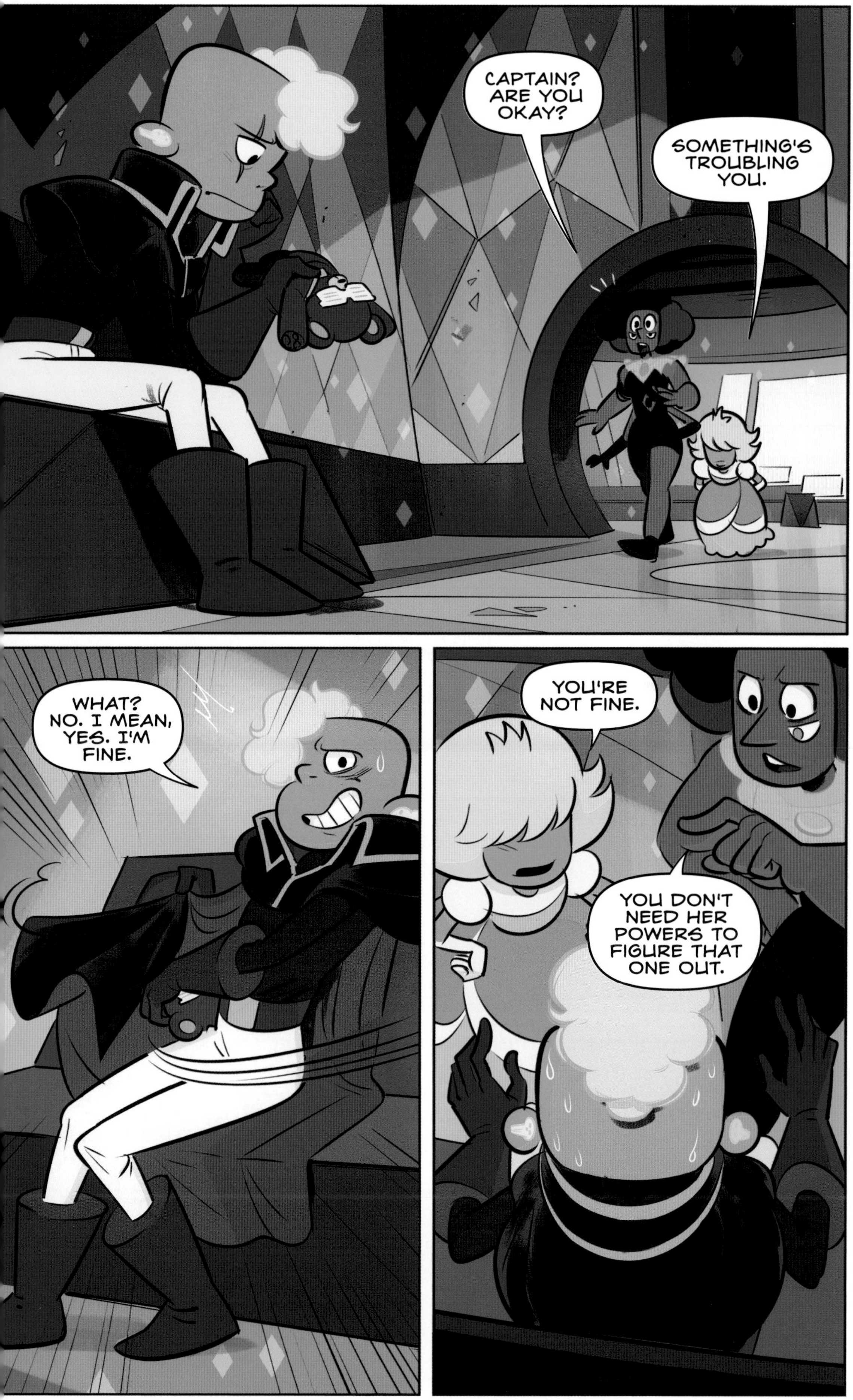
CAPTAIN? ARE YOU OKAY?
SOMETHING'S TROUBLING YOU.
WHAT? NO. I MEAN, YES. I'M FINE.
YOU'RE NOT FINE.
YOU DON'T NEED HER POWERS TO FIGURE THAT ONE OUT.

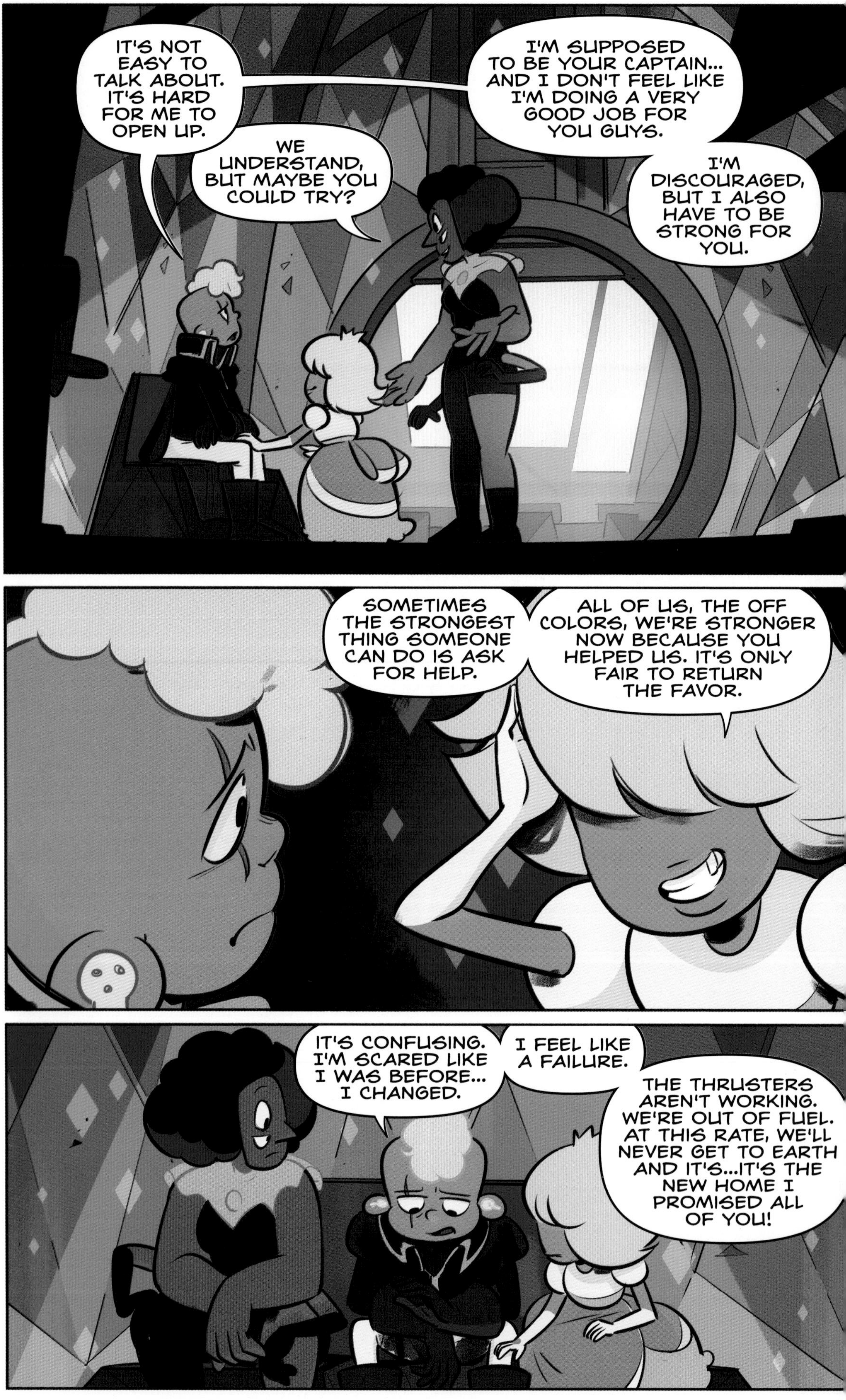
IT'S NOT EASY TO TALK ABOUT. IT'S HARD FOR ME TO OPEN UP.
I'M SUPPOSED TO BE YOUR CAPTAIN... AND I DON'T FEEL LIKE I'M DOING A VERY GOOD JOB FOR YOU GUYS.
WE UNDERSTAND, BUT MAYBE YOU COULD TRY?
I'M DISCOURAGED, BUT I ALSO HAVE TO BE STRONG FOR YOU.
SOMETIMES THE STRONGEST THING SOMEONE CAN DO IS ASK FOR HELP.
ALL OF US, THE OFF COLORS, WE'RE STRONGER NOW BECAUSE YOU HELPED US. IT'S ONLY FAIR TO RETURN THE FAVOR.
IT'S CONFUSING. I'M SCARED LIKE I WAS BEFORE... I CHANGED.
I FEEL LIKE A FAILURE.
THE THRUSTERS AREN'T WORKING. WE'RE OUT OF FUEL. AT THIS RATE, WE'LL NEVER GET TO EARTH AND IT'S...IT'S THE NEW HOME I PROMISED ALL OF YOU!

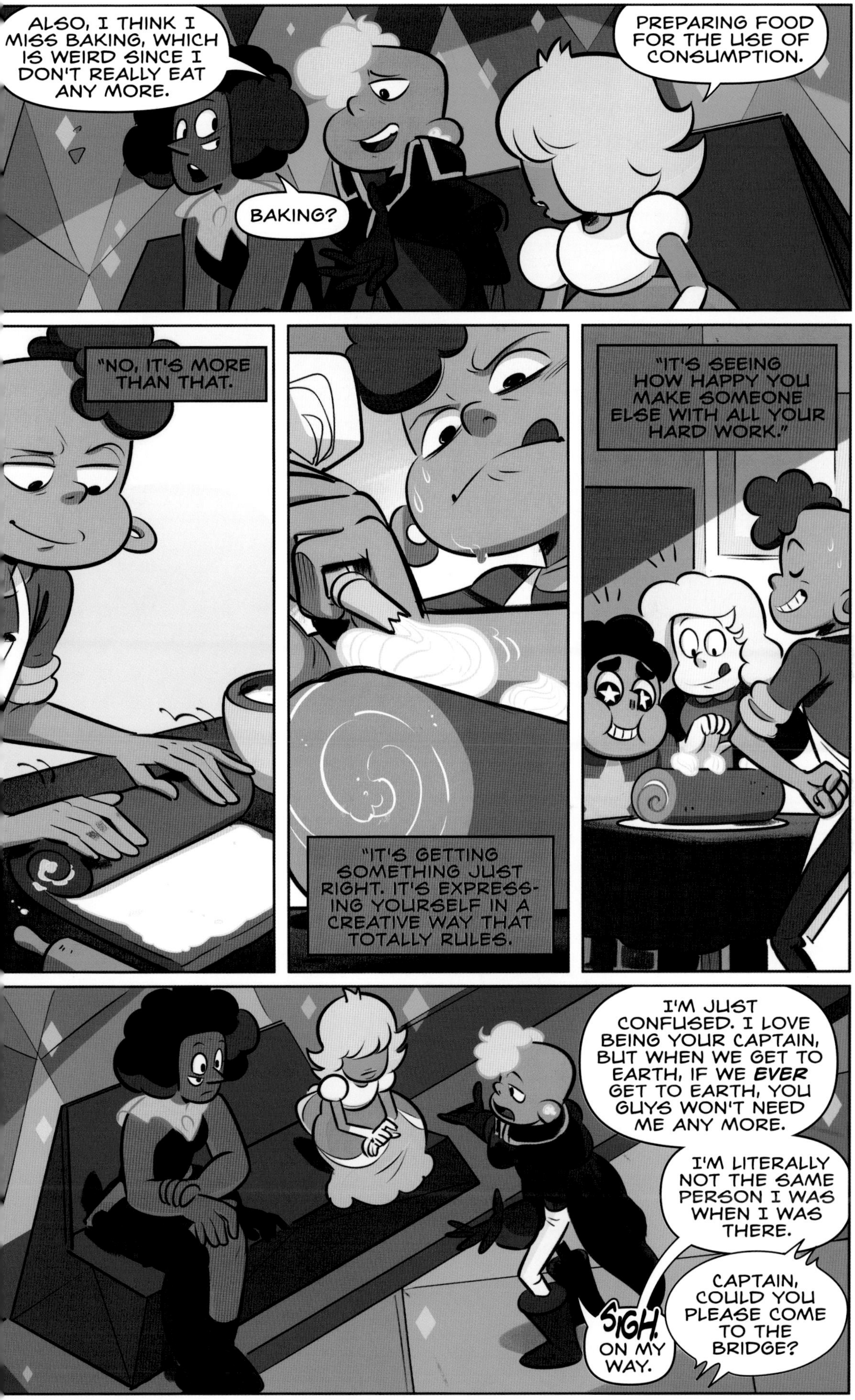
ALSO, I THINK I MISS BAKING, WHICH IS WEIRD SINCE I DON'T REALLY EAT ANY MORE.
PREPARING FOOD FOR THE USE OF CONSUMPTION.
BAKING?
"NO, IT'S MORE THAN THAT.
"IT'S GETTING SOMETHING JUST RIGHT. IT'S EXPRESS-ING YOURSELF IN A CREATIVE WAY THAT TOTALLY RULES.
"IT'S SEEING HOW HAPPY YOU MAKE SOMEONE ELSE WITH ALL YOUR HARD WORK."
I'M JUST CONFUSED. I LOVE BEING YOUR CAPTAIN, BUT WHEN WE GET TO EARTH, IF WE *EVER* GET TO EARTH, YOU GUYS WON'T NEED ME ANY MORE.
I'M LITERALLY NOT THE SAME PERSON I WAS WHEN I WAS THERE.
CAPTAIN, COULD YOU PLEASE COME TO THE BRIDGE?
SIGH. ON MY WAY.

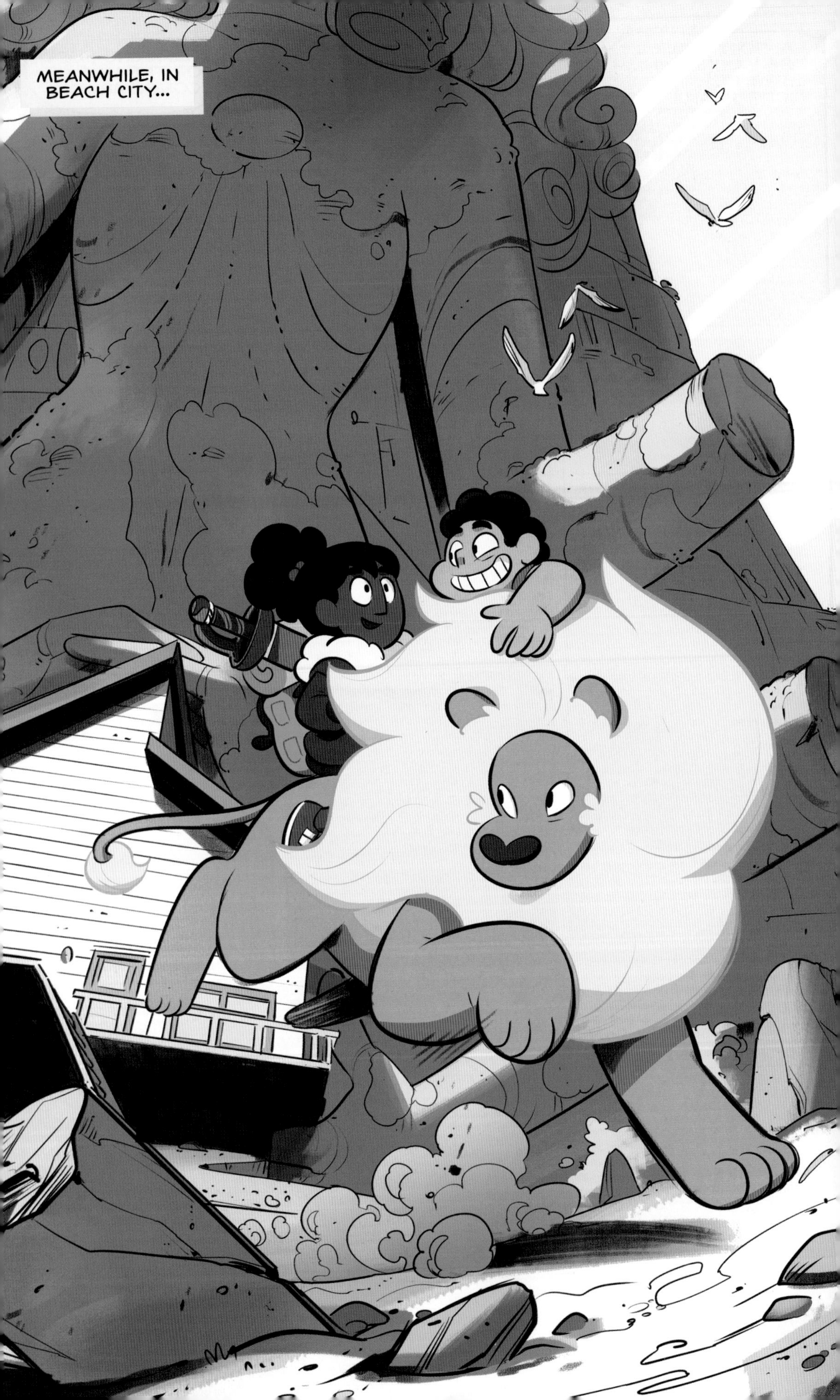
MEANWHILE, IN BEACH CITY...

PUTTING TOGETHER A CARE PACKAGE IS SO NICE OF YOU, STEVEN. I'M SURE LARS IS REALLY GOING TO APPRECIATE IT.

I'VE BROUGHT HIM ONE BEFORE.

YEAH, BUT I MEAN, JUST THINKING OF HIM AND LETTING HIM KNOW HE ISN'T FORGOTTEN.

IT'S SWEET. AND CARE PACKAGES ARE FUN AND FULL OF UNEXPECTED SURPRISES.

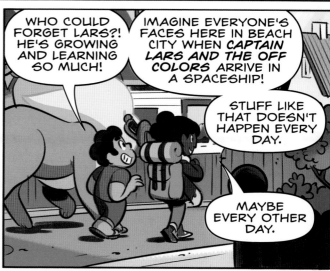

WHO COULD FORGET LARS?! HE'S GROWING AND LEARNING SO MUCH!

IMAGINE EVERYONE'S FACES HERE IN BEACH CITY WHEN *CAPTAIN LARS AND THE OFF COLORS* ARRIVE IN A SPACESHIP!

STUFF LIKE THAT DOESN'T HAPPEN EVERY DAY.

MAYBE EVERY OTHER DAY.

YOU'RE SO RIGHT!

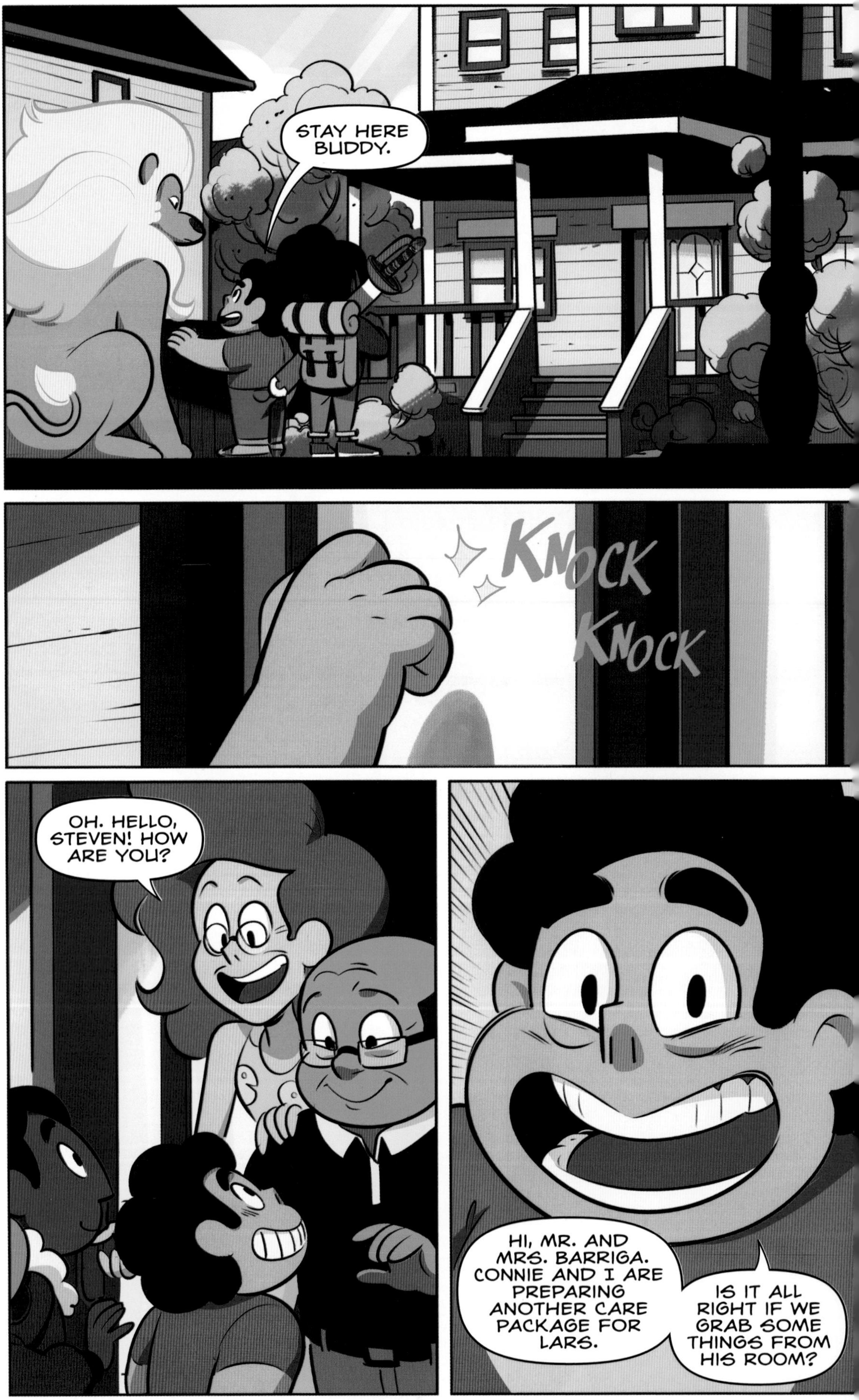
STAY HERE BUDDY.
KNOCK
KNOCK
OH. HELLO, STEVEN! HOW ARE YOU?
HI, MR. AND MRS. BARRIGA. CONNIE AND I ARE PREPARING ANOTHER CARE PACKAGE FOR LARS.
IS IT ALL RIGHT IF WE GRAB SOME THINGS FROM HIS ROOM?

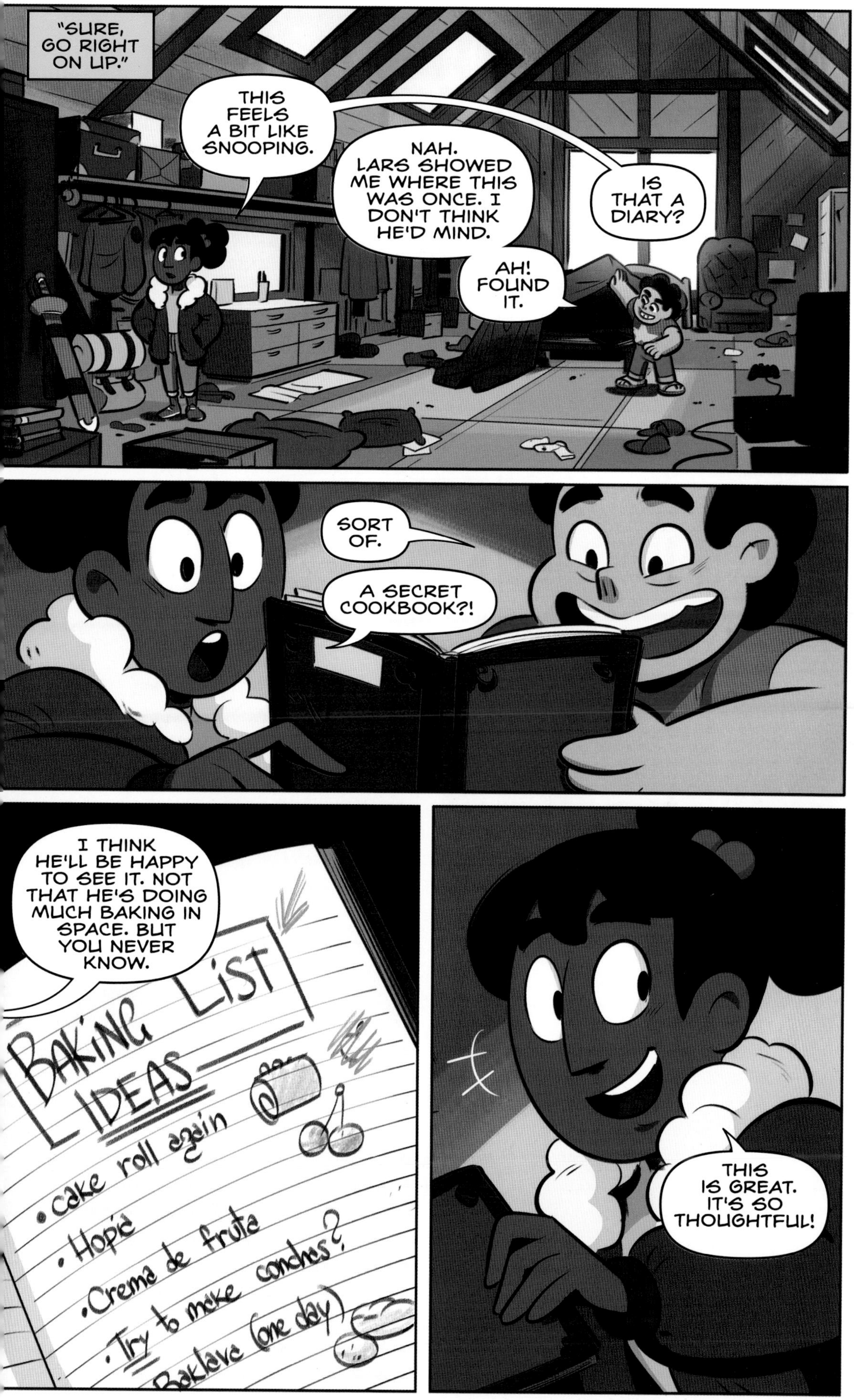
"SURE, GO RIGHT ON UP."
THIS FEELS A BIT LIKE SNOOPING.
NAH. LARS SHOWED ME WHERE THIS WAS ONCE. I DON'T THINK HE'D MIND.
IS THAT A DIARY?
AH! FOUND IT.
SORT OF.
A SECRET COOKBOOK?!
I THINK HE'LL BE HAPPY TO SEE IT. NOT THAT HE'S DOING MUCH BAKING IN SPACE. BUT YOU NEVER KNOW.
BAKING LIST IDEAS
• cake roll again
• Hopíe
• Crema de fruta
• Try to make conches?
• Baklava (one day)
THIS IS GREAT. IT'S SO THOUGHTFUL!

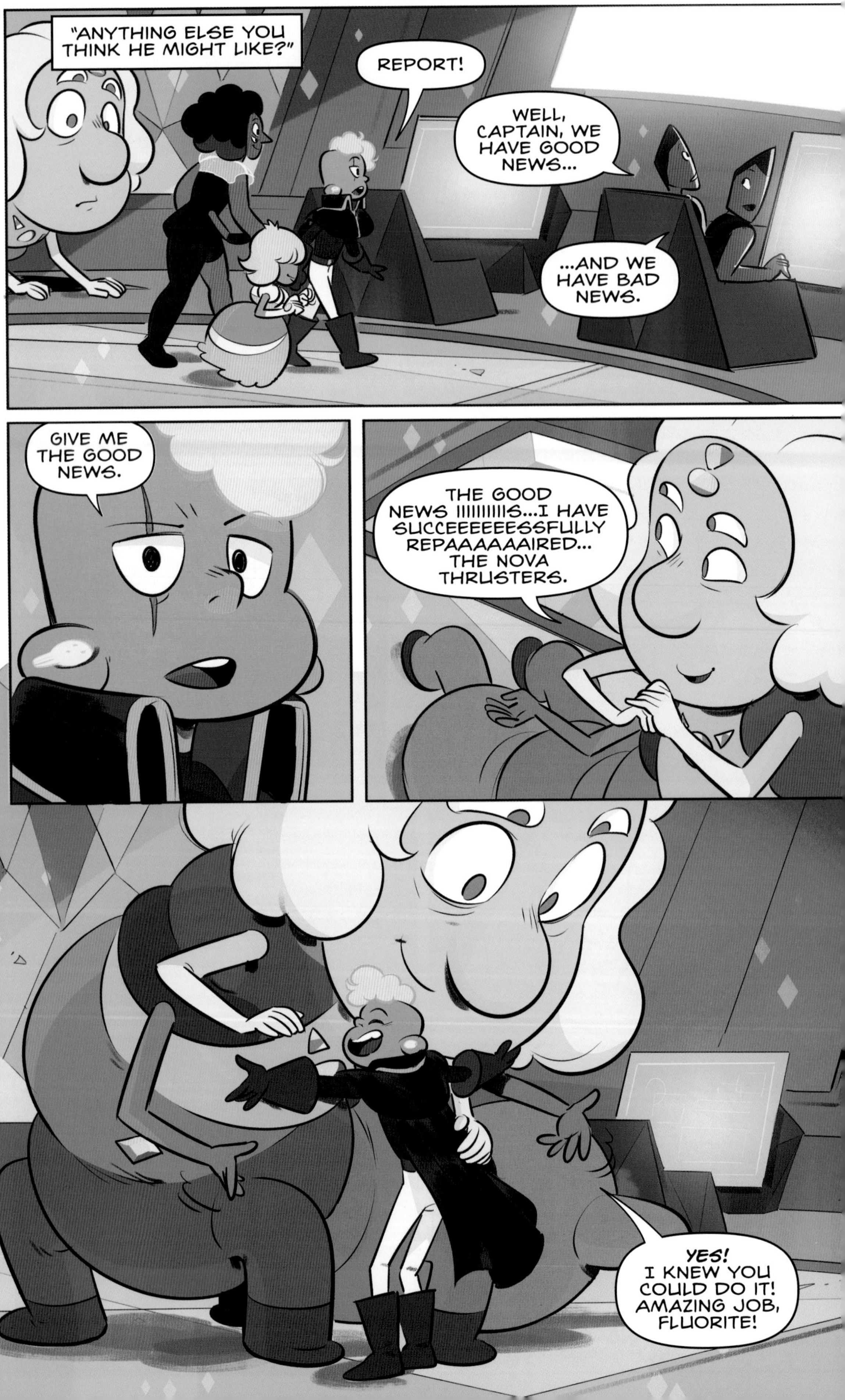
"ANYTHING ELSE YOU THINK HE MIGHT LIKE?"
REPORT!
WELL, CAPTAIN, WE HAVE GOOD NEWS...
...AND WE HAVE BAD NEWS.
GIVE ME THE GOOD NEWS.
THE GOOD NEWS IIIIIIIIIIS...I HAVE SUCCEEEEEEESSFULLY REPAAAAAAIRED... THE NOVA THRUSTERS.
YES! I KNEW YOU COULD DO IT! AMAZING JOB, FLUORITE!

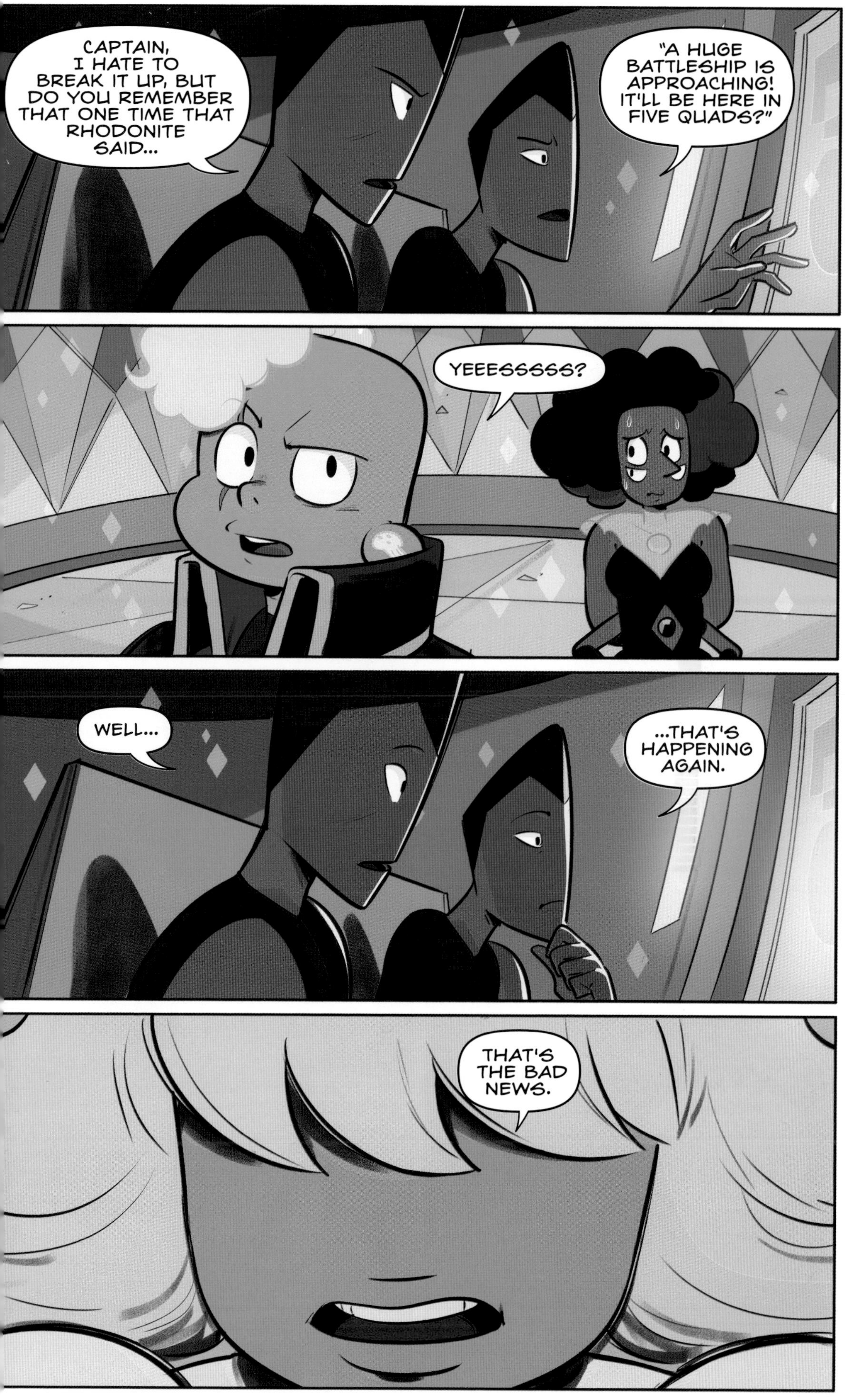

CAPTAIN, I HATE TO BREAK IT UP, BUT DO YOU REMEMBER THAT ONE TIME THAT RHODONITE SAID...
"A HUGE BATTLESHIP IS APPROACHING! IT'LL BE HERE IN FIVE QUADS?"
YEEESSSSS?
WELL...
...THAT'S HAPPENING AGAIN.
THAT'S THE BAD NEWS.

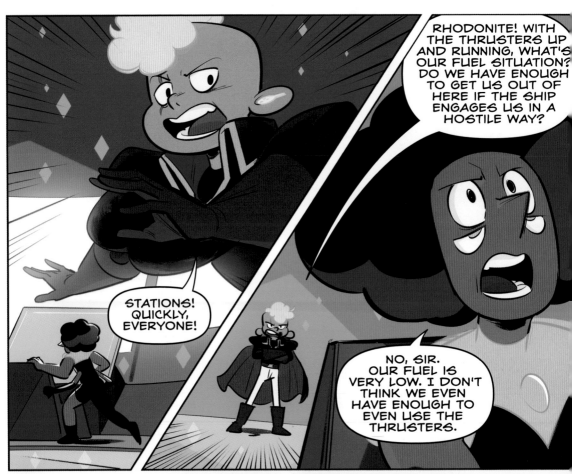

RHODONITE! WITH THE THRUSTERS UP AND RUNNING, WHAT'S OUR FUEL SITUATION? DO WE HAVE ENOUGH TO GET US OUT OF HERE IF THE SHIP ENGAGES US IN A HOSTILE WAY?

STATIONS! QUICKLY, EVERYONE!

NO, SIR. OUR FUEL IS VERY LOW. I DON'T THINK WE EVEN HAVE ENOUGH TO EVEN USE THE THRUSTERS.

ARE WE ABLE TO DETECT THE SHIP? WHO IT BELONGS TO?

WE CAN, BUT I DON'T THINK YOU'RE GOING TO LIKE IT.

ON SCREEN.

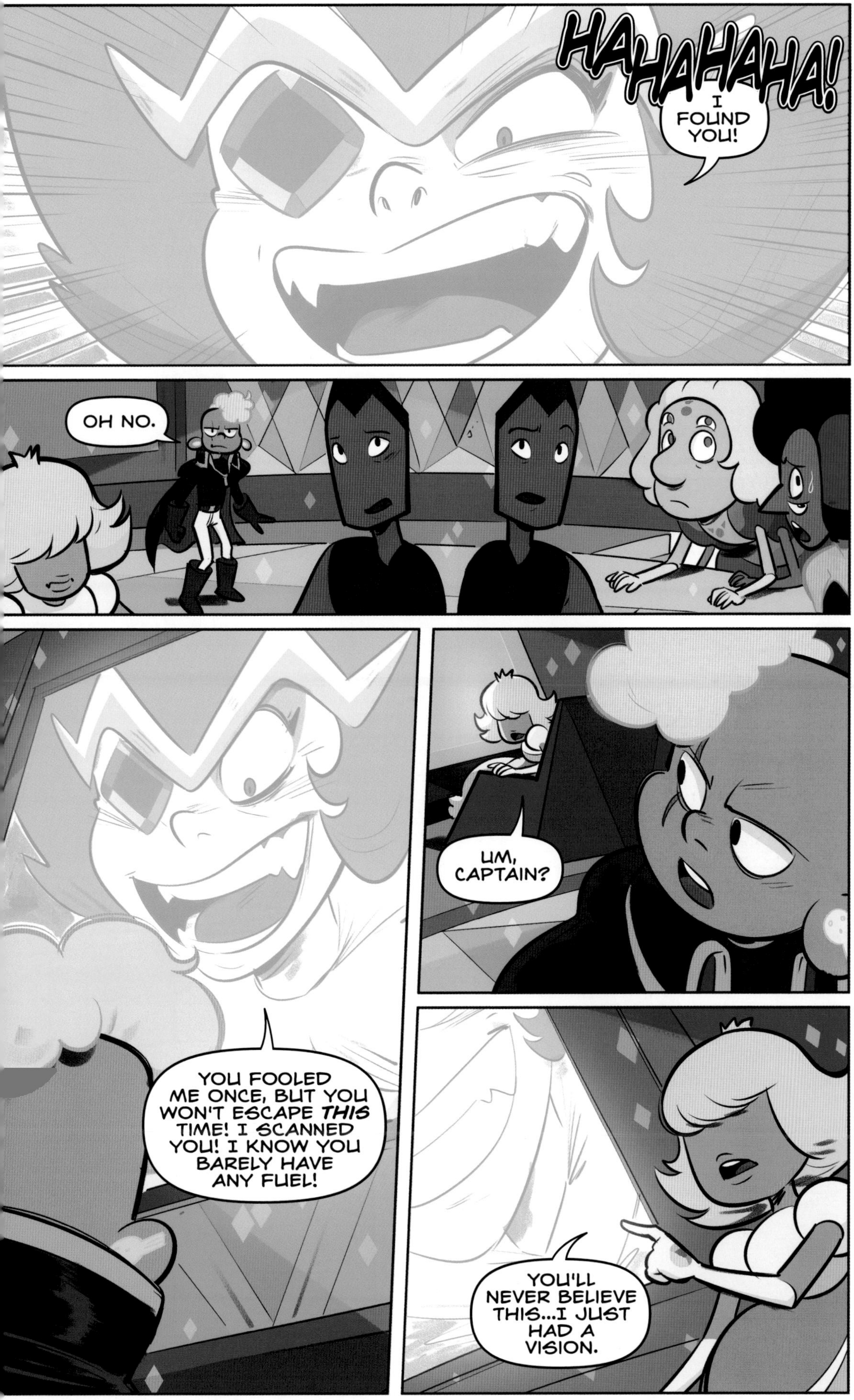
HAHAHAHA!
I FOUND YOU!
OH NO.
YOU FOOLED ME ONCE, BUT YOU WON'T ESCAPE *THIS* TIME! I SCANNED YOU! I KNOW YOU BARELY HAVE ANY FUEL!
UM, CAPTAIN?
YOU'LL NEVER BELIEVE THIS...I JUST HAD A VISION.

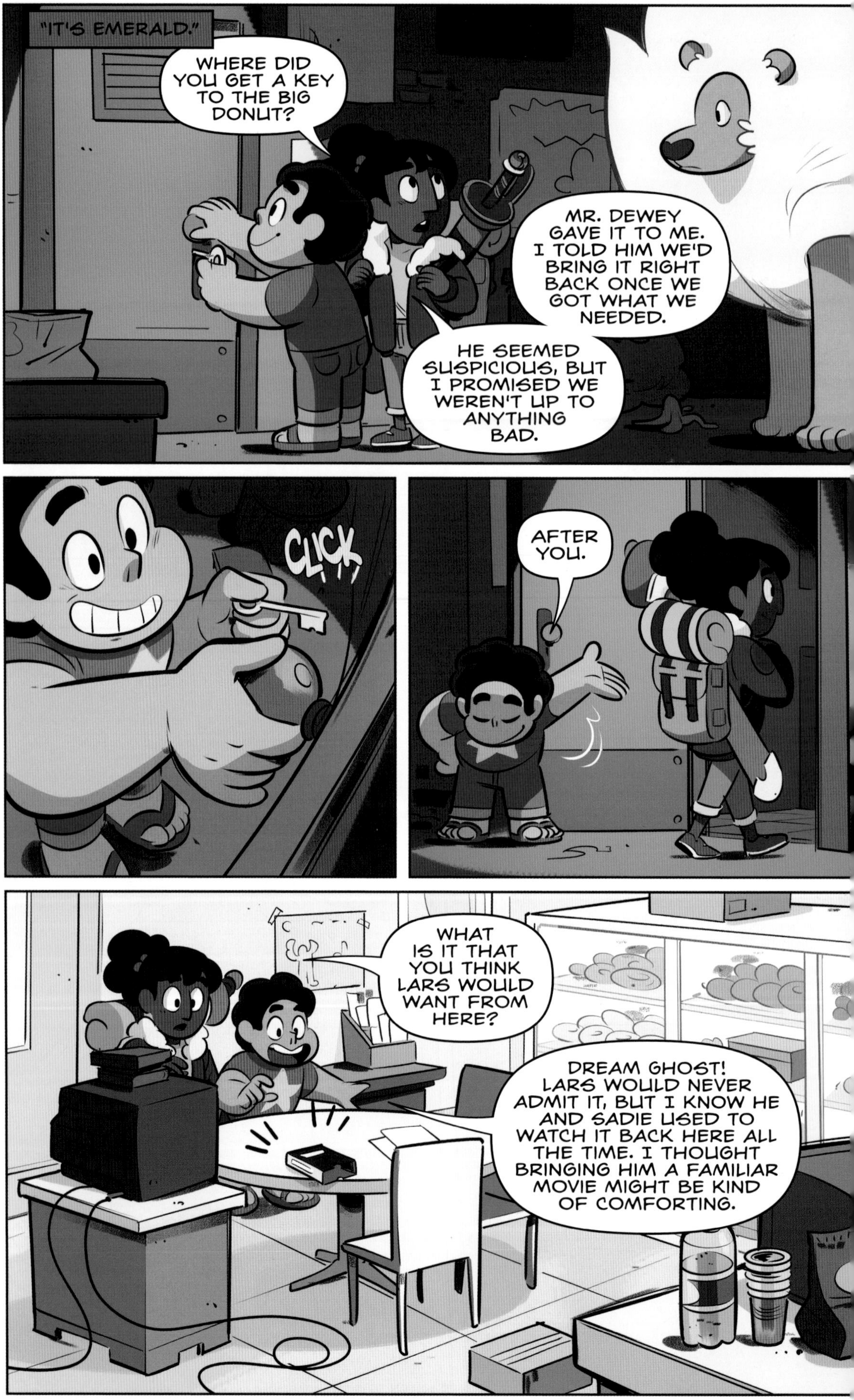
"IT'S EMERALD."
WHERE DID YOU GET A KEY TO THE BIG DONUT?
MR. DEWEY GAVE IT TO ME. I TOLD HIM WE'D BRING IT RIGHT BACK ONCE WE GOT WHAT WE NEEDED.
HE SEEMED SUSPICIOUS, BUT I PROMISED WE WEREN'T UP TO ANYTHING BAD.
CLICK
AFTER YOU.
WHAT IS IT THAT YOU THINK LARS WOULD WANT FROM HERE?
DREAM GHOST! LARS WOULD NEVER ADMIT IT, BUT I KNOW HE AND SADIE USED TO WATCH IT BACK HERE ALL THE TIME. I THOUGHT BRINGING HIM A FAMILIAR MOVIE MIGHT BE KIND OF COMFORTING.

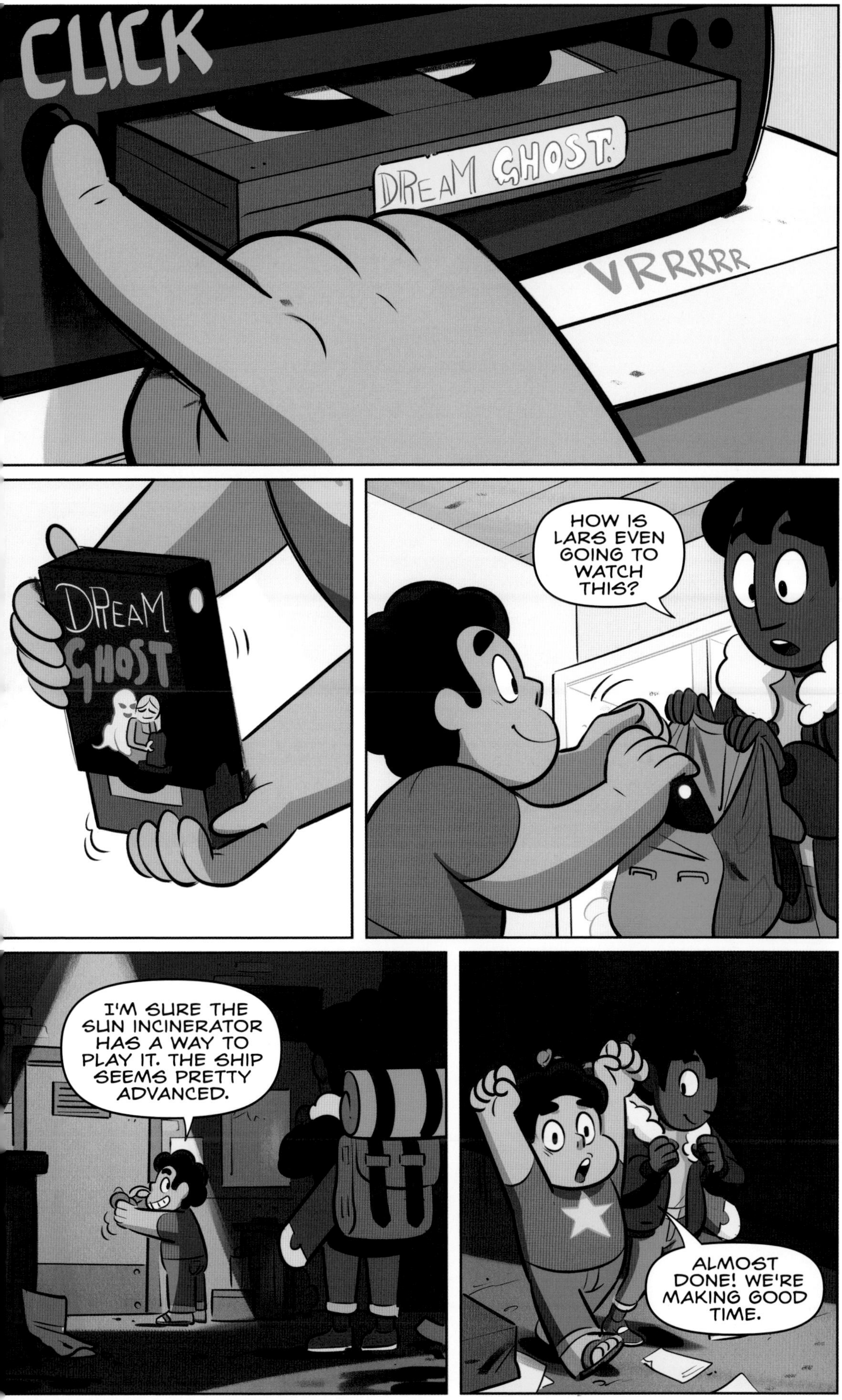
CLICK
DREAM GHOST
VRRRRR
DREAM GHOST
HOW IS LARS EVEN GOING TO WATCH THIS?
I'M SURE THE SUN INCINERATOR HAS A WAY TO PLAY IT. THE SHIP SEEMS PRETTY ADVANCED.
ALMOST DONE! WE'RE MAKING GOOD TIME.

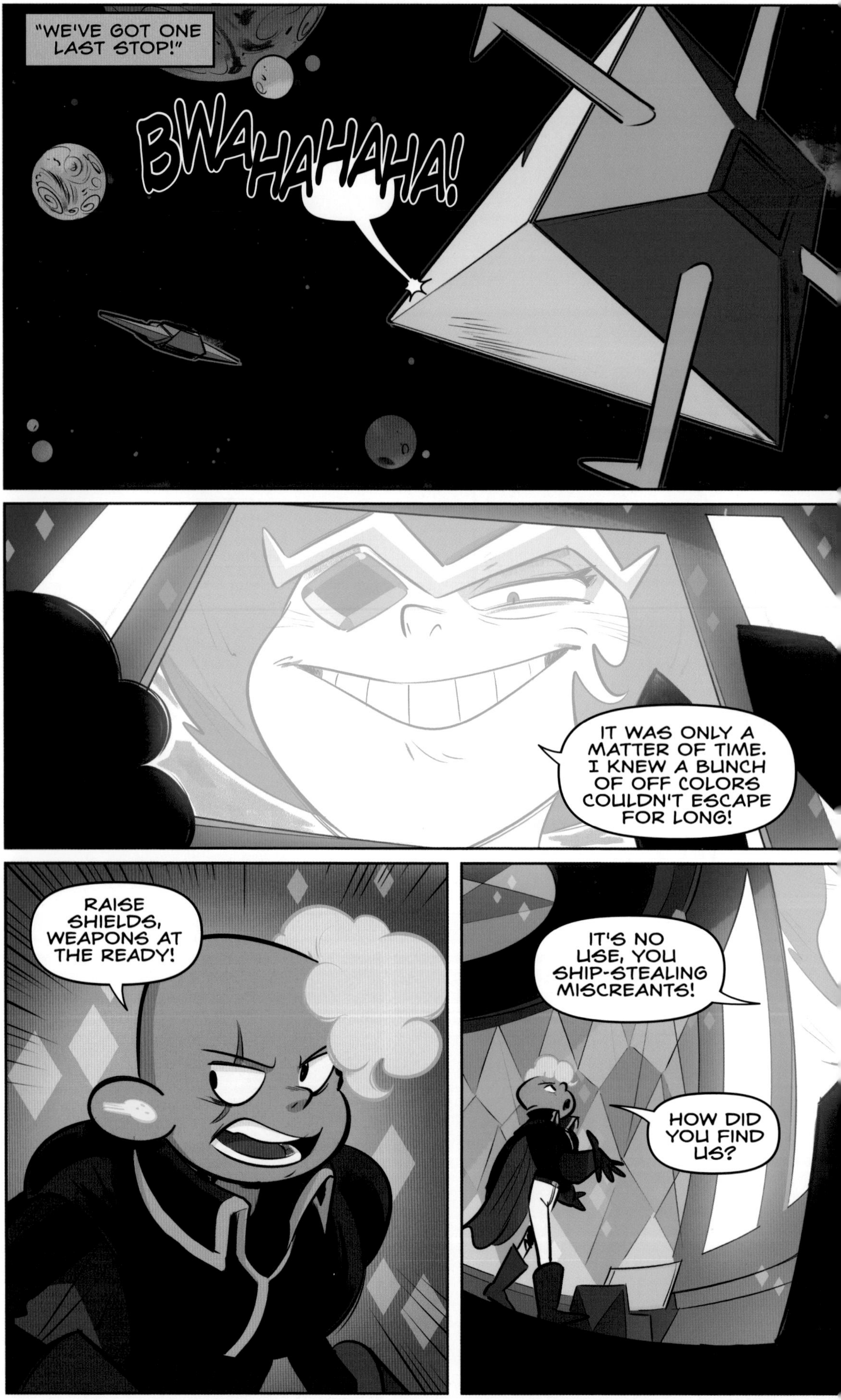

"WE'VE GOT ONE LAST STOP!"
BWAHAHAHAHA!
IT WAS ONLY A MATTER OF TIME. I KNEW A BUNCH OF OFF COLORS COULDN'T ESCAPE FOR LONG!
RAISE SHIELDS, WEAPONS AT THE READY!
IT'S NO USE, YOU SHIP-STEALING MISCREANTS!
HOW DID YOU FIND US?

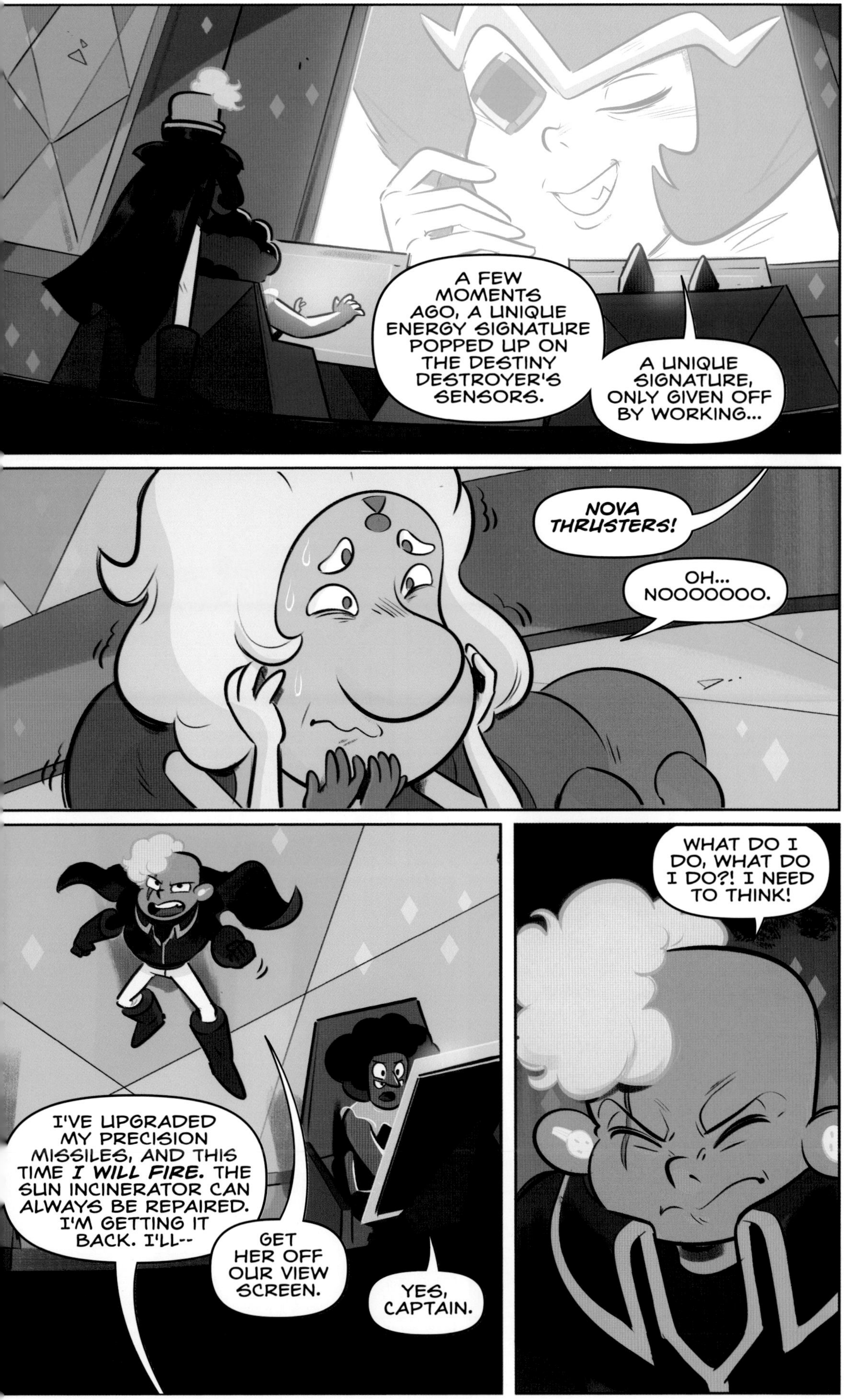
A FEW MOMENTS AGO, A UNIQUE ENERGY SIGNATURE POPPED UP ON THE DESTINY DESTROYER'S SENSORS.
A UNIQUE SIGNATURE, ONLY GIVEN OFF BY WORKING...
NOVA THRUSTERS!
OH... NOOOOOOO.
I'VE UPGRADED MY PRECISION MISSILES, AND THIS TIME I WILL FIRE. THE SUN INCINERATOR CAN ALWAYS BE REPAIRED. I'M GETTING IT BACK. I'LL--
GET HER OFF OUR VIEW SCREEN.
YES, CAPTAIN.
WHAT DO I DO, WHAT DO I DO?! I NEED TO THINK!

SADIE WAS IN TROUBLE AND I DIDN'T DO ANYTHING! ACTUALLY, WAIT. I DID DO SOMETHING! I RAN AND HID. JUST LIKE I ALWAYS DO. JUST LIKE I RAN FROM THE POTLUCK.

BUT YOU WERE ABDUCTED, THAT'S NOT YOUR FAULT.

NO, I TRASHED MY ROLL AND RAN AWAY. THEN I WAS ABDUCTED.

WHY COULDN'T I JUST LET PEOPLE EAT MY FOOD?

CAPTAIN, EMERALD IS CHARGING HER WEAPONS!

WE CAN'T OUTRUN HER WITH NO FUEL.

SCAN FOR ASTEROID BELTS, NEBULAS, ANYTHING THAT MIGHT HELP MASK OUR SIGNATURE.

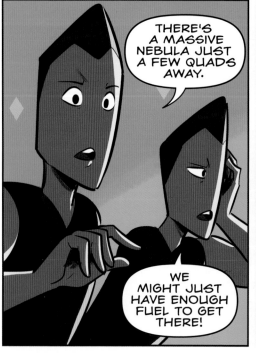

THERE'S A MASSIVE NEBULA JUST A FEW QUADS AWAY.

WE MIGHT JUST HAVE ENOUGH FUEL TO GET THERE!

PUNCH IT.

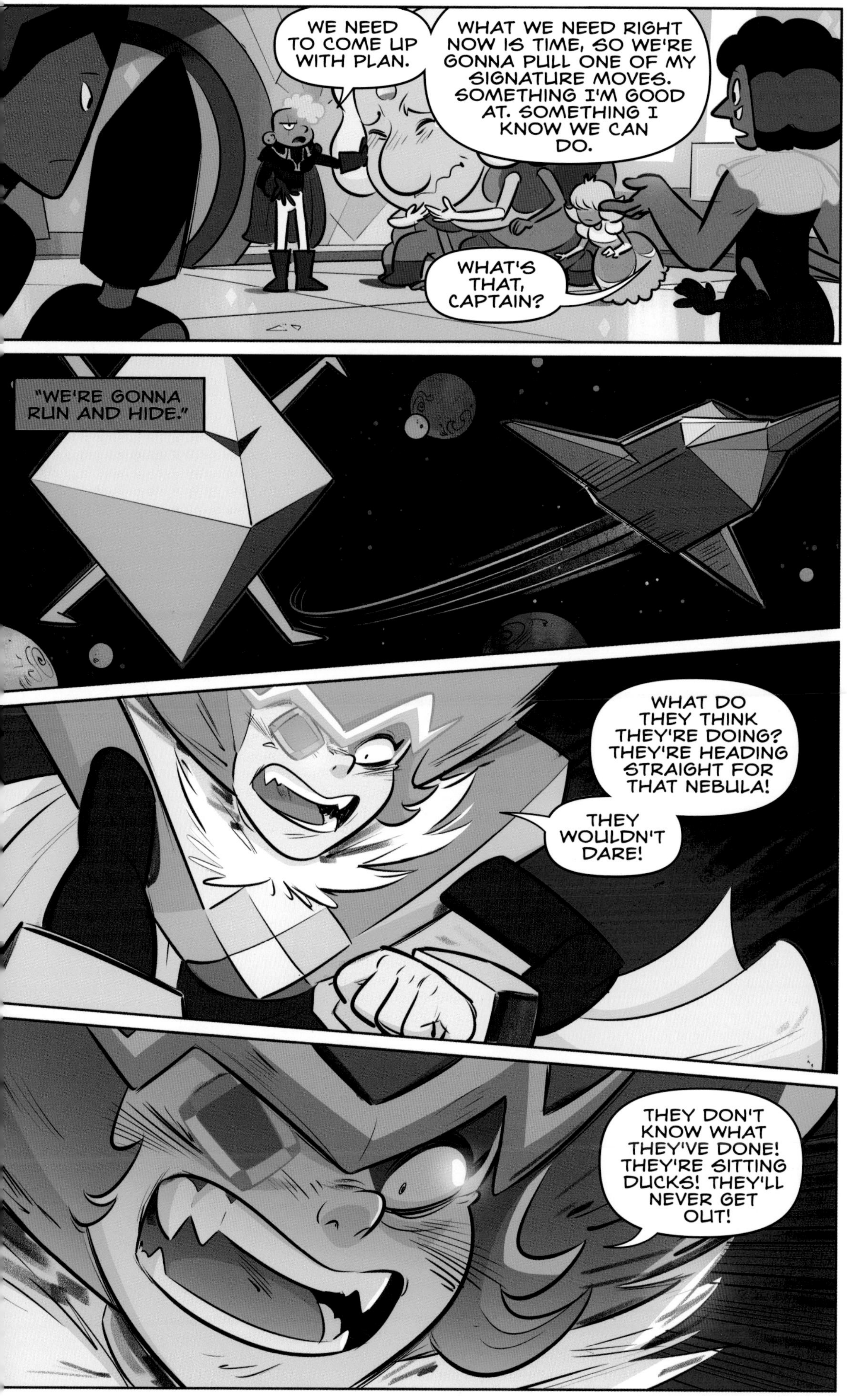
WE NEED TO COME UP WITH PLAN.
WHAT WE NEED RIGHT NOW IS TIME, SO WE'RE GONNA PULL ONE OF MY SIGNATURE MOVES. SOMETHING I'M GOOD AT. SOMETHING I KNOW WE CAN DO.
WHAT'S THAT, CAPTAIN?
"WE'RE GONNA RUN AND HIDE."
WHAT DO THEY THINK THEY'RE DOING? THEY'RE HEADING STRAIGHT FOR THAT NEBULA!
THEY WOULDN'T DARE!
THEY DON'T KNOW WHAT THEY'VE DONE! THEY'RE SITTING DUCKS! THEY'LL NEVER GET OUT!

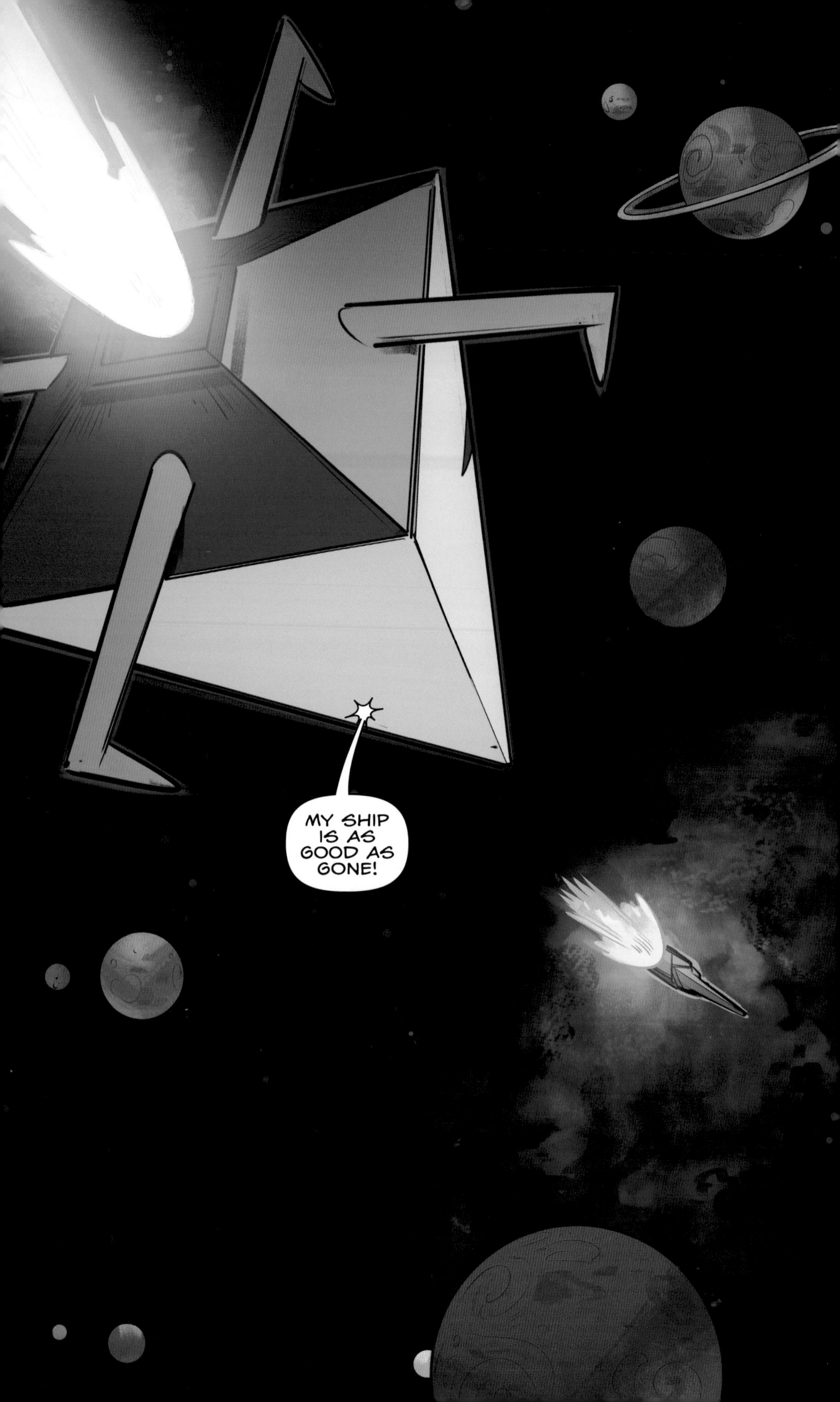
MY SHIP IS AS GOOD AS GONE!

Issue Twenty-Five Preorder Cover
FRANCESCA PERRONE

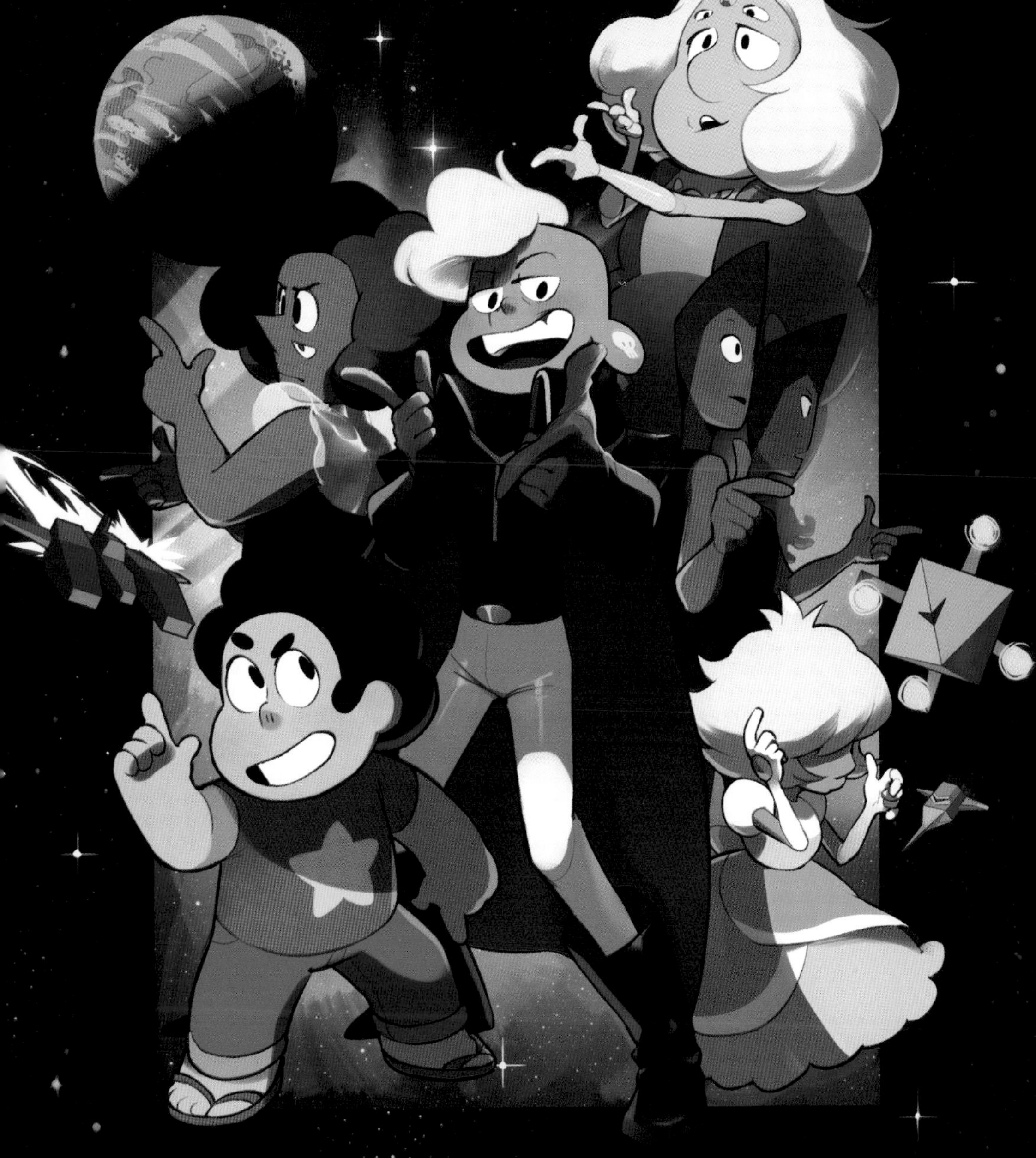

Issue Twenty-Six Main Cover
MISSY PEÑA

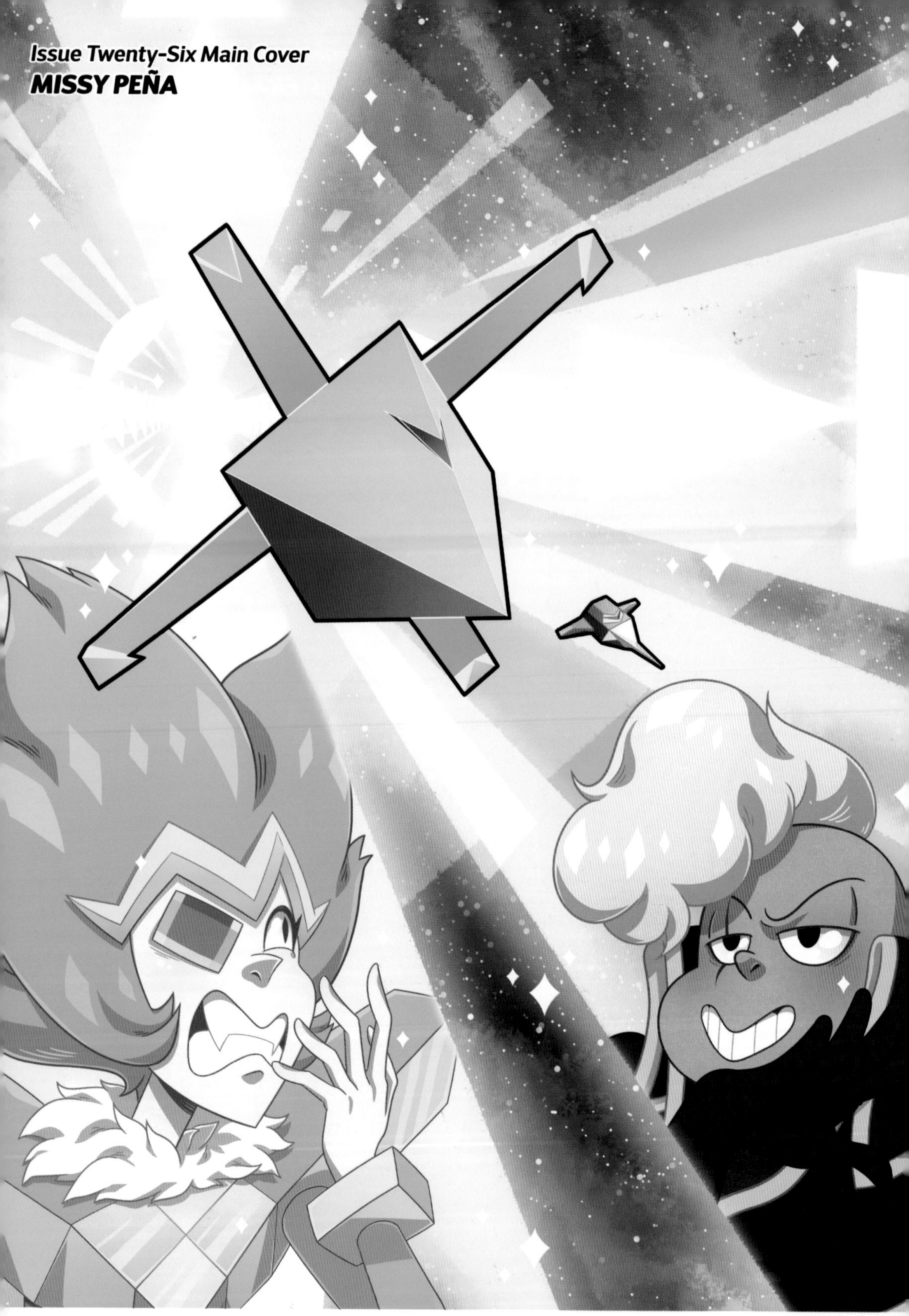

CHAPTER TWENTY-SIX

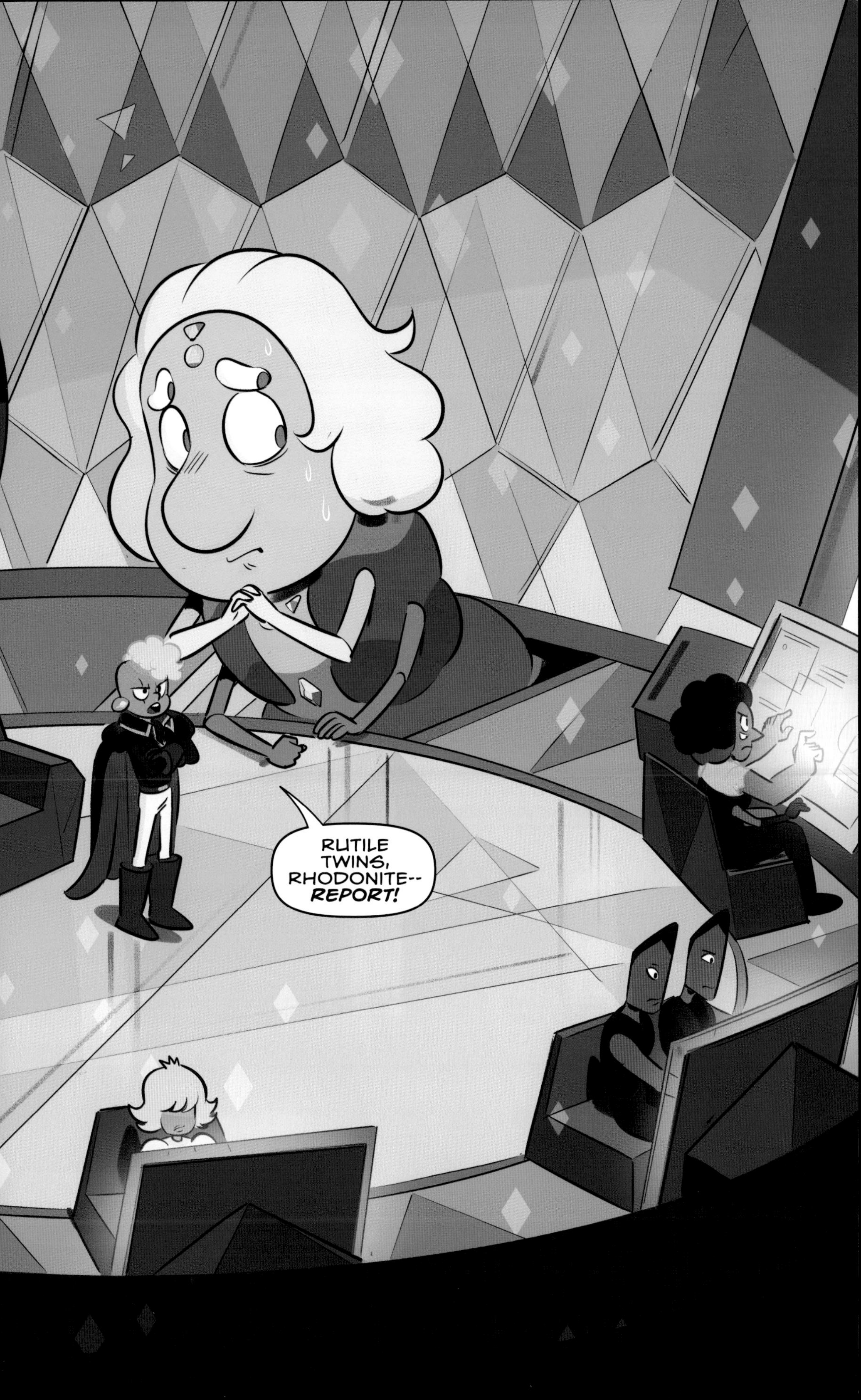
RUTILE TWINS, RHODONITE-- REPORT!

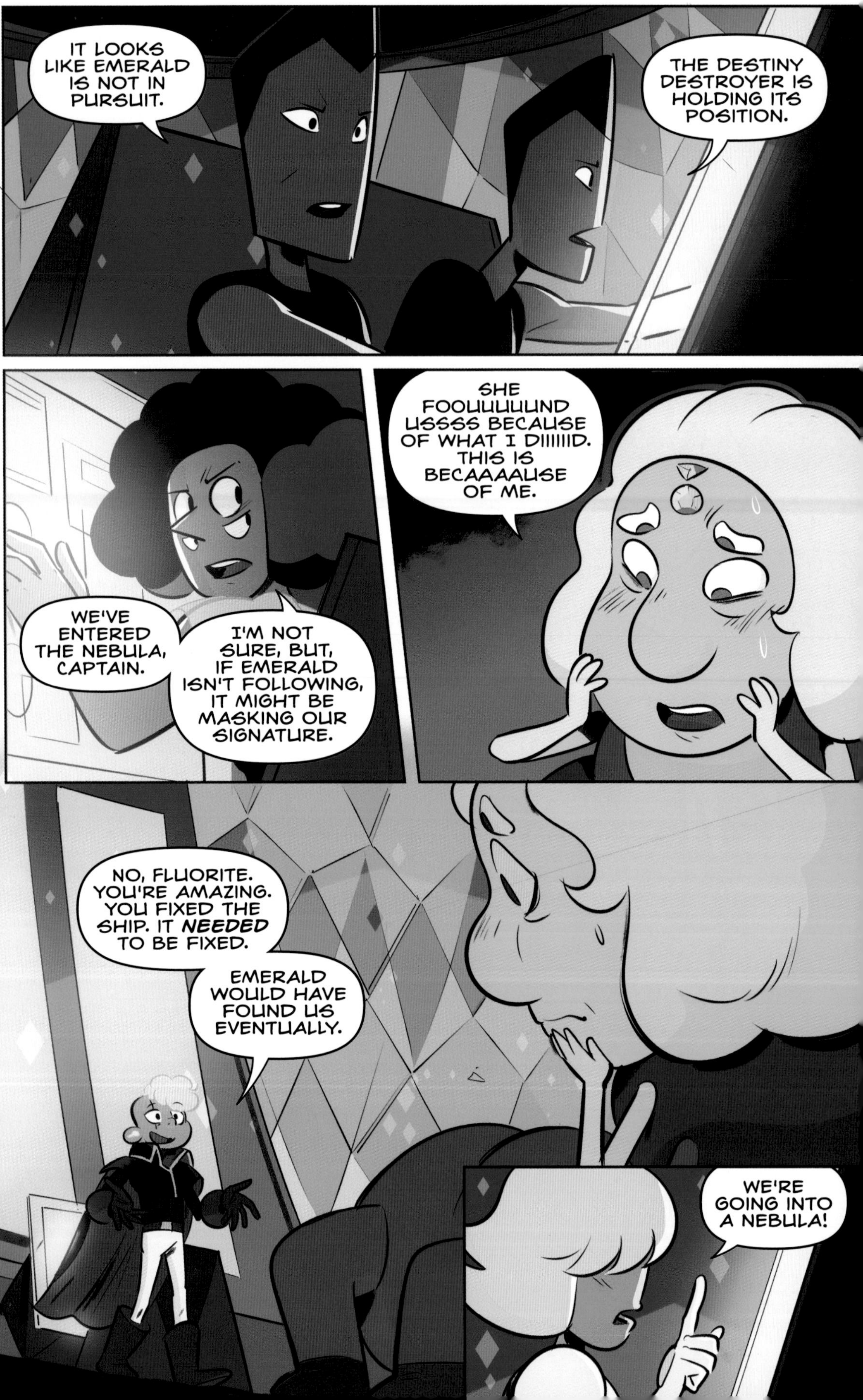
IT LOOKS LIKE EMERALD IS NOT IN PURSUIT.
THE DESTINY DESTROYER IS HOLDING ITS POSITION.
WE'VE ENTERED THE NEBULA, CAPTAIN.
I'M NOT SURE, BUT, IF EMERALD ISN'T FOLLOWING, IT MIGHT BE MASKING OUR SIGNATURE.
SHE FOOUUUUUUND USSSS BECAUSE OF WHAT I DIIIIIID. THIS IS BECAAAAUSE OF ME.
NO, FLUORITE. YOU'RE AMAZING. YOU FIXED THE SHIP. IT *NEEDED* TO BE FIXED.
EMERALD WOULD HAVE FOUND US EVENTUALLY.
WE'RE GOING INTO A NEBULA!

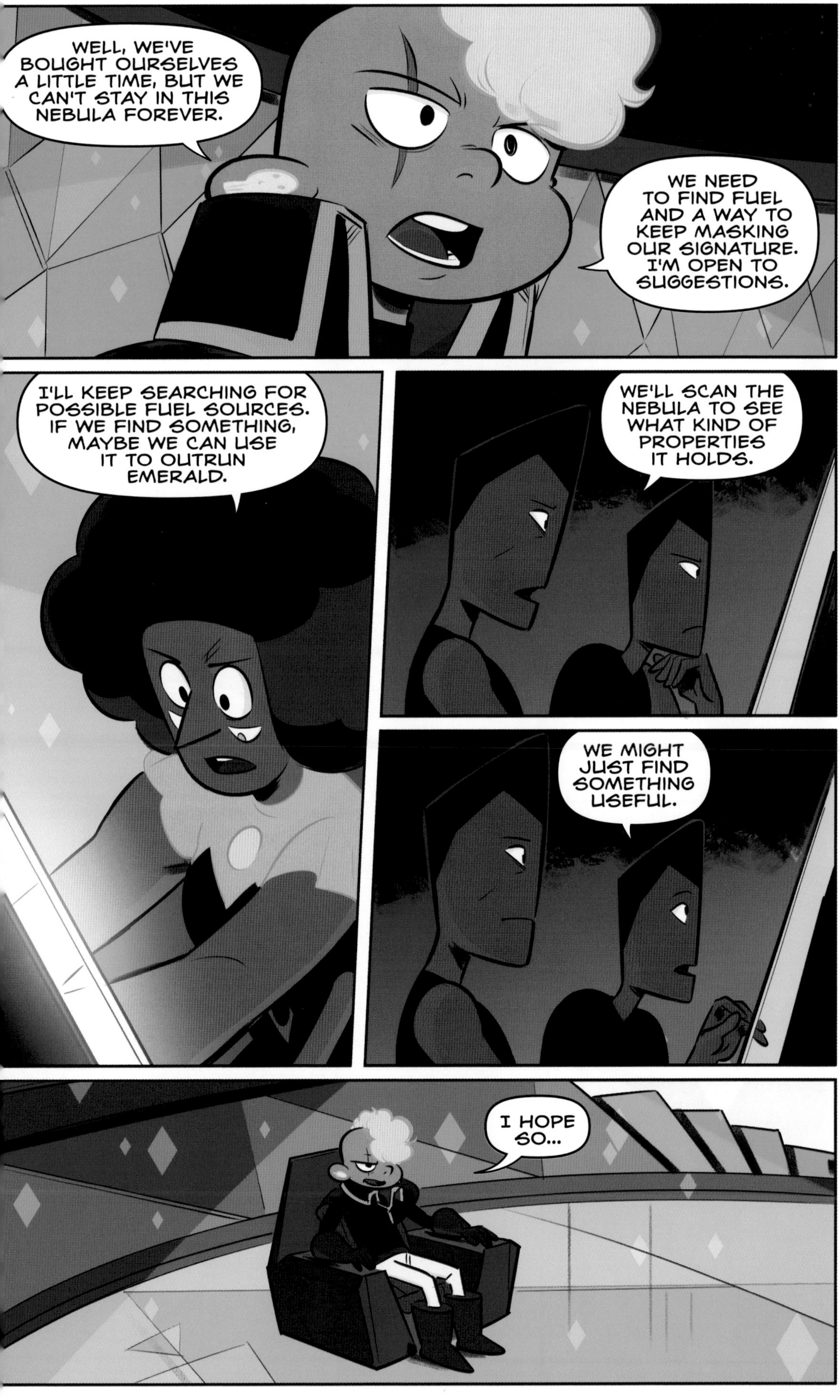
WELL, WE'VE BOUGHT OURSELVES A LITTLE TIME, BUT WE CAN'T STAY IN THIS NEBULA FOREVER.
WE NEED TO FIND FUEL AND A WAY TO KEEP MASKING OUR SIGNATURE. I'M OPEN TO SUGGESTIONS.
I'LL KEEP SEARCHING FOR POSSIBLE FUEL SOURCES. IF WE FIND SOMETHING, MAYBE WE CAN USE IT TO OUTRUN EMERALD.
WE'LL SCAN THE NEBULA TO SEE WHAT KIND OF PROPERTIES IT HOLDS.
WE MIGHT JUST FIND SOMETHING USEFUL.
I HOPE SO...

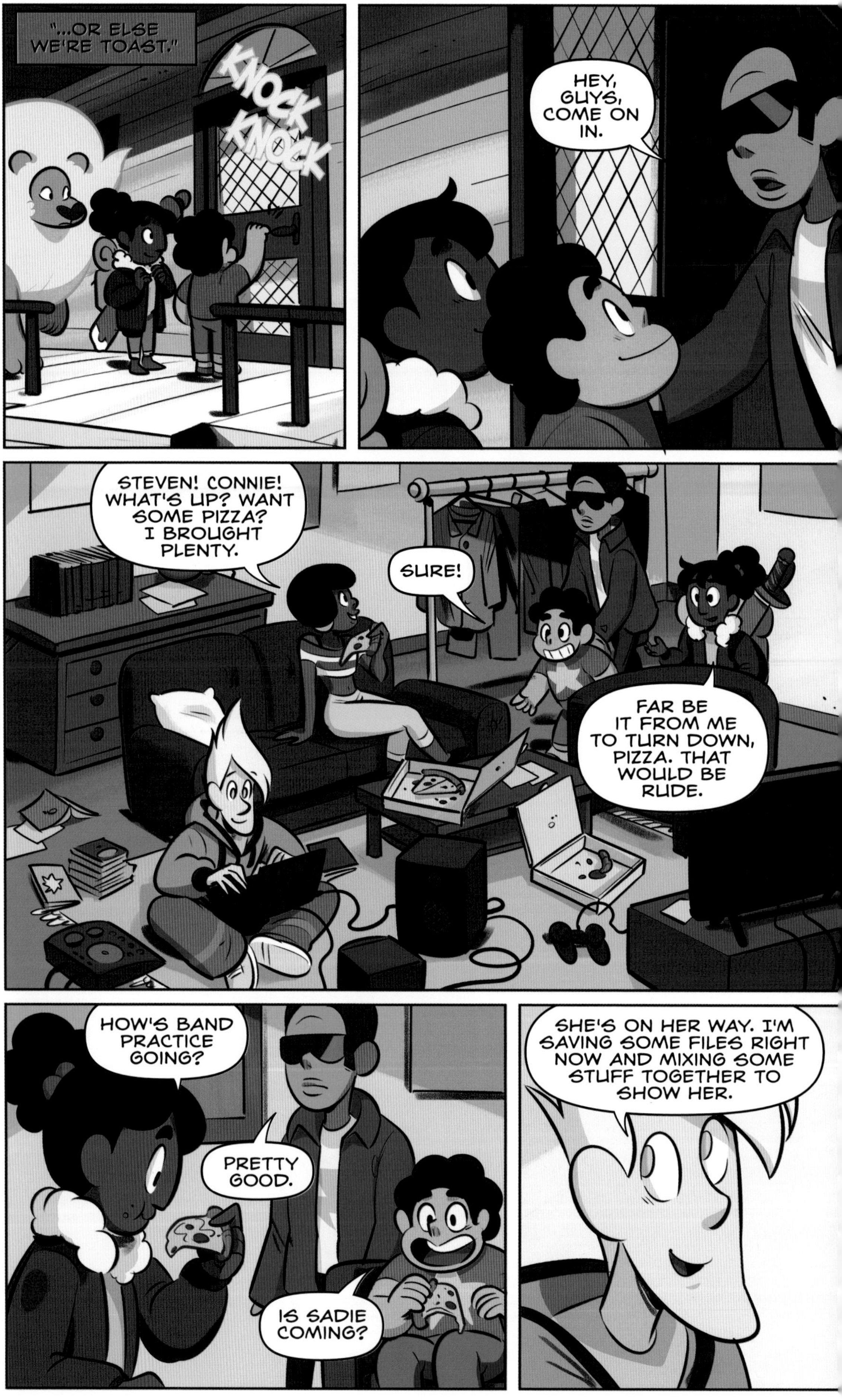
"...OR ELSE WE'RE TOAST."
KNOCK KNOCK
HEY, GUYS, COME ON IN.
STEVEN! CONNIE! WHAT'S UP? WANT SOME PIZZA? I BROUGHT PLENTY.
SURE!
FAR BE IT FROM ME TO TURN DOWN, PIZZA. THAT WOULD BE RUDE.
HOW'S BAND PRACTICE GOING?
PRETTY GOOD.
IS SADIE COMING?
SHE'S ON HER WAY. I'M SAVING SOME FILES RIGHT NOW AND MIXING SOME STUFF TOGETHER TO SHOW HER.

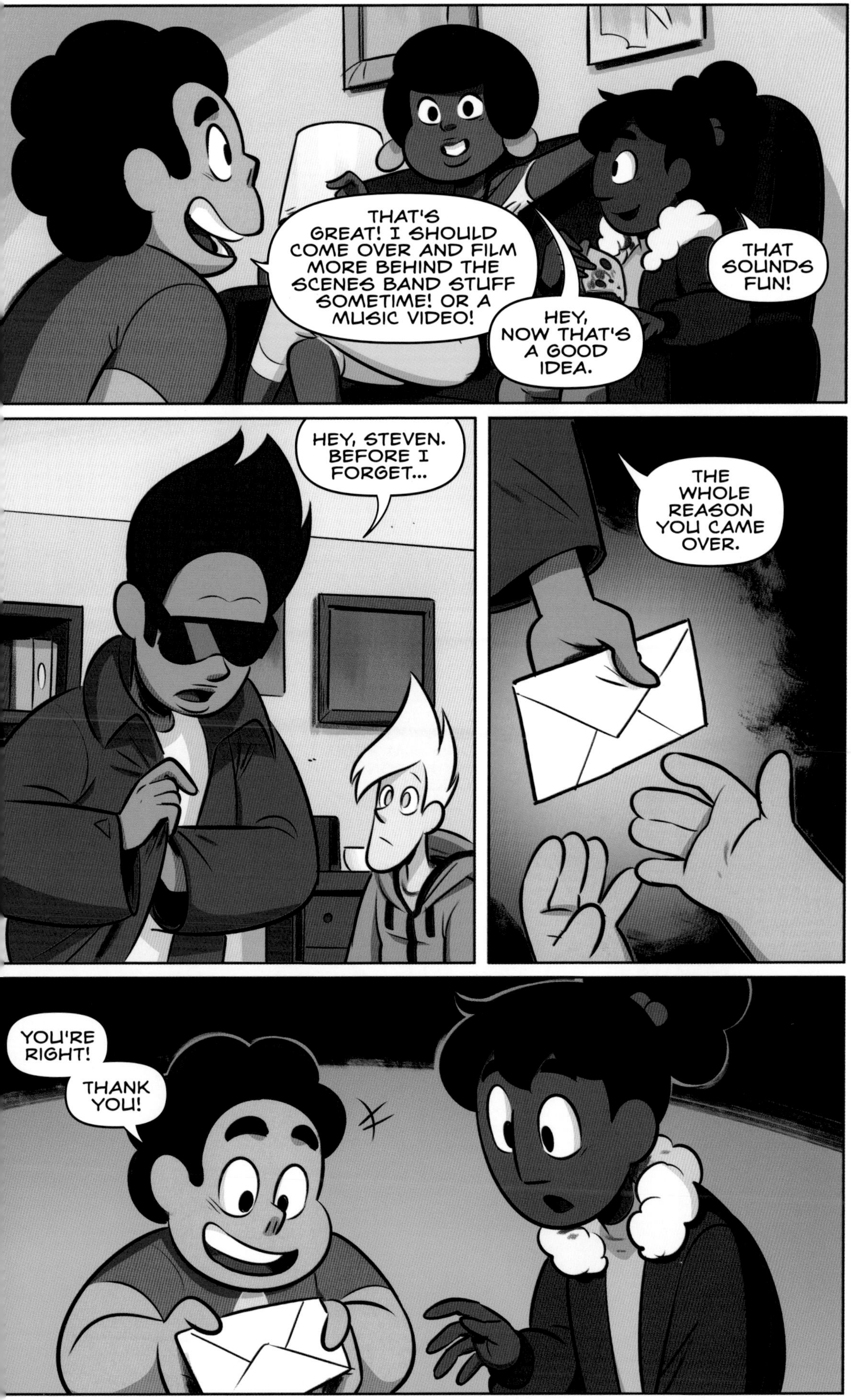
THAT'S GREAT! I SHOULD COME OVER AND FILM MORE BEHIND THE SCENES BAND STUFF SOMETIME! OR A MUSIC VIDEO!
HEY, NOW THAT'S A GOOD IDEA.
THAT SOUNDS FUN!
HEY, STEVEN. BEFORE I FORGET...
THE WHOLE REASON YOU CAME OVER.
YOU'RE RIGHT!
THANK YOU!

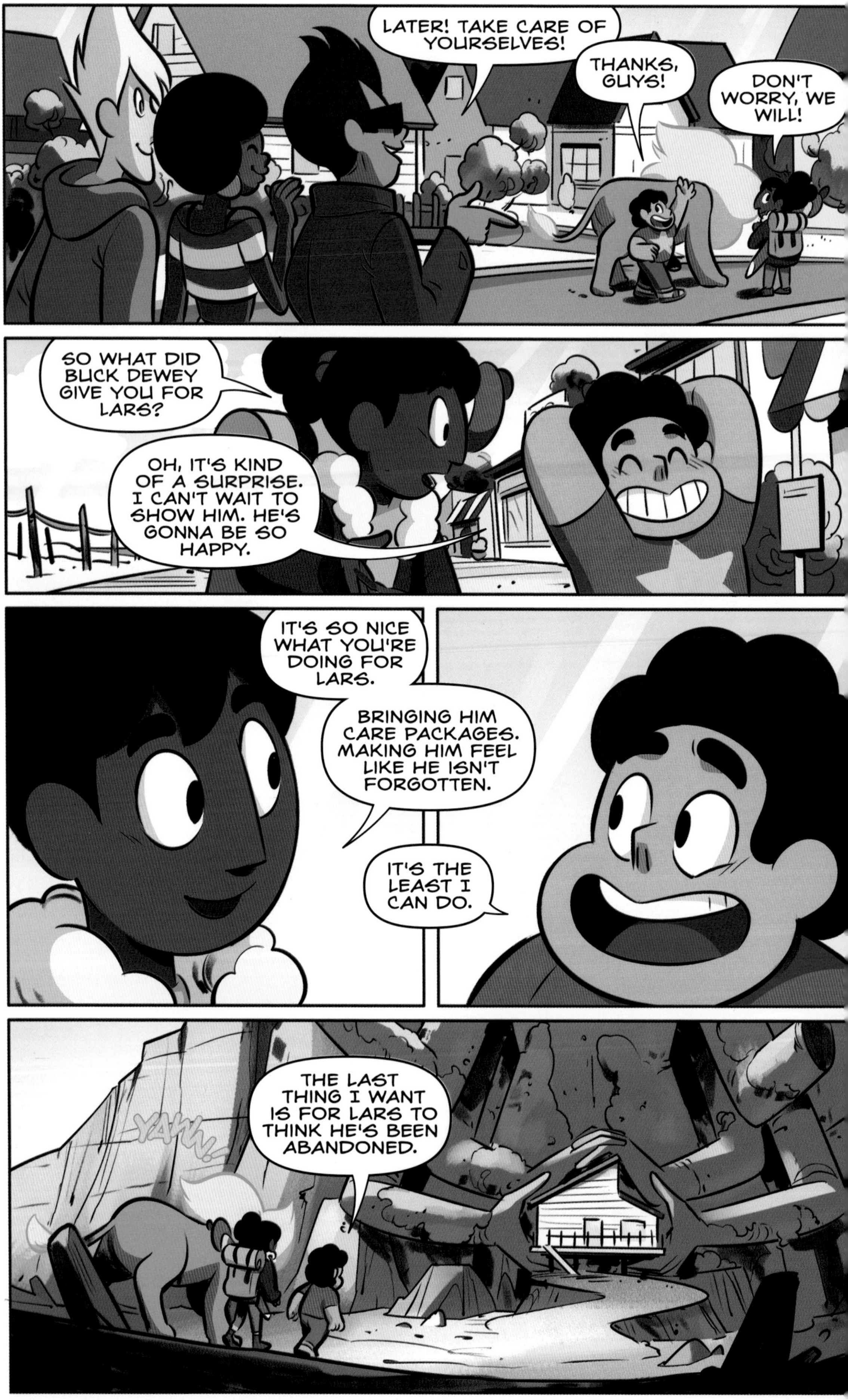
LATER! TAKE CARE OF YOURSELVES!
THANKS, GUYS!
DON'T WORRY, WE WILL!
SO WHAT DID BUCK DEWEY GIVE YOU FOR LARS?
OH, IT'S KIND OF A SURPRISE. I CAN'T WAIT TO SHOW HIM. HE'S GONNA BE SO HAPPY.
IT'S SO NICE WHAT YOU'RE DOING FOR LARS.
BRINGING HIM CARE PACKAGES. MAKING HIM FEEL LIKE HE ISN'T FORGOTTEN.
IT'S THE LEAST I CAN DO.
YAWN!
THE LAST THING I WANT IS FOR LARS TO THINK HE'S BEEN ABANDONED.

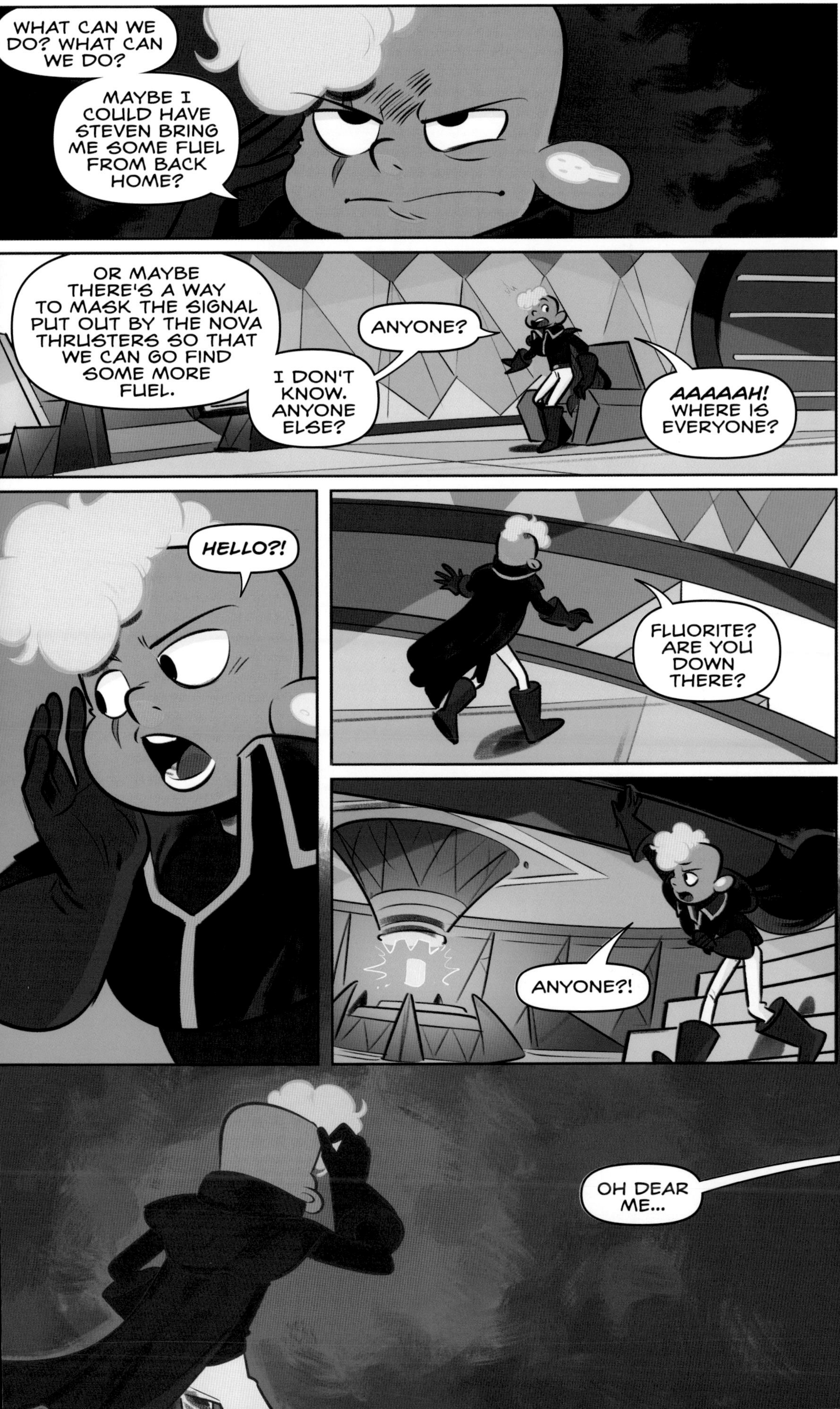
WHAT CAN WE DO? WHAT CAN WE DO?
MAYBE I COULD HAVE STEVEN BRING ME SOME FUEL FROM BACK HOME?
OR MAYBE THERE'S A WAY TO MASK THE SIGNAL PUT OUT BY THE NOVA THRUSTERS SO THAT WE CAN GO FIND SOME MORE FUEL.
I DON'T KNOW. ANYONE ELSE?
ANYONE?
AAAAAH! WHERE IS EVERYONE?
HELLO?!
FLUORITE? ARE YOU DOWN THERE?
ANYONE?!
OH DEAR ME...

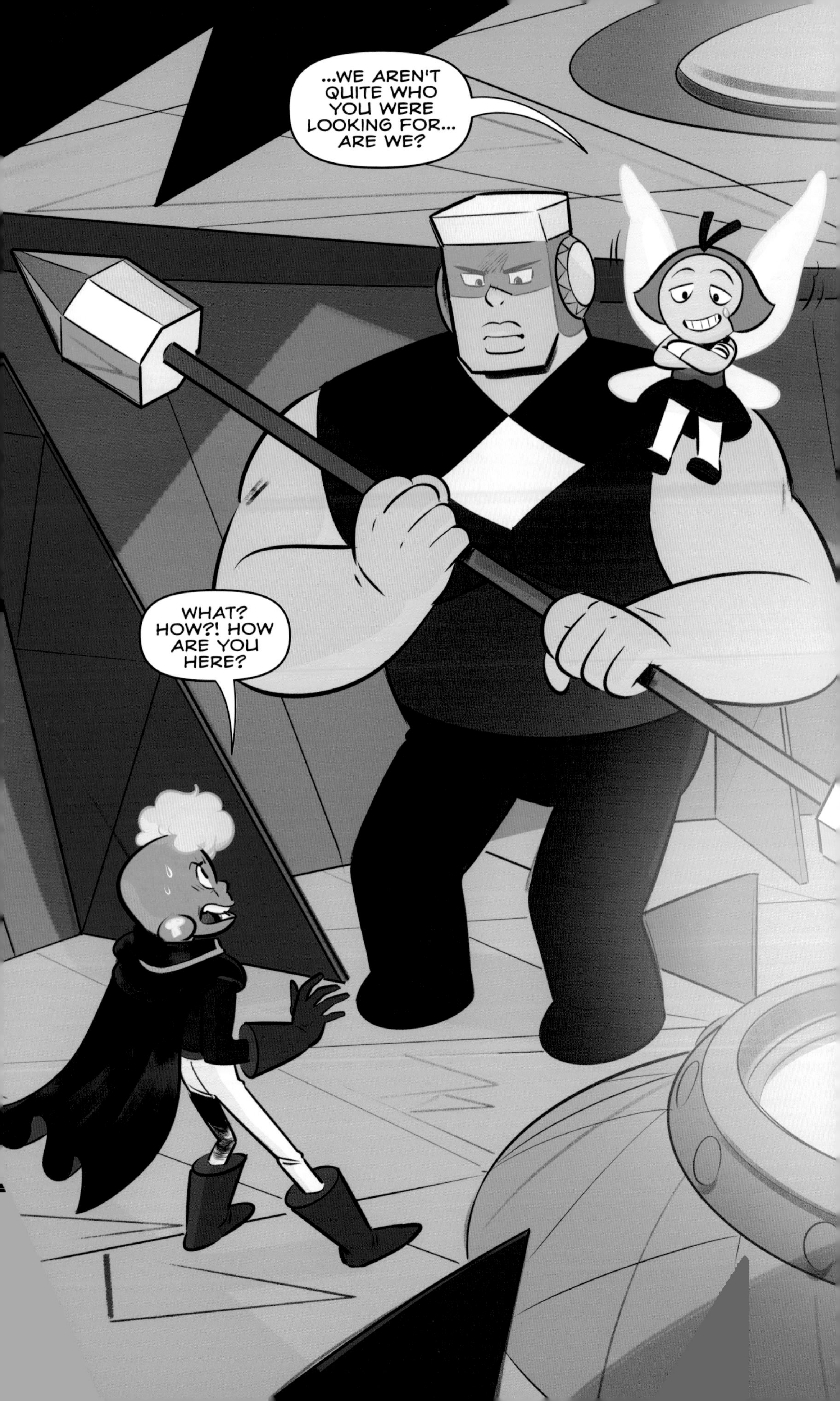
...WE AREN'T QUITE WHO YOU WERE LOOKING FOR... ARE WE?
WHAT? HOW?! HOW ARE YOU HERE?

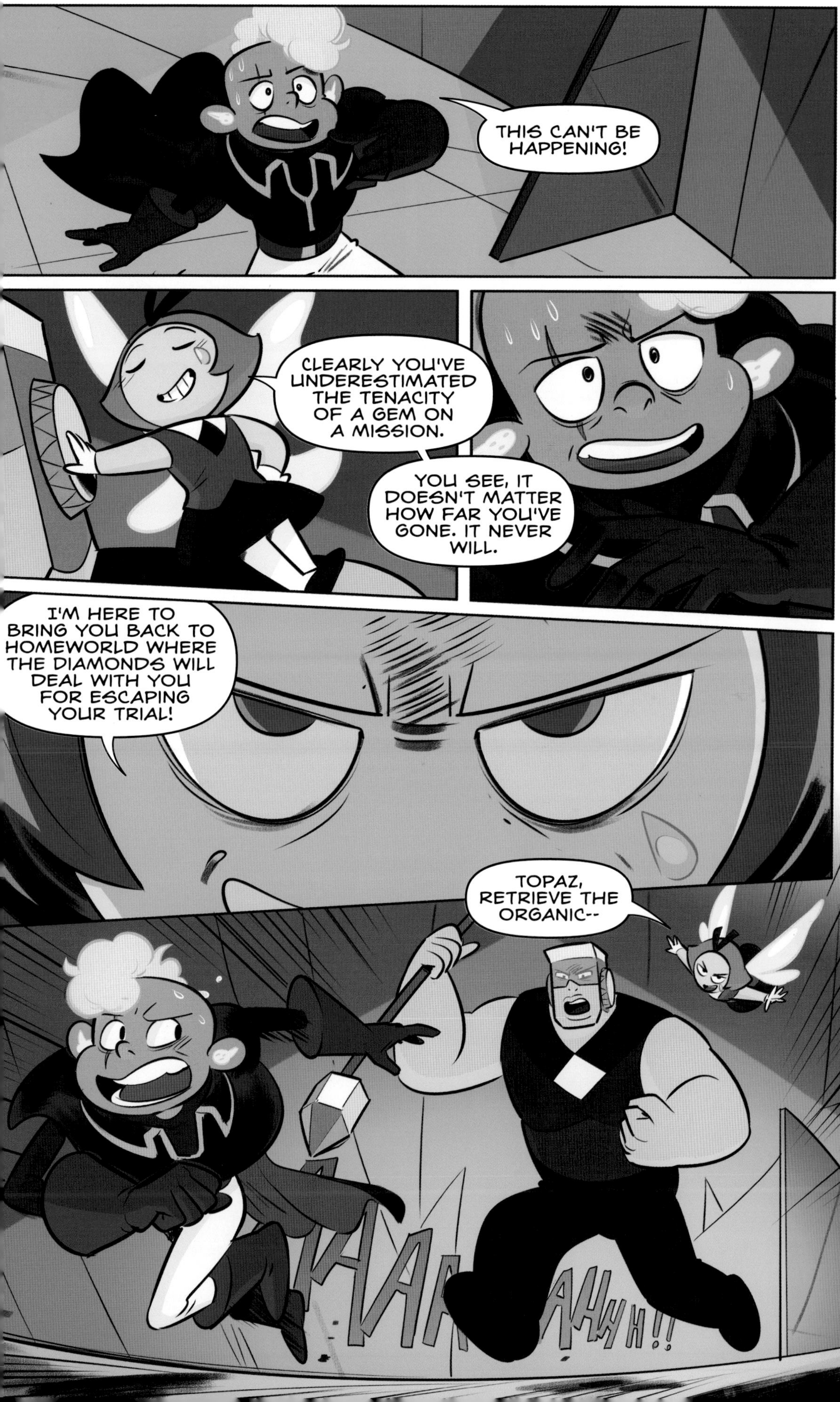
THIS CAN'T BE HAPPENING!
CLEARLY YOU'VE UNDERESTIMATED THE TENACITY OF A GEM ON A MISSION.
YOU SEE, IT DOESN'T MATTER HOW FAR YOU'VE GONE. IT NEVER WILL.
I'M HERE TO BRING YOU BACK TO HOMEWORLD WHERE THE DIAMONDS WILL DEAL WITH YOU FOR ESCAPING YOUR TRIAL!
TOPAZ, RETRIEVE THE ORGANIC--
AAAHHH!!

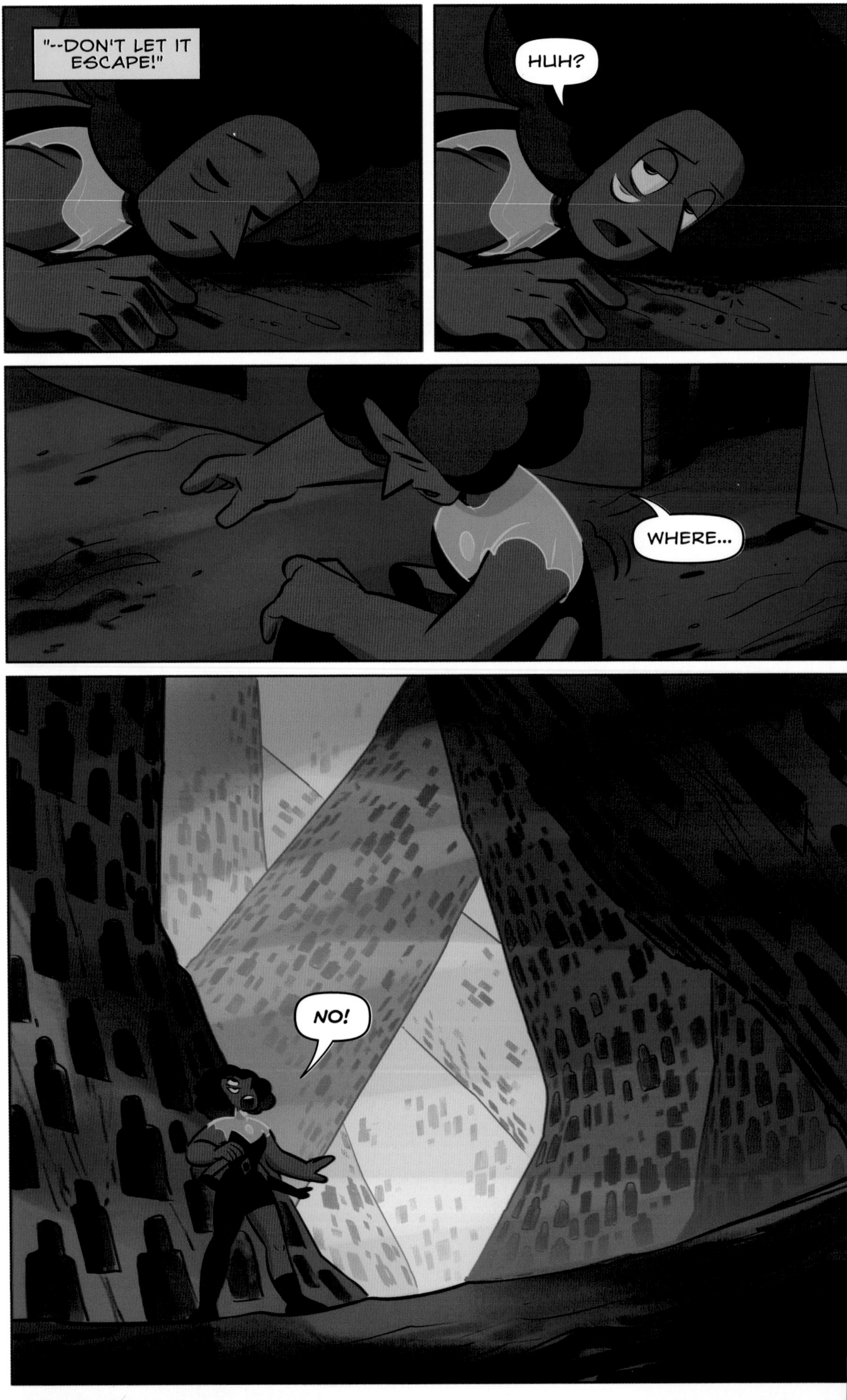
"--DON'T LET IT ESCAPE!"
HUH?
WHERE...
NO!

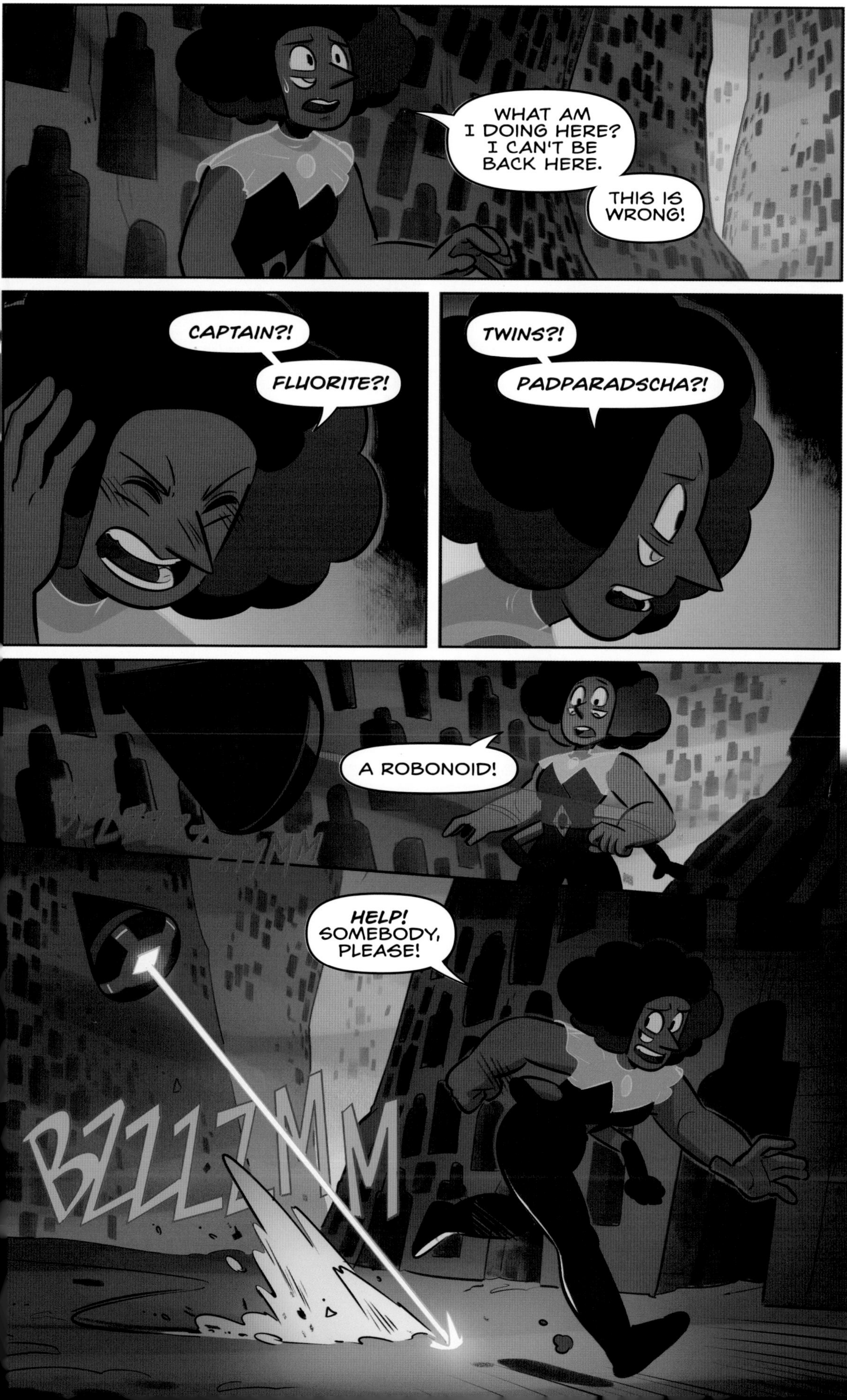
WHAT AM I DOING HERE? I CAN'T BE BACK HERE.
THIS IS WRONG!
CAPTAIN?!
FLUORITE?!
TWINS?!
PADPARADSCHA?!
A ROBONOID!
HELP! SOMEBODY, PLEASE!
BZZZMM

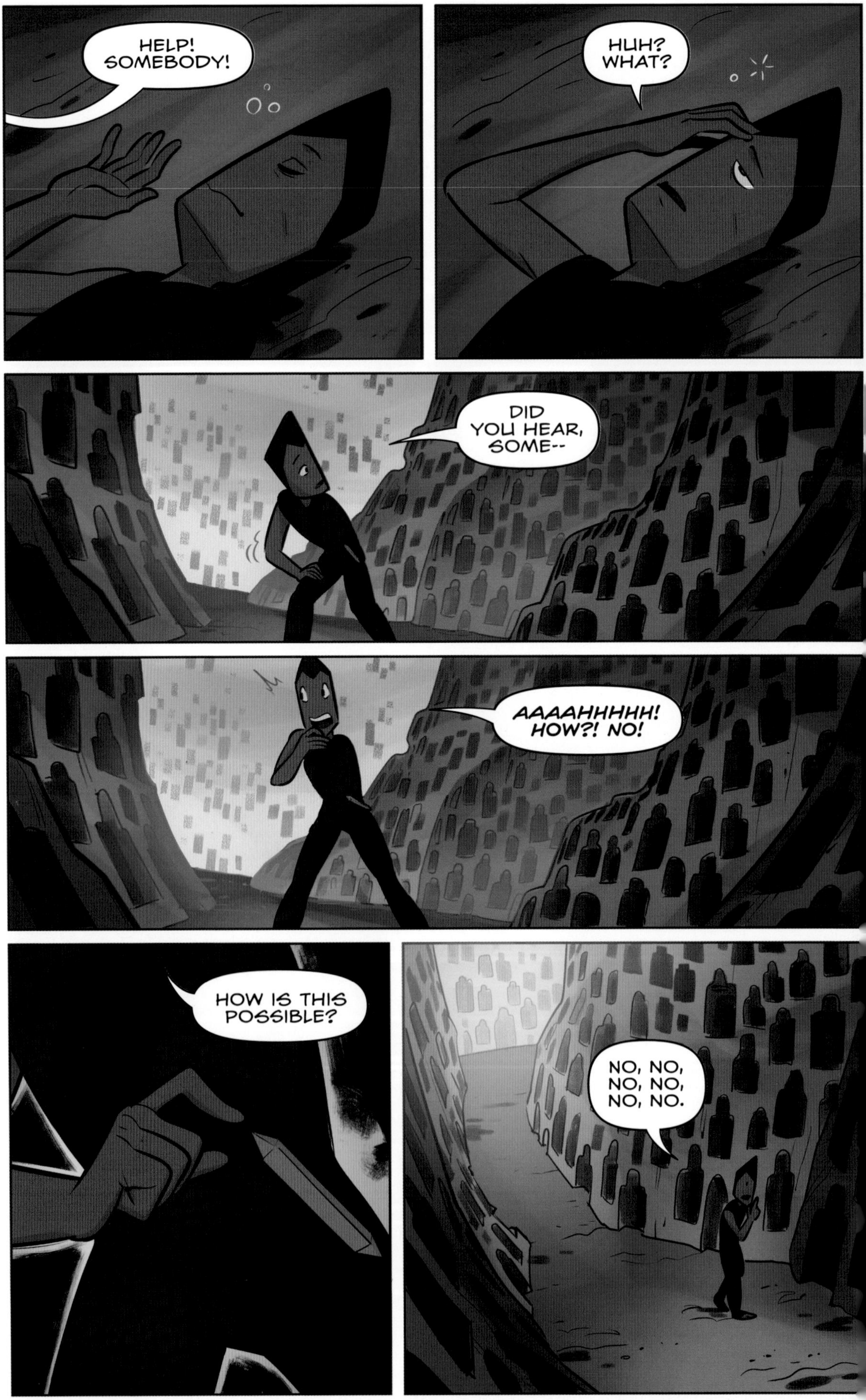
HELP! SOMEBODY!
HUH? WHAT?
DID YOU HEAR, SOME--
AAAAHHHHH! HOW?! NO!
HOW IS THIS POSSIBLE?
NO, NO, NO, NO, NO, NO.

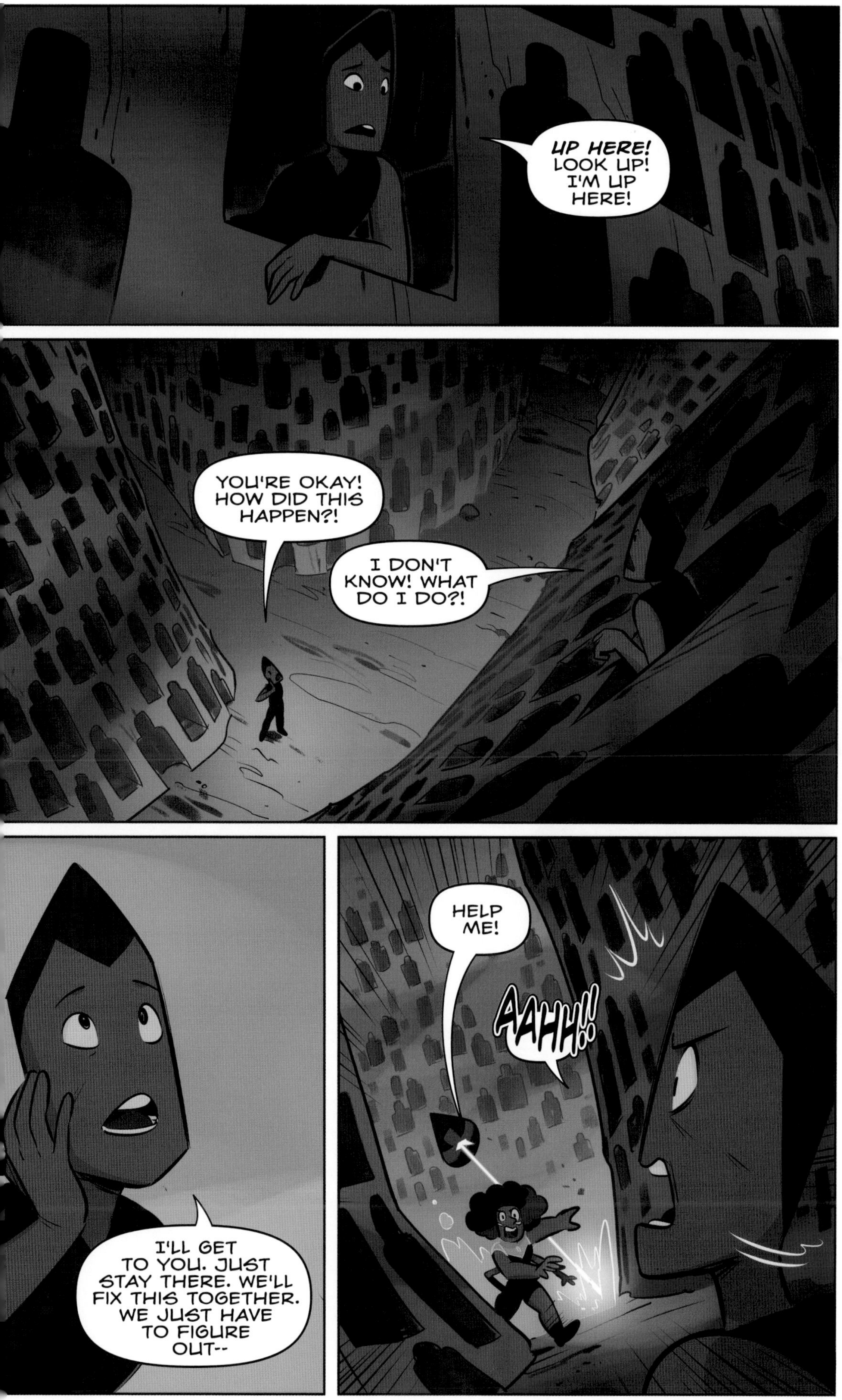
UP HERE! LOOK UP! I'M UP HERE!
YOU'RE OKAY! HOW DID THIS HAPPEN?!
I DON'T KNOW! WHAT DO I DO?!
I'LL GET TO YOU. JUST STAY THERE. WE'LL FIX THIS TOGETHER. WE JUST HAVE TO FIGURE OUT--
HELP ME!
AAHH!!

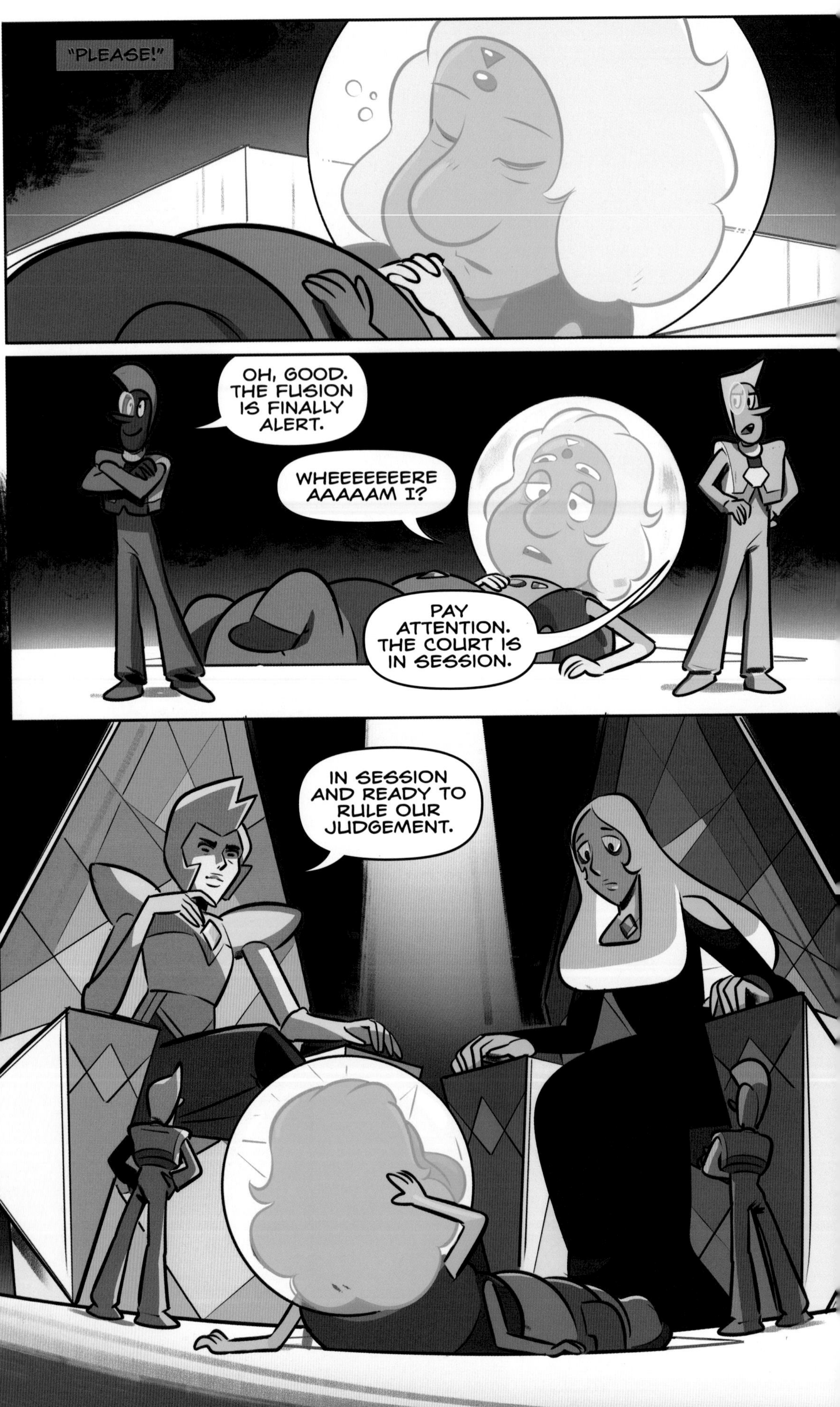
"PLEASE!"
OH, GOOD. THE FUSION IS FINALLY ALERT.
WHEEEEEEERE AAAAAM I?
PAY ATTENTION. THE COURT IS IN SESSION.
IN SESSION AND READY TO RULE OUR JUDGEMENT.

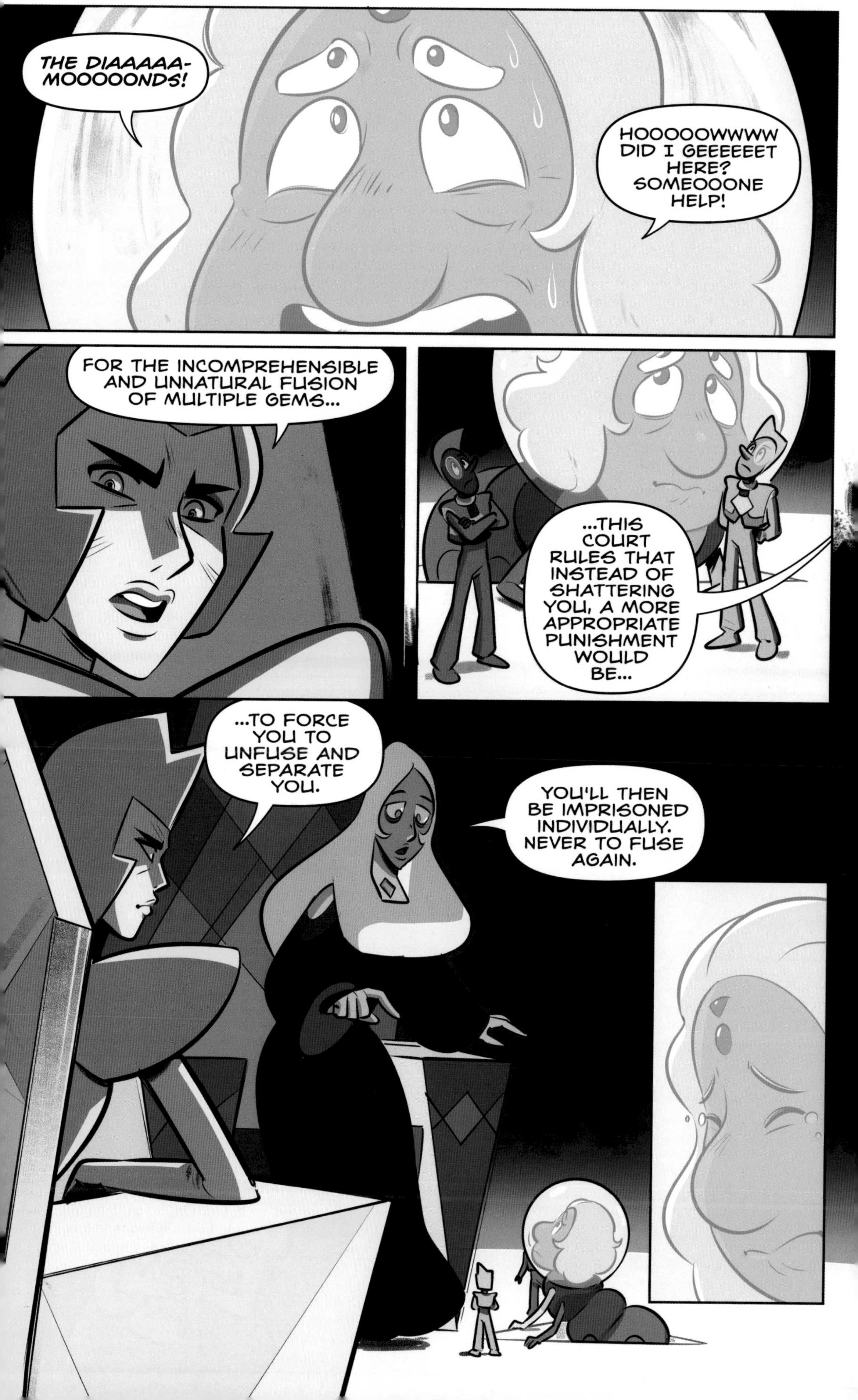
THE DIAAAAA-MOOOOONDS!
HOOOOOWWWW DID I GEEEEEET HERE? SOMEOOONE HELP!
FOR THE INCOMPREHENSIBLE AND UNNATURAL FUSION OF MULTIPLE GEMS...
...THIS COURT RULES THAT INSTEAD OF SHATTERING YOU, A MORE APPROPRIATE PUNISHMENT WOULD BE...
...TO FORCE YOU TO UNFUSE AND SEPARATE YOU.
YOU'LL THEN BE IMPRISONED INDIVIDUALLY. NEVER TO FUSE AGAIN.

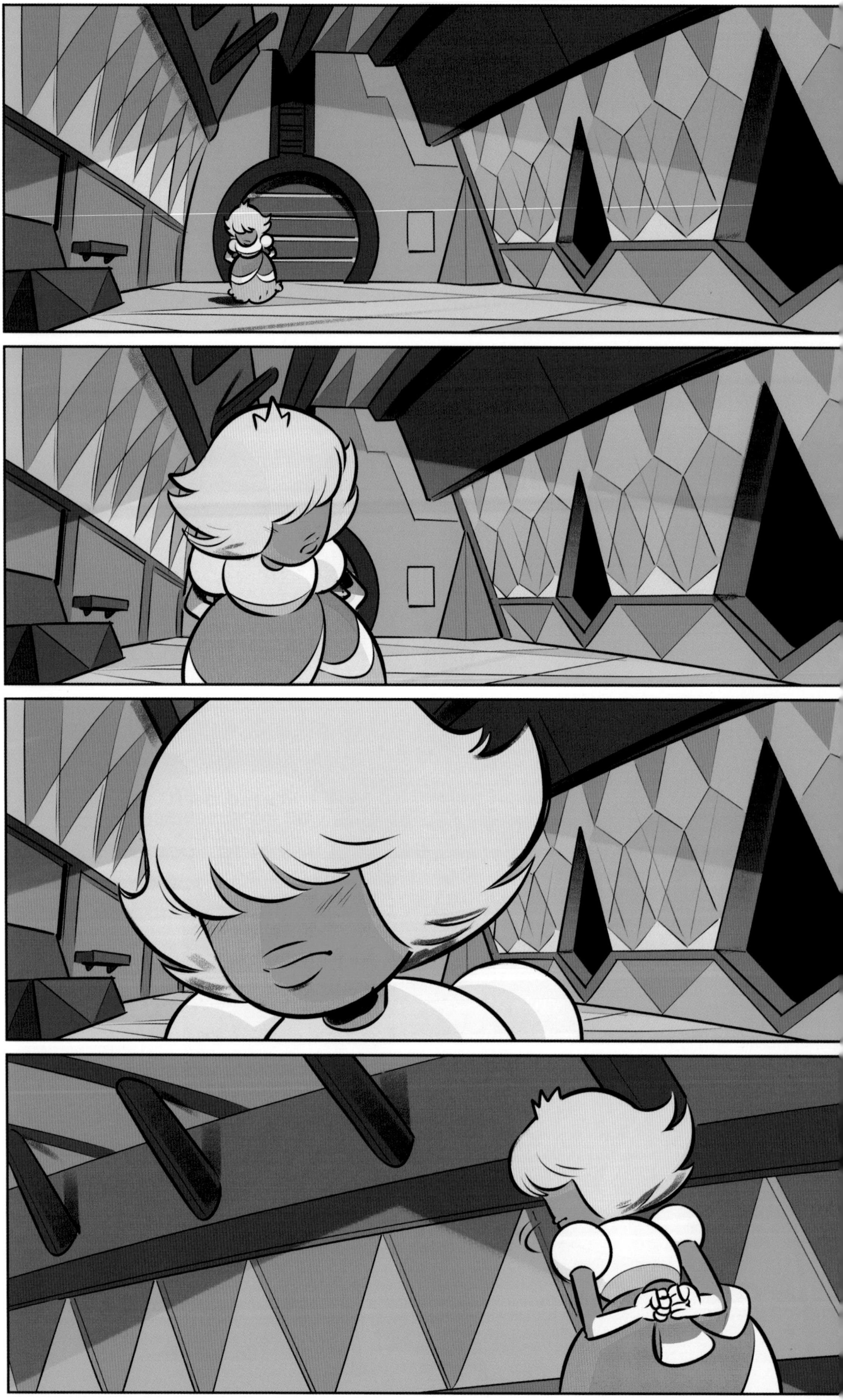

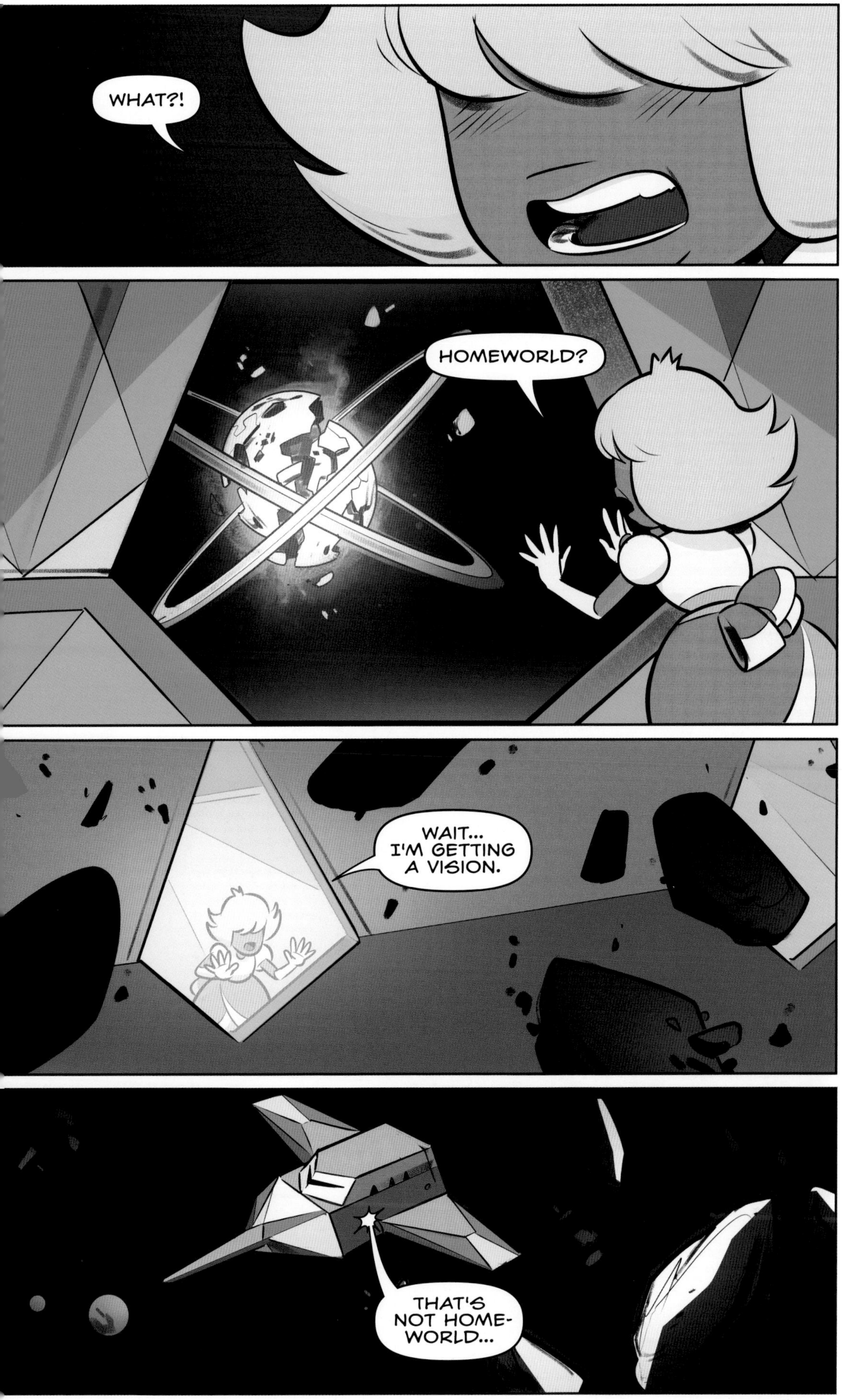
WHAT?!
HOMEWORLD?
WAIT... I'M GETTING A VISION.
THAT'S NOT HOME-WORLD...

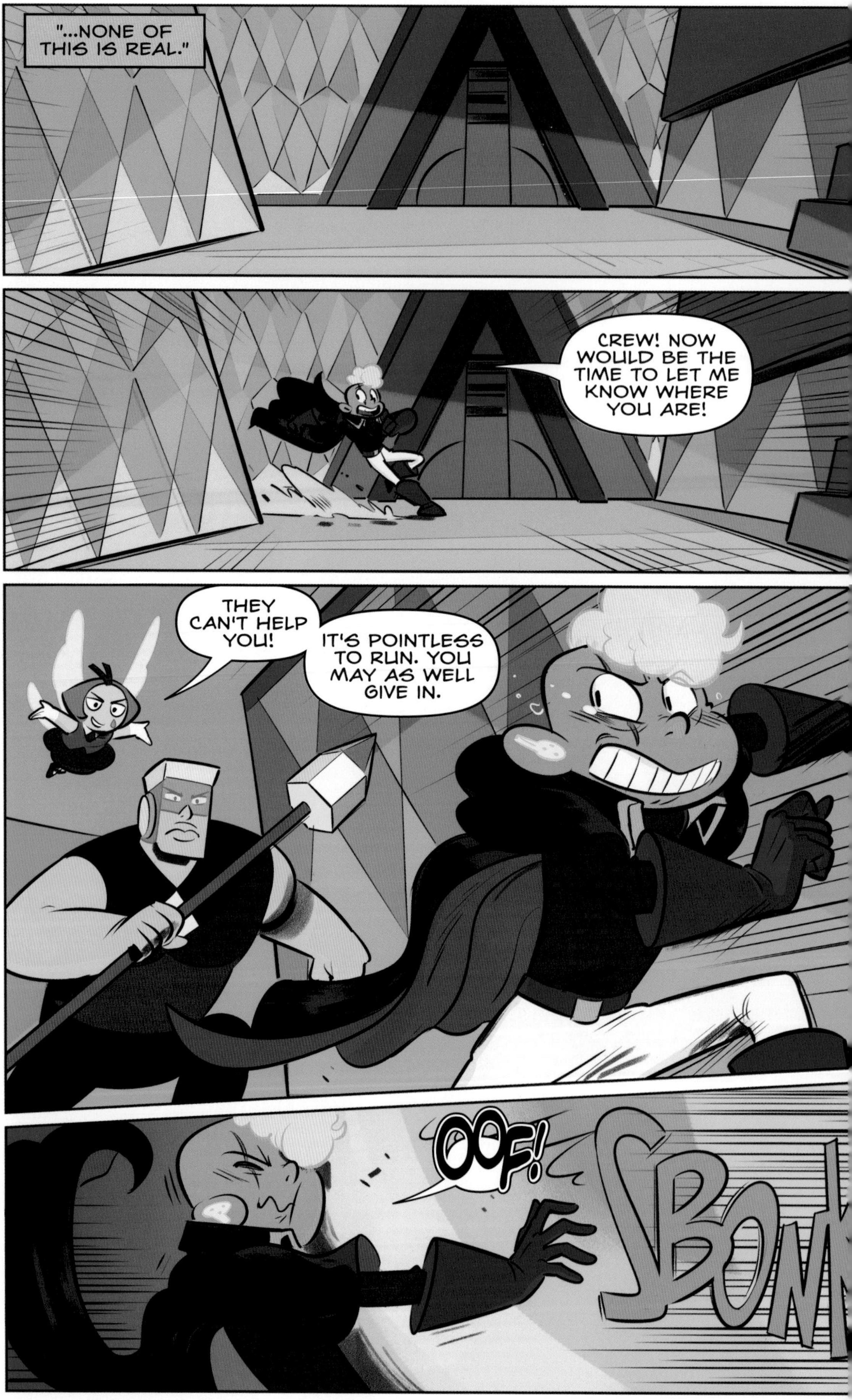
"...NONE OF
THIS IS REAL."
CREW! NOW
WOULD BE THE
TIME TO LET ME
KNOW WHERE
YOU ARE!
THEY
CAN'T HELP
YOU!
IT'S POINTLESS
TO RUN. YOU
MAY AS WELL
GIVE IN.
OOF!

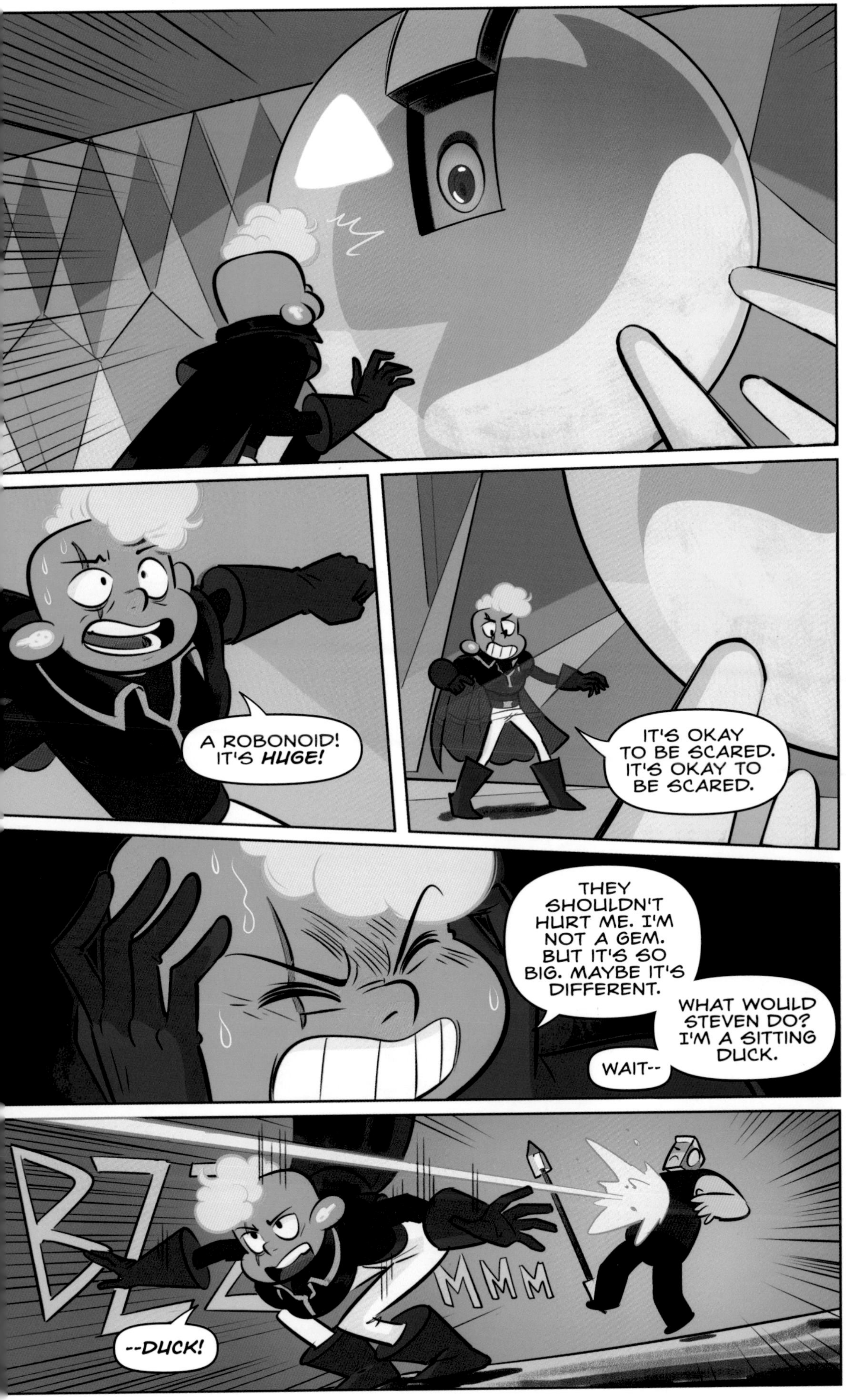
A ROBONOID! IT'S *HUGE!*
IT'S OKAY TO BE SCARED. IT'S OKAY TO BE SCARED.
THEY SHOULDN'T HURT ME. I'M NOT A GEM. BUT IT'S SO BIG. MAYBE IT'S DIFFERENT.
WHAT WOULD STEVEN DO? I'M A SITTING DUCK.
WAIT--
BZZMMM
--DUCK!

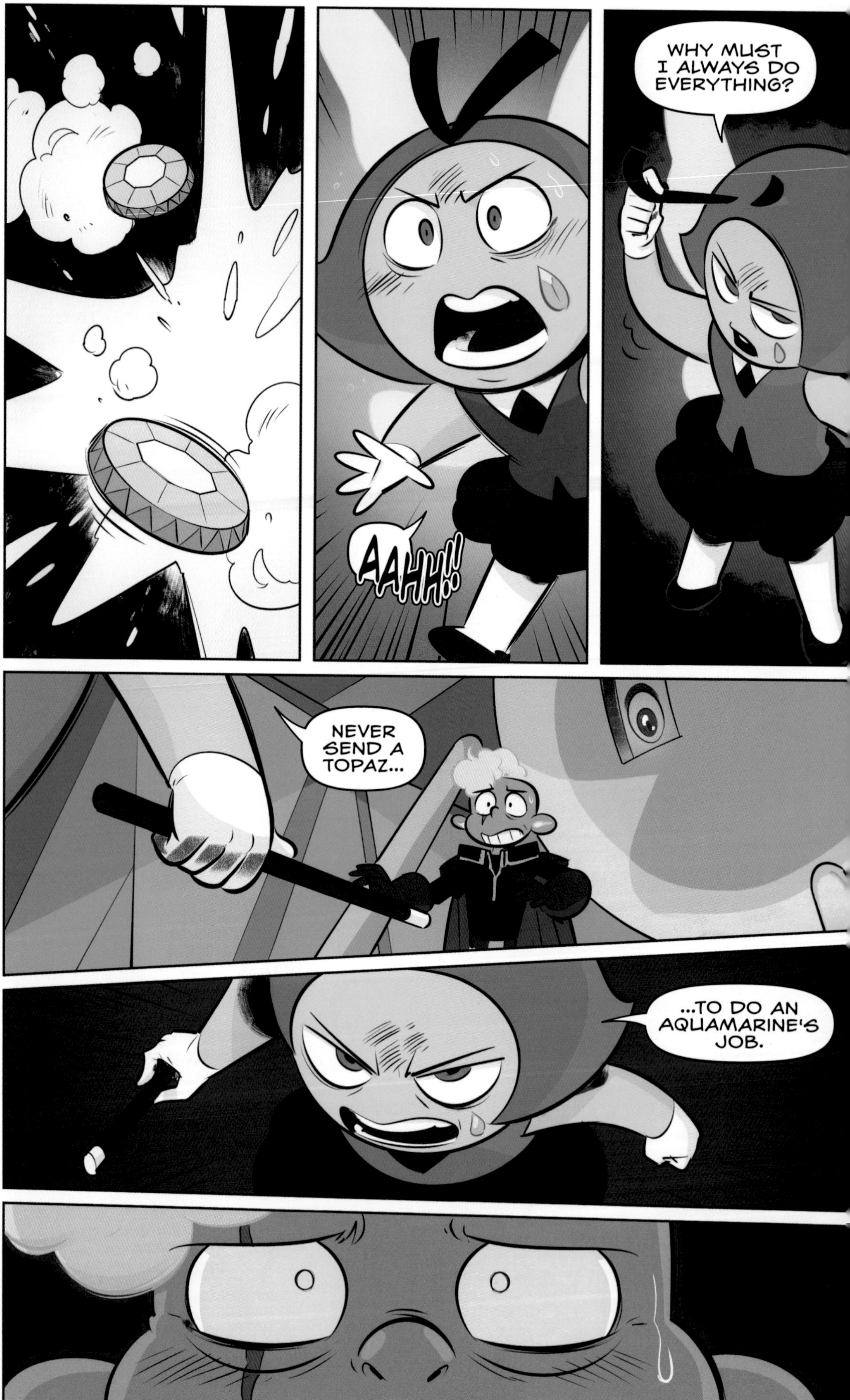
AAHH!!
WHY MUST I ALWAYS DO EVERYTHING?
NEVER SEND A TOPAZ...
...TO DO AN AQUAMARINE'S JOB.

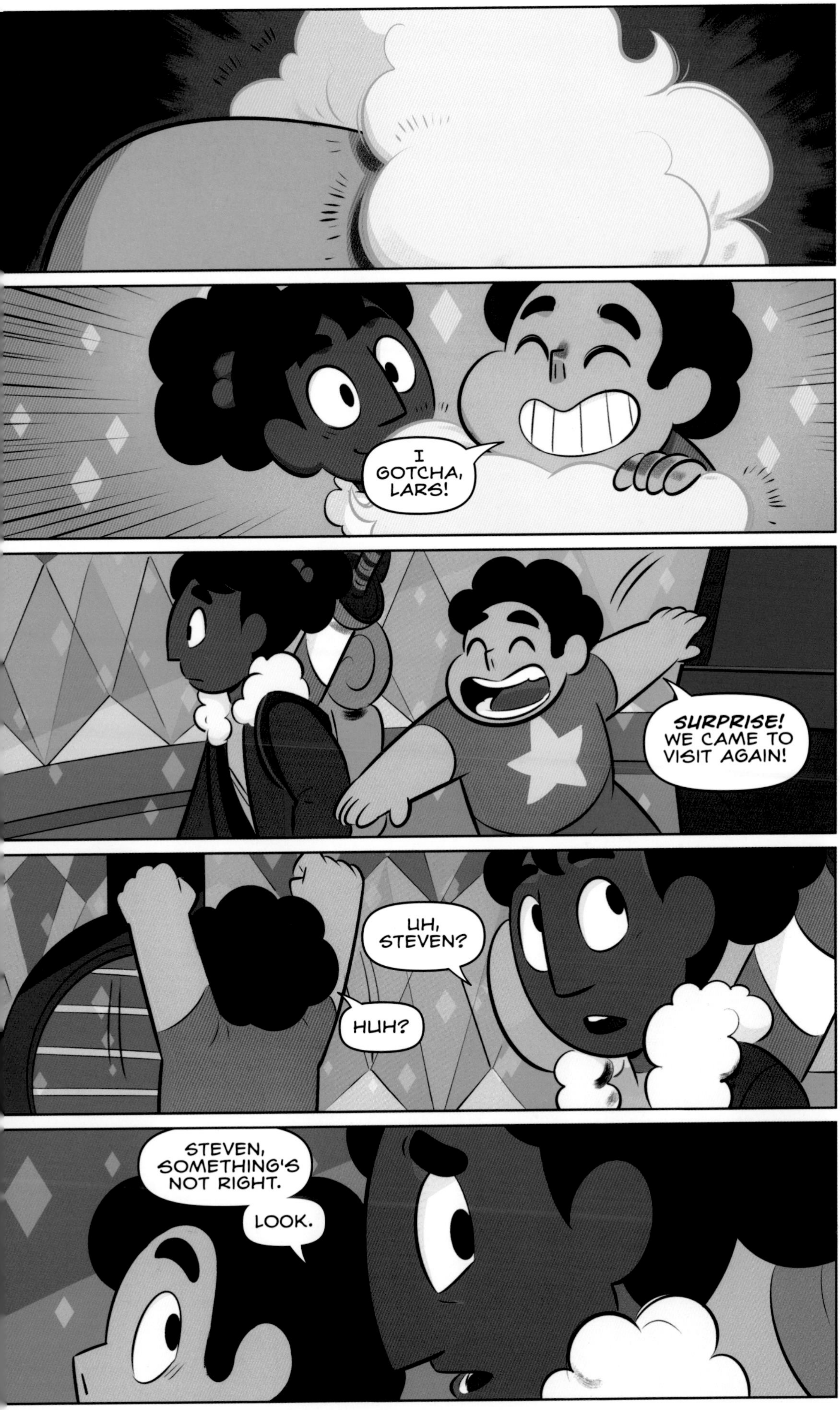
I GOTCHA, LARS!
SURPRISE! WE CAME TO VISIT AGAIN!
UH, STEVEN?
HUH?
STEVEN, SOMETHING'S NOT RIGHT.
LOOK.

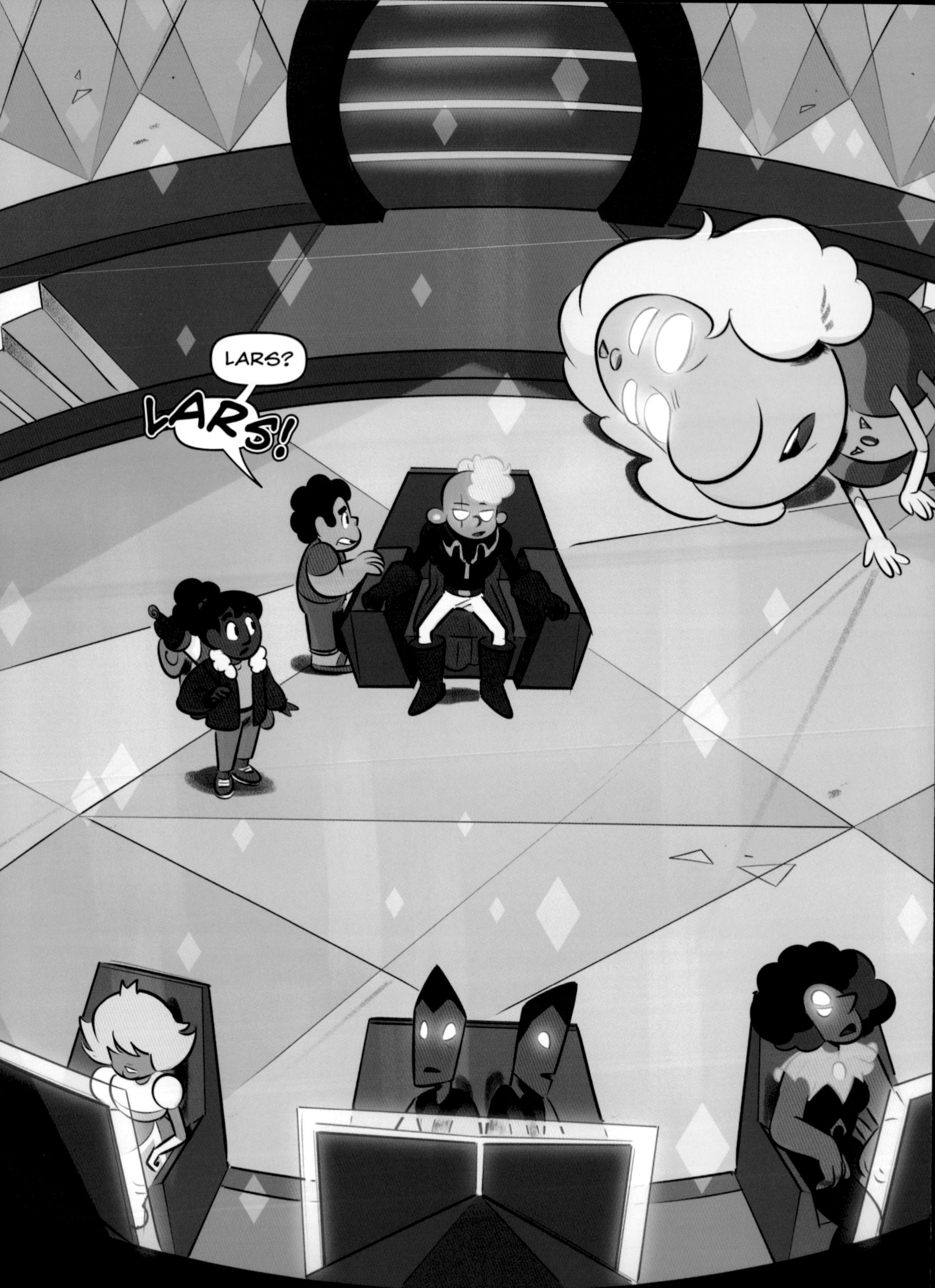
LARS?
LARS!

Issue Twenty-Six Preorder Cover
FRANCESCA PERRONE

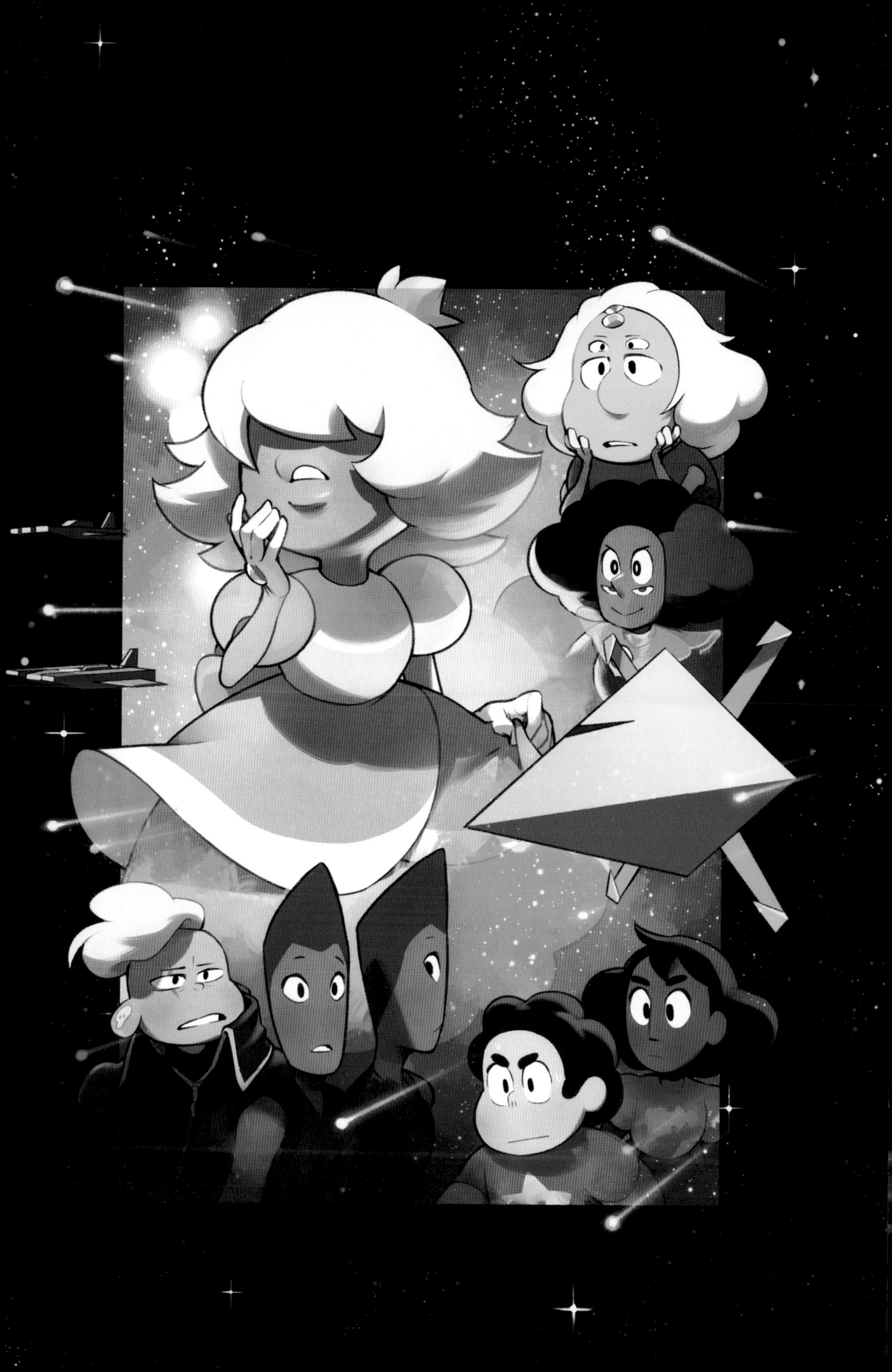

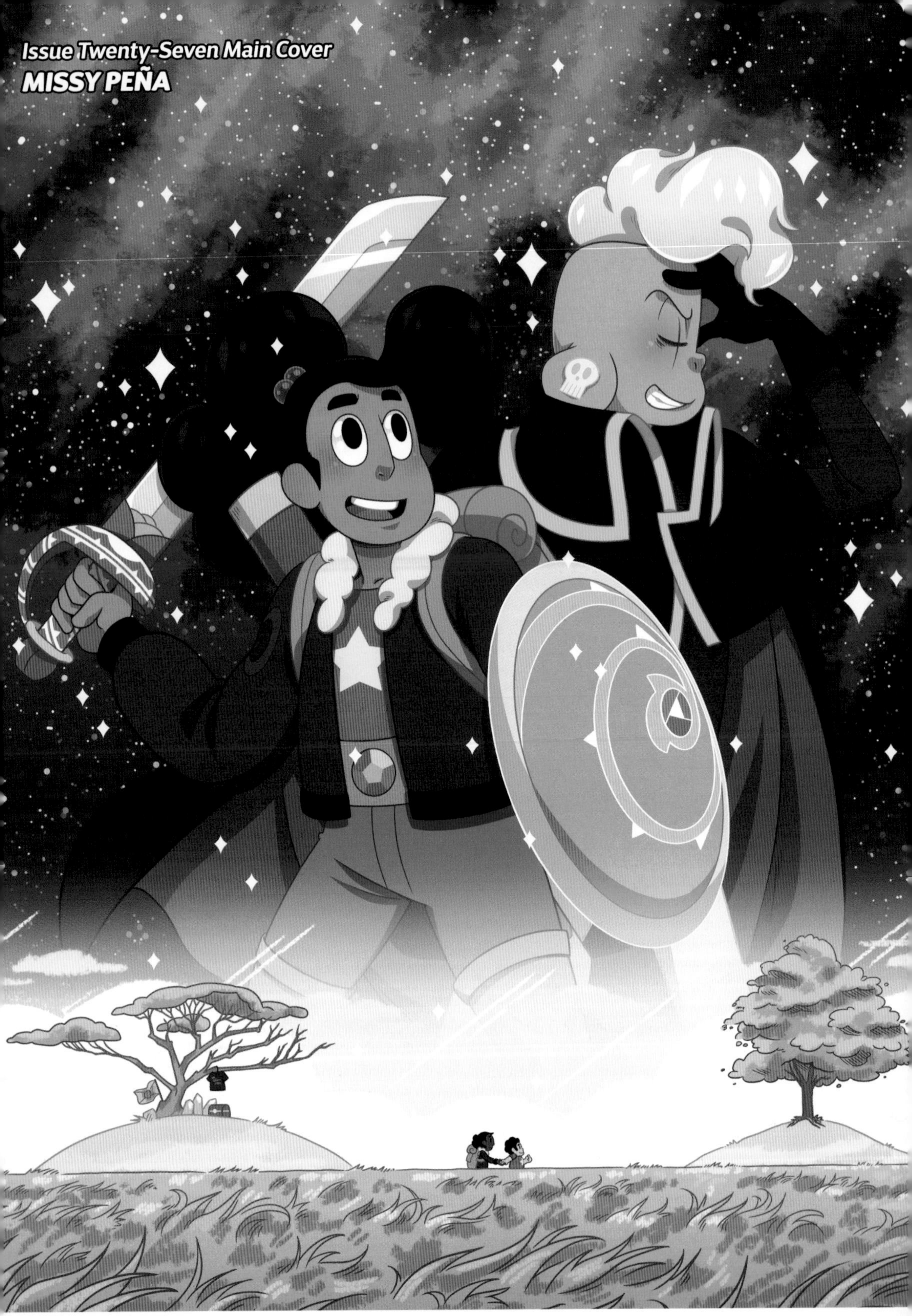

Issue Twenty-Seven Main Cover
MISSY PEÑA

CHAPTER TWENTY-SEVEN

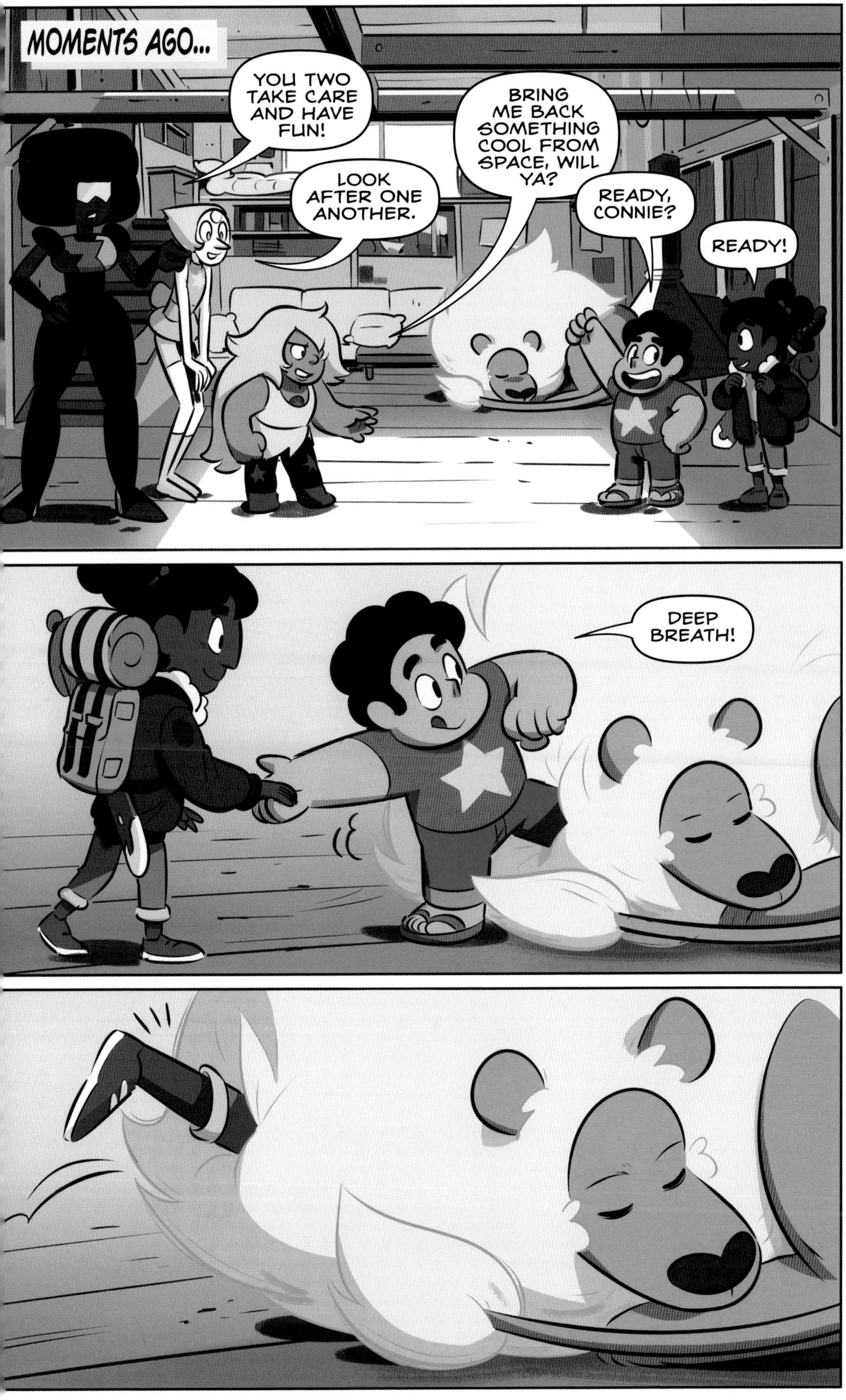

MOMENTS AGO...
YOU TWO TAKE CARE AND HAVE FUN!
LOOK AFTER ONE ANOTHER.
BRING ME BACK SOMETHING COOL FROM SPACE, WILL YA?
READY, CONNIE?
READY!
DEEP BREATH!

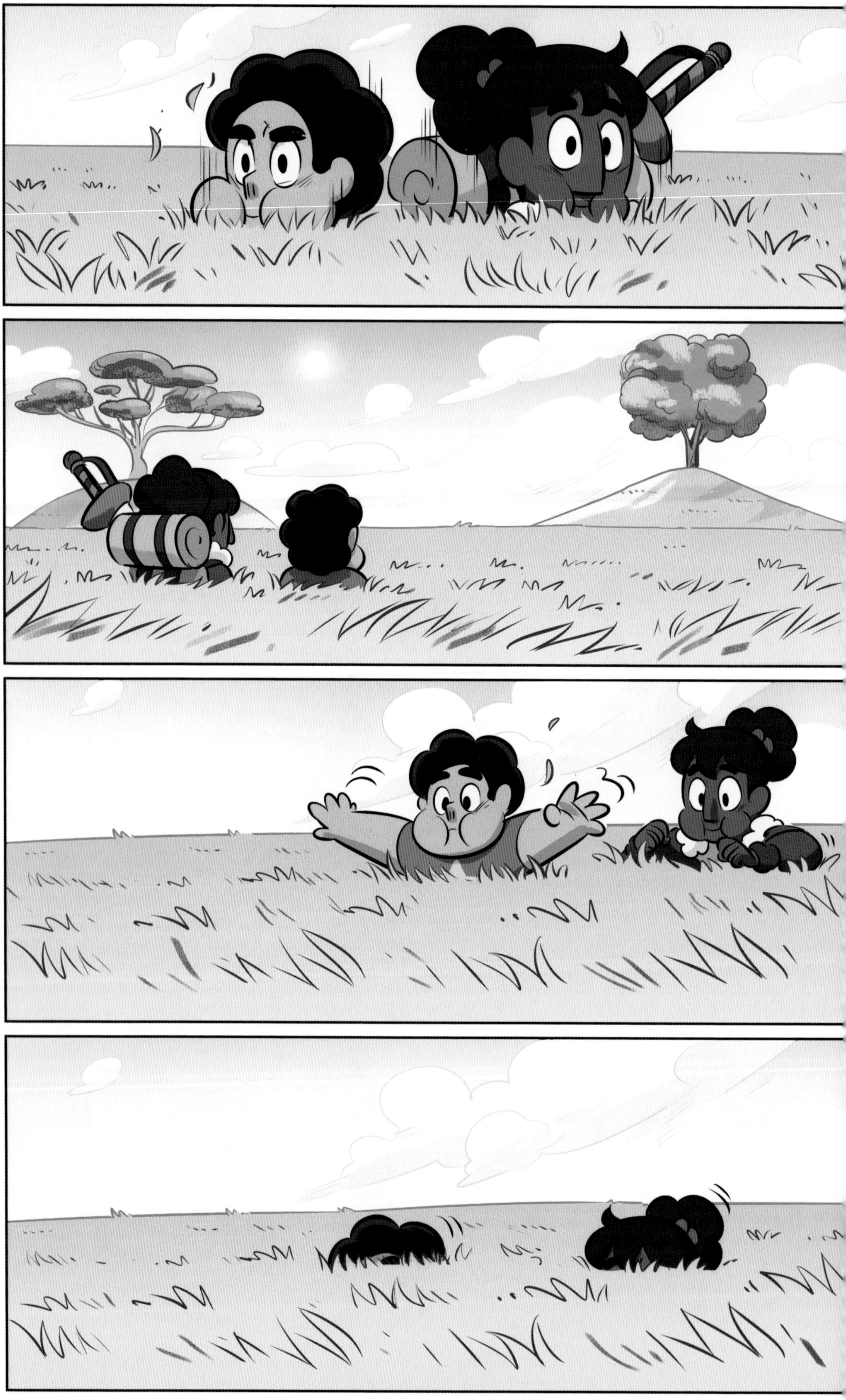

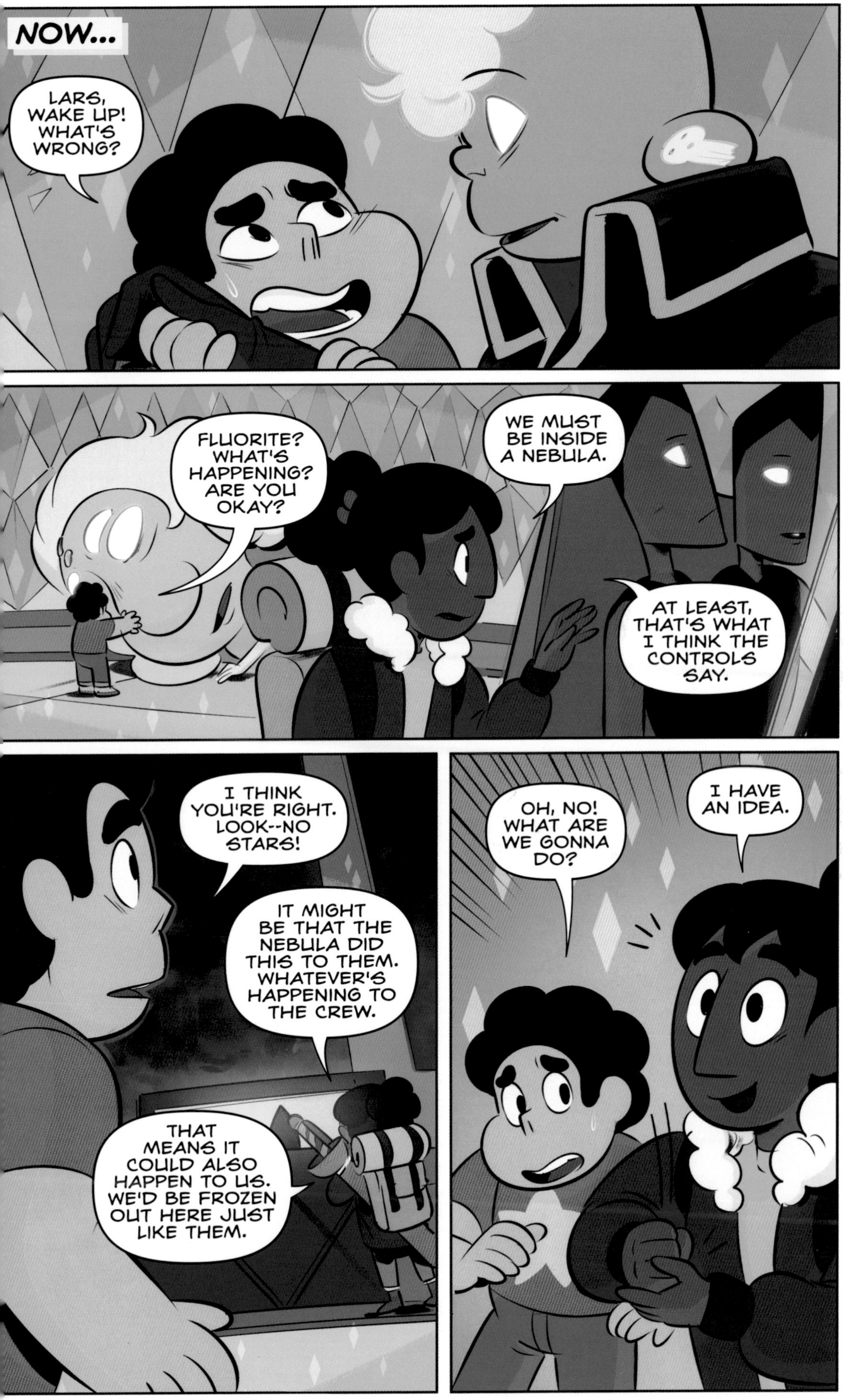
NOW...
LARS, WAKE UP! WHAT'S WRONG?
FLUORITE? WHAT'S HAPPENING? ARE YOU OKAY?
WE MUST BE INSIDE A NEBULA.
AT LEAST, THAT'S WHAT I THINK THE CONTROLS SAY.
I THINK YOU'RE RIGHT. LOOK--NO STARS!
IT MIGHT BE THAT THE NEBULA DID THIS TO THEM. WHATEVER'S HAPPENING TO THE CREW.
THAT MEANS IT COULD ALSO HAPPEN TO US. WE'D BE FROZEN OUT HERE JUST LIKE THEM.
OH, NO! WHAT ARE WE GONNA DO?
I HAVE AN IDEA.

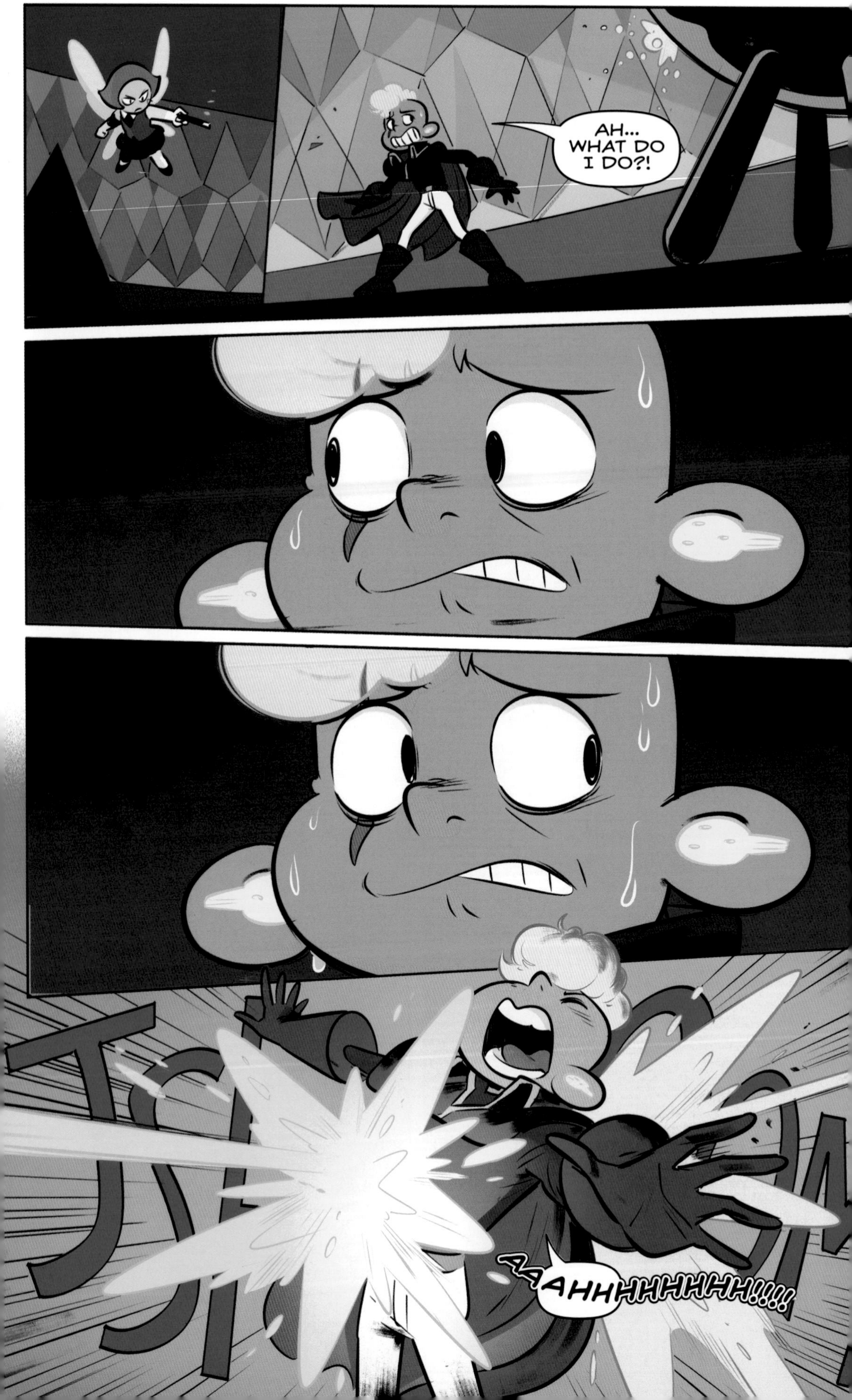
AH... WHAT DO I DO?!
AAAHHHHHHHHH!!!!

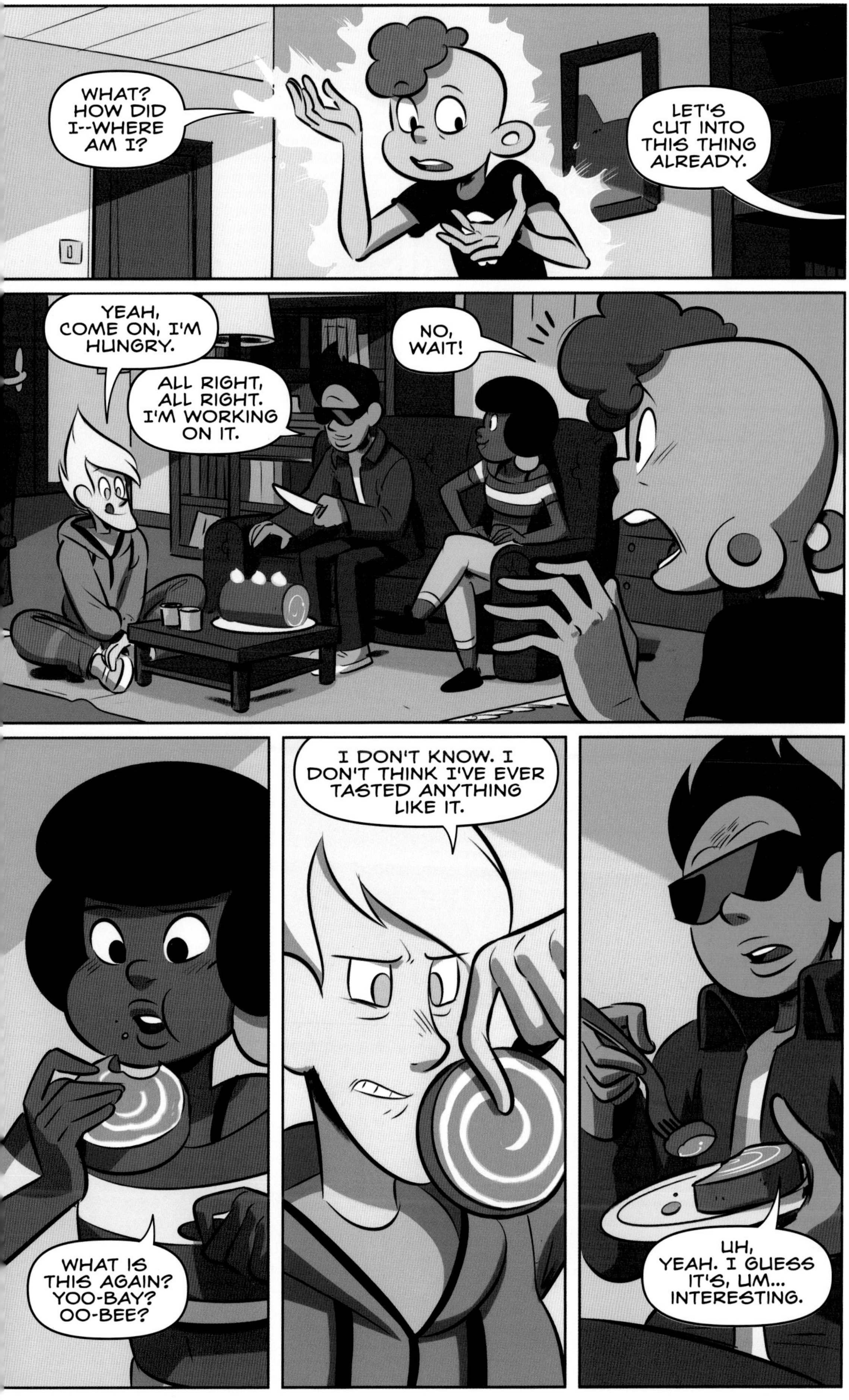
WHAT? HOW DID I--WHERE AM I?
LET'S CUT INTO THIS THING ALREADY.
YEAH, COME ON, I'M HUNGRY.
ALL RIGHT, ALL RIGHT. I'M WORKING ON IT.
NO, WAIT!
WHAT IS THIS AGAIN? YOO-BAY? OO-BEE?
I DON'T KNOW. I DON'T THINK I'VE EVER TASTED ANYTHING LIKE IT.
UH, YEAH. I GUESS IT'S, UM... INTERESTING.

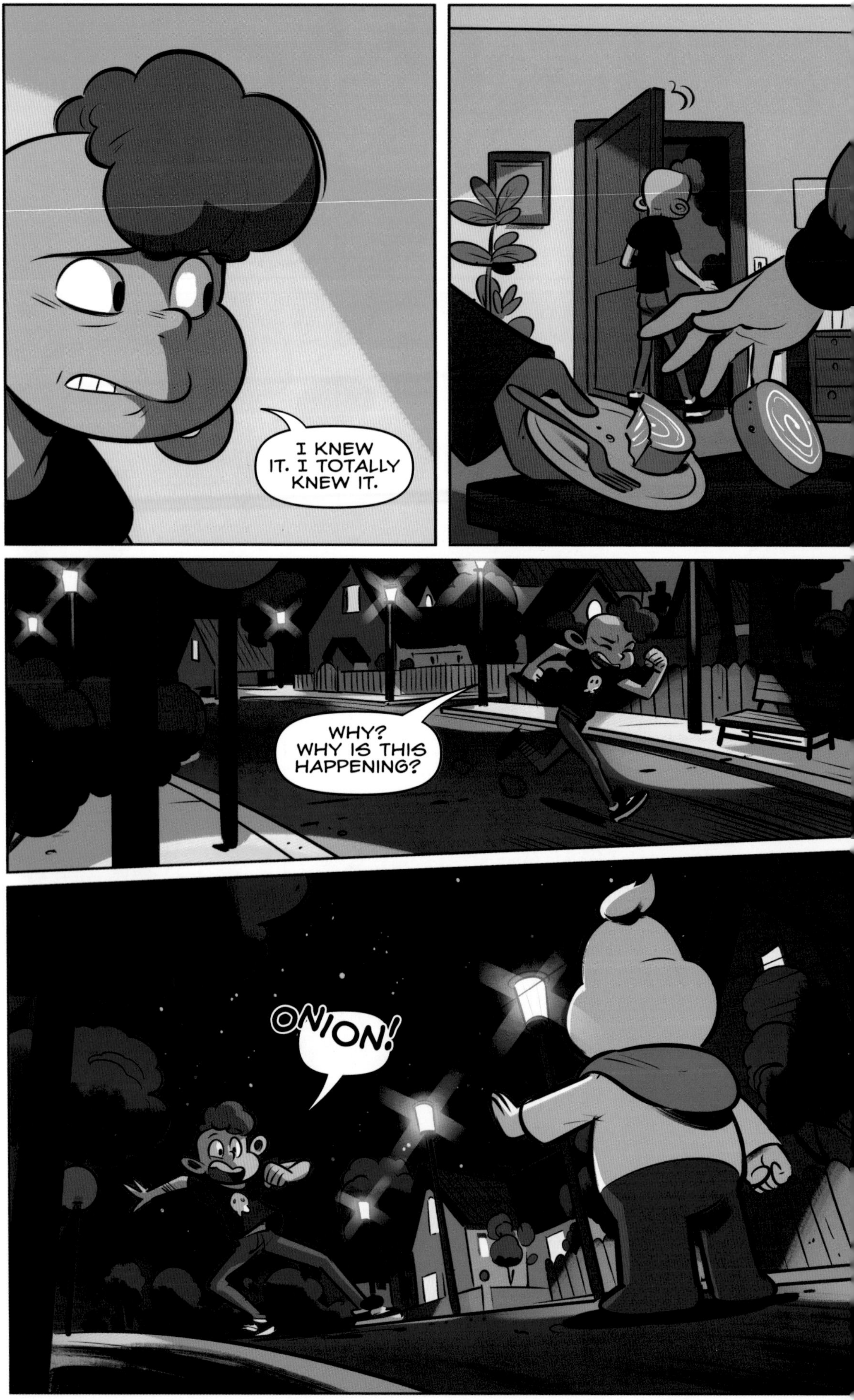
I KNEW IT. I TOTALLY KNEW IT.
WHY? WHY IS THIS HAPPENING?
ONION!

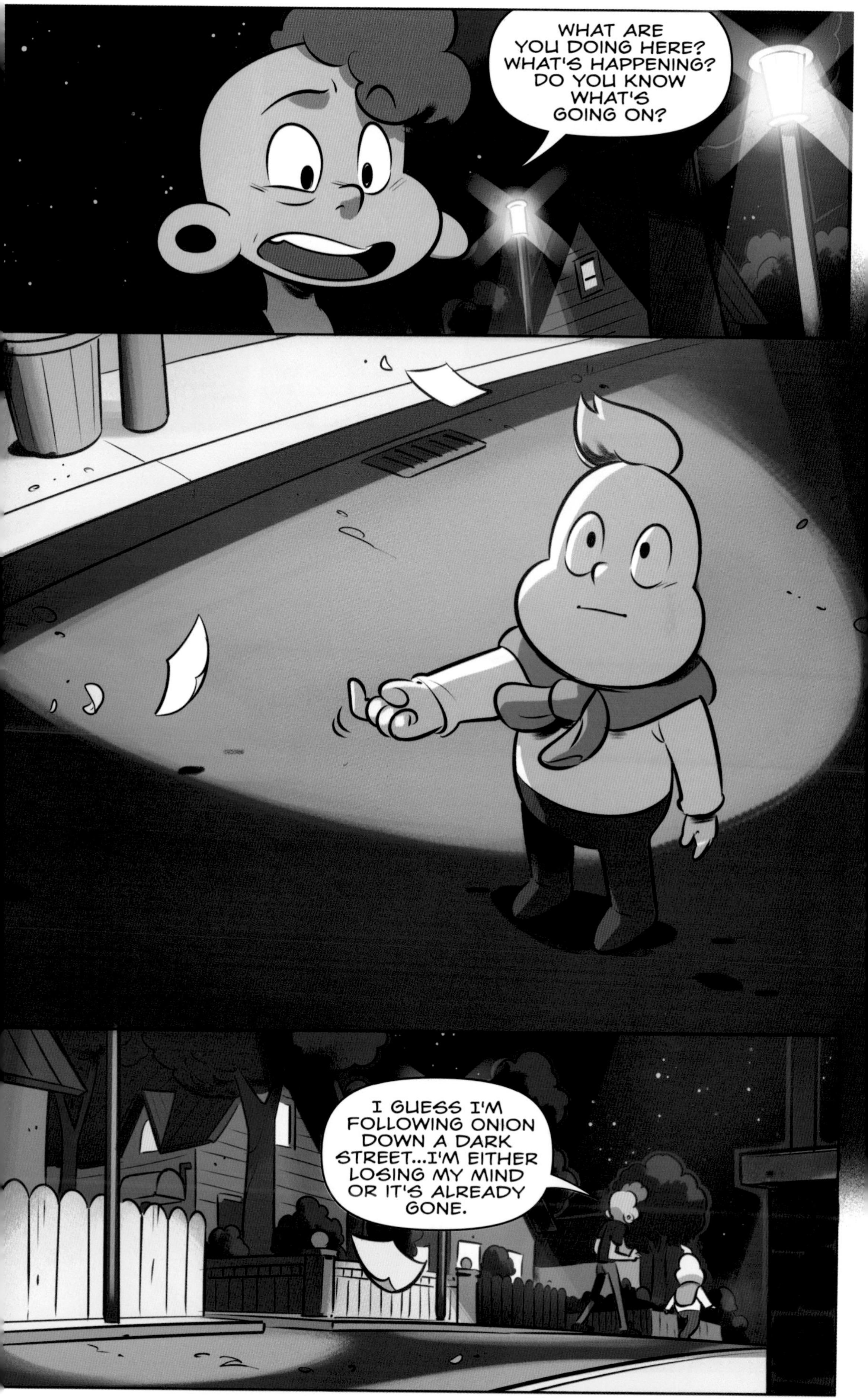
WHAT ARE YOU DOING HERE? WHAT'S HAPPENING? DO YOU KNOW WHAT'S GOING ON?
I GUESS I'M FOLLOWING ONION DOWN A DARK STREET...I'M EITHER LOSING MY MIND OR IT'S ALREADY GONE.

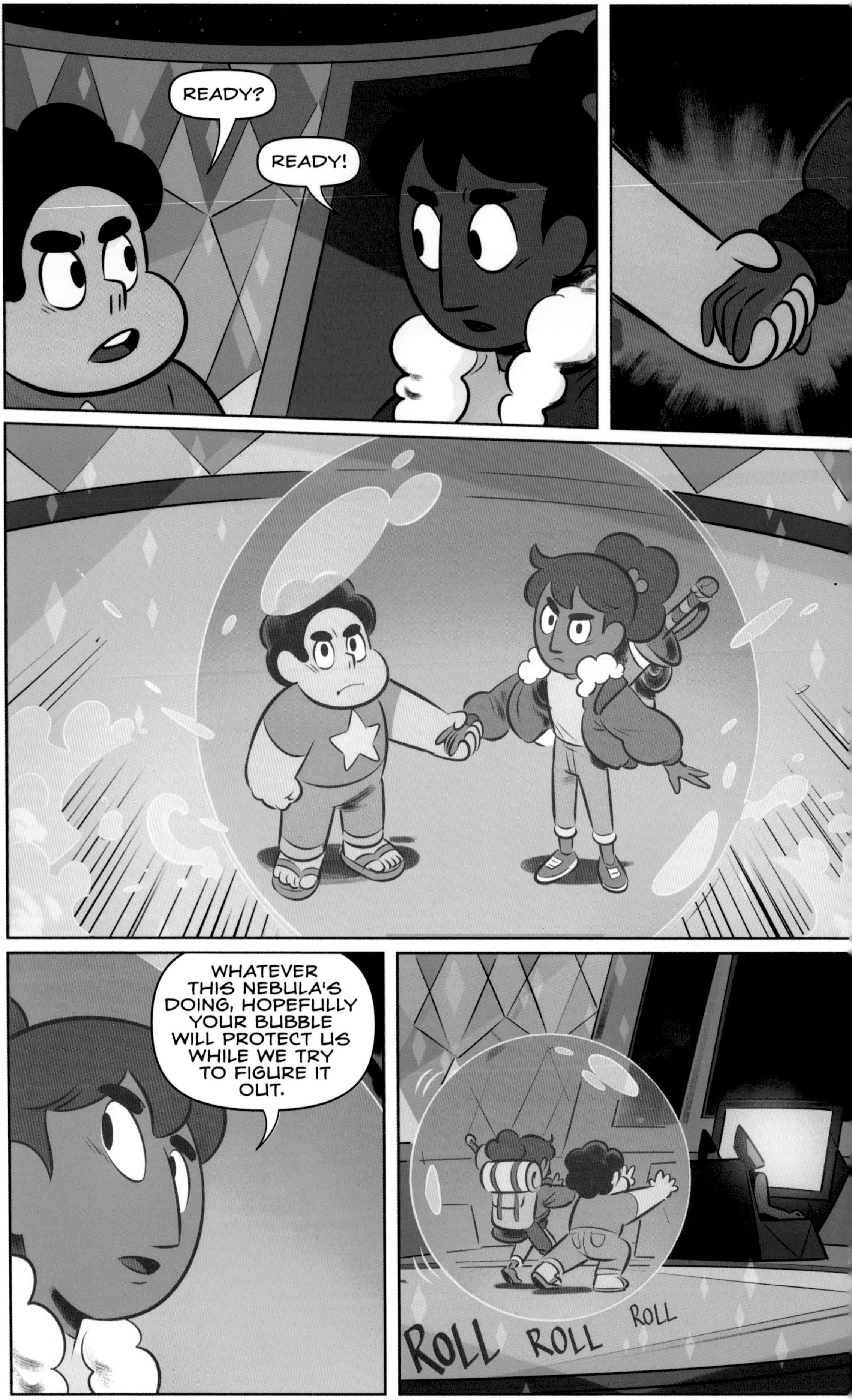
READY?
READY!
WHATEVER THIS NEBULA'S DOING, HOPEFULLY YOUR BUBBLE WILL PROTECT US WHILE WE TRY TO FIGURE IT OUT.
ROLL
ROLL
ROLL

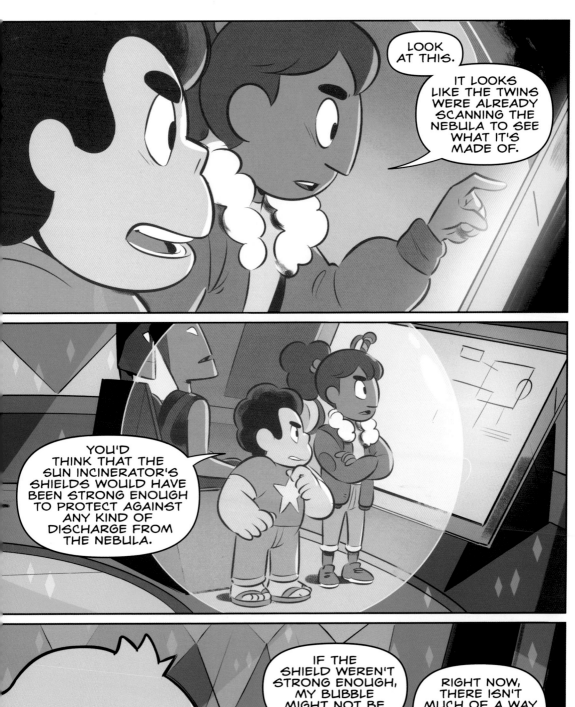

LOOK AT THIS.

IT LOOKS LIKE THE TWINS WERE ALREADY SCANNING THE NEBULA TO SEE WHAT IT'S MADE OF.

YOU'D THINK THAT THE SUN INCINERATOR'S SHIELDS WOULD HAVE BEEN STRONG ENOUGH TO PROTECT AGAINST ANY KIND OF DISCHARGE FROM THE NEBULA.

IF THE SHIELD WEREN'T STRONG ENOUGH, MY BUBBLE MIGHT NOT BE EITHER.

RIGHT NOW, THERE ISN'T MUCH OF A WAY FOR US TO KNOW, SO WE GOTTA WORK FAST.

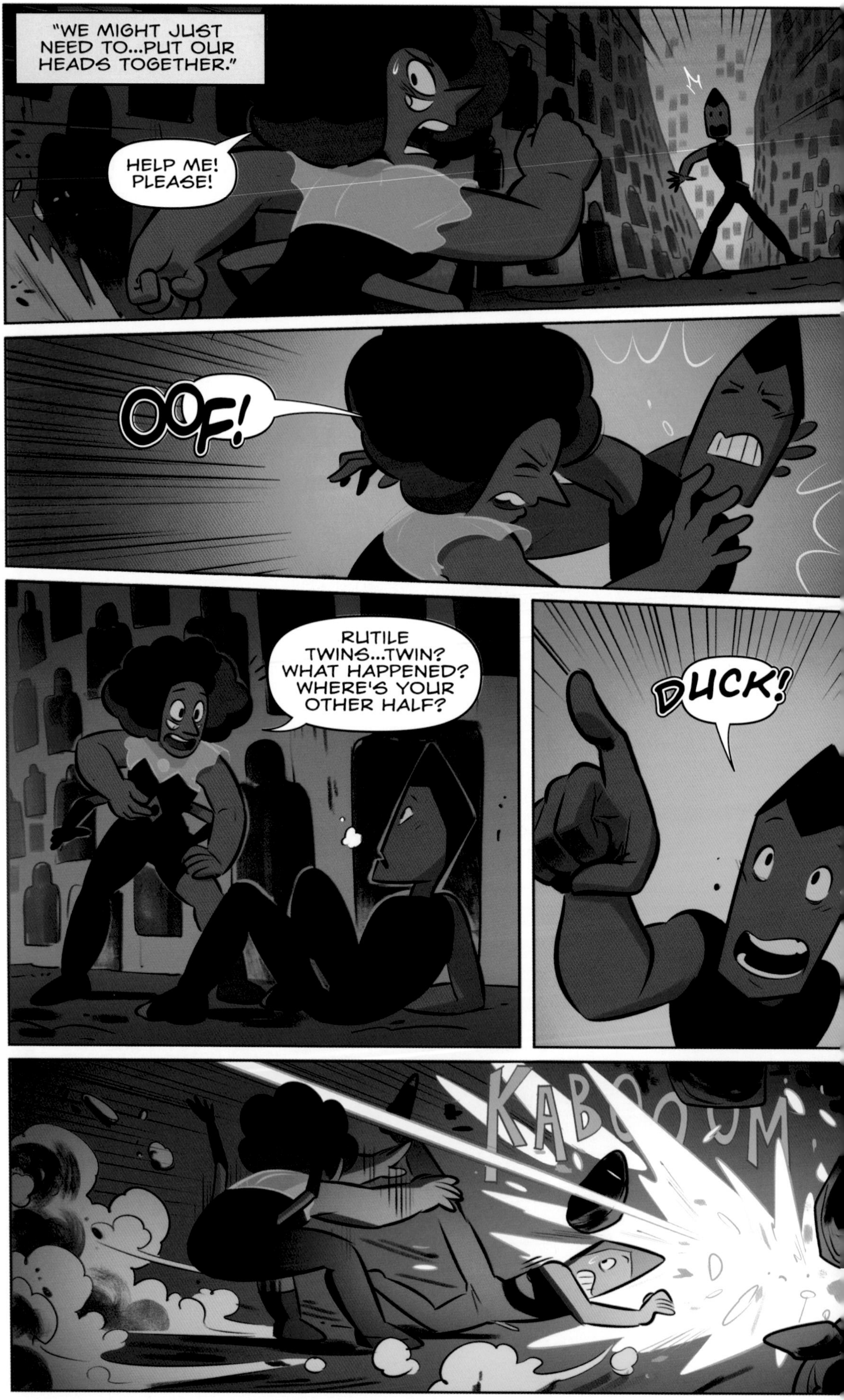
"WE MIGHT JUST NEED TO...PUT OUR HEADS TOGETHER."
HELP ME! PLEASE!
OOF!
RUTILE TWINS...TWIN? WHAT HAPPENED? WHERE'S YOUR OTHER HALF?
DUCK!
KABOOOM

GRAB A WEAPON.

HEEEEYAAAUGH!

KRAAASH!

I DON'T THINK I CAN DO THIS!

YES, YOU CAN! AND YOU DON'T HAVE TO DO IT ALONE!

WE'RE GONNA GET OUT OF HERE, BUT FIRST WE GOTTA GET TO MY TWIN.

UP THERE!

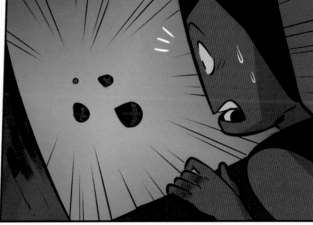

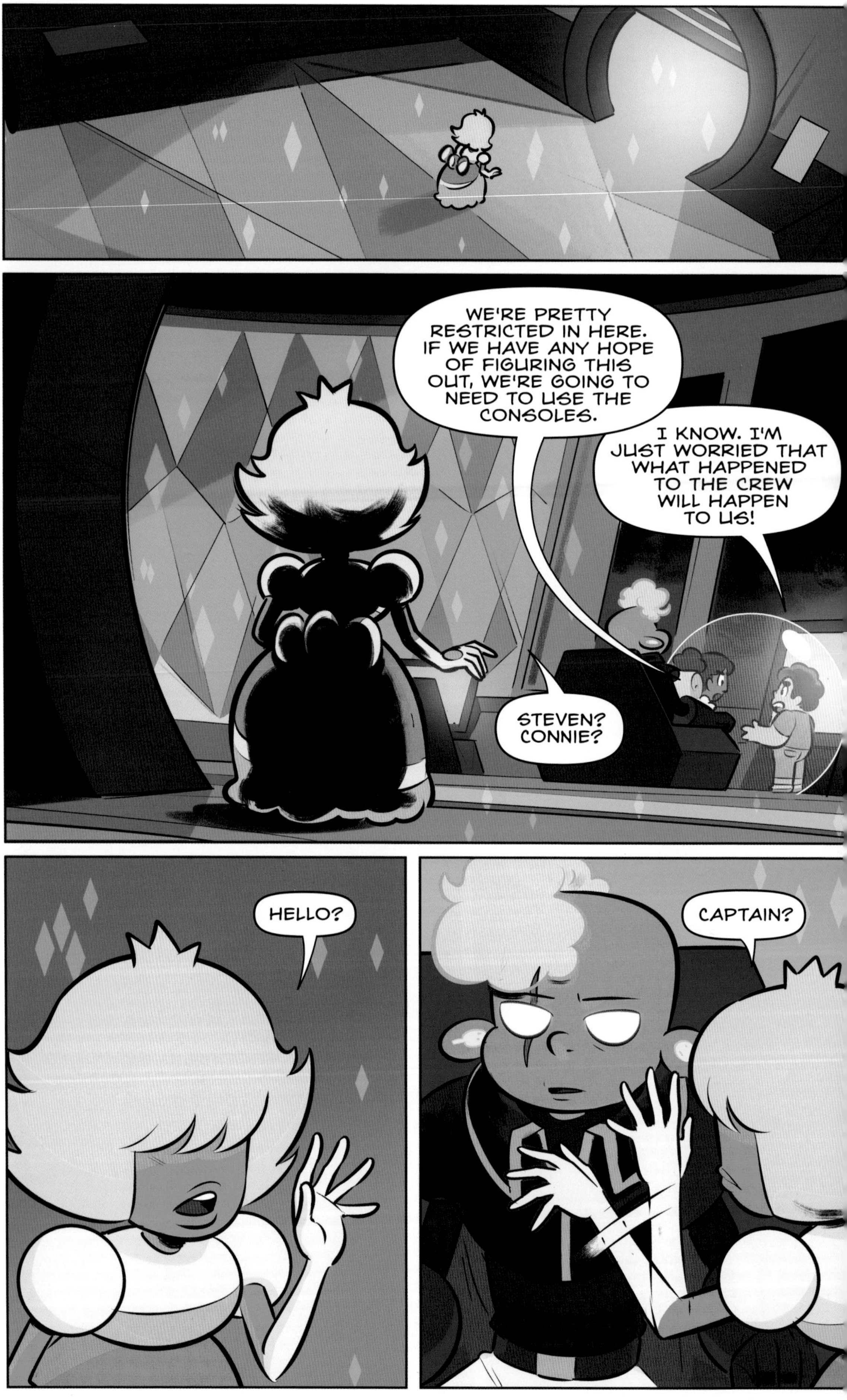
WE'RE PRETTY RESTRICTED IN HERE. IF WE HAVE ANY HOPE OF FIGURING THIS OUT, WE'RE GOING TO NEED TO USE THE CONSOLES.
I KNOW. I'M JUST WORRIED THAT WHAT HAPPENED TO THE CREW WILL HAPPEN TO US!
STEVEN? CONNIE?
HELLO?
CAPTAIN?

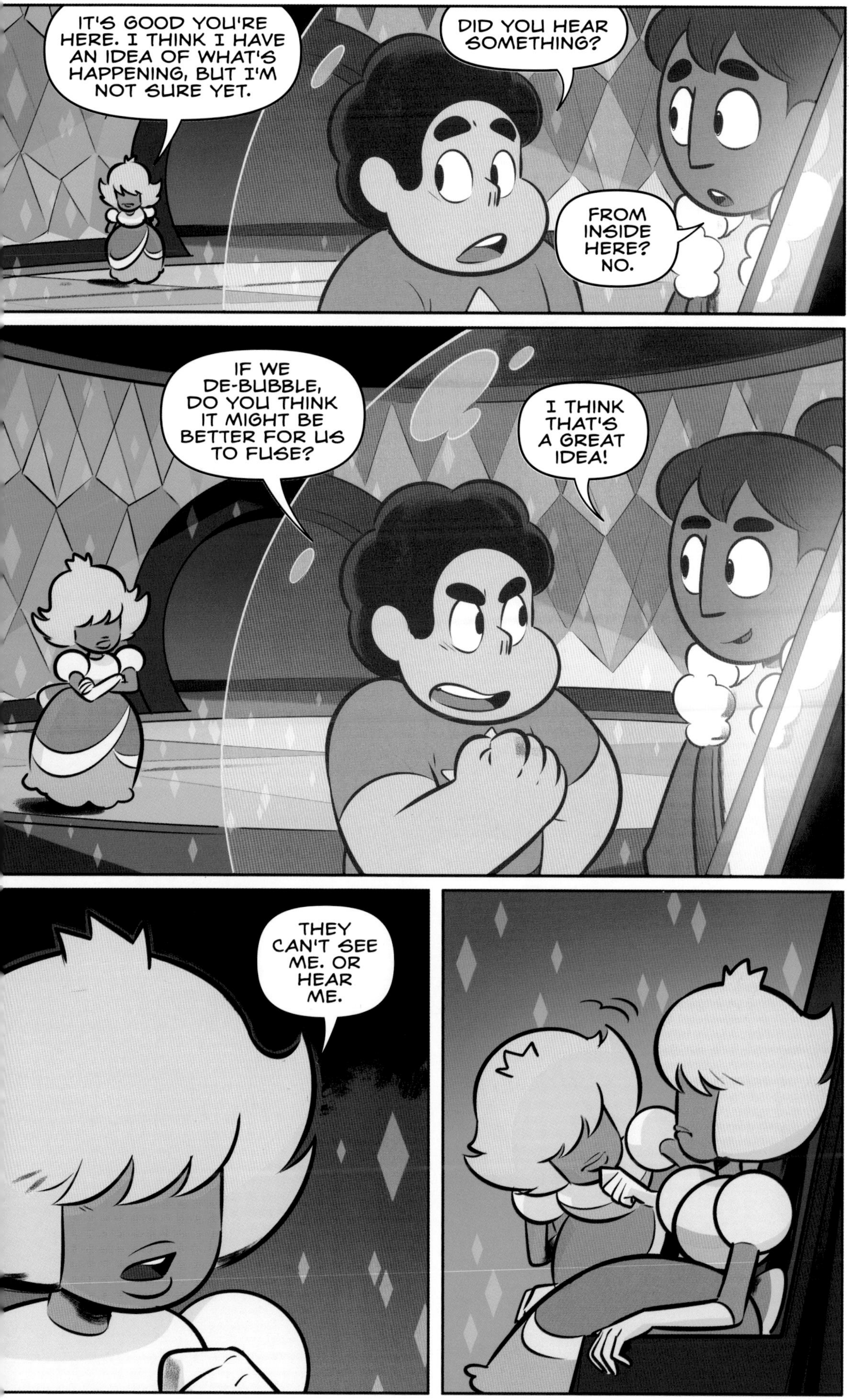
IT'S GOOD YOU'RE HERE. I THINK I HAVE AN IDEA OF WHAT'S HAPPENING, BUT I'M NOT SURE YET.
DID YOU HEAR SOMETHING?
FROM INSIDE HERE? NO.
IF WE DE-BUBBLE, DO YOU THINK IT MIGHT BE BETTER FOR US TO FUSE?
I THINK THAT'S A GREAT IDEA!
THEY CAN'T SEE ME. OR HEAR ME.

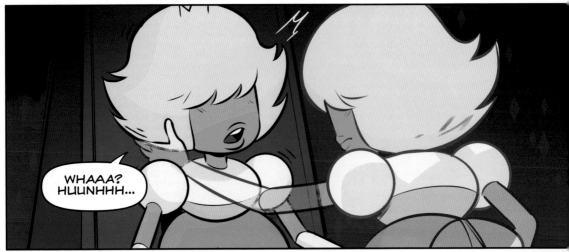

WHAAA? HUUNHHH...

MAYBE TOGETHER WE'LL BE STRONG ENOUGH TO RESIST THE NEBULA.

IT'S WORTH A SHOT. YOU MIGHT BE RIGHT.

SHE IS RIGHT.

HERE WE GO!

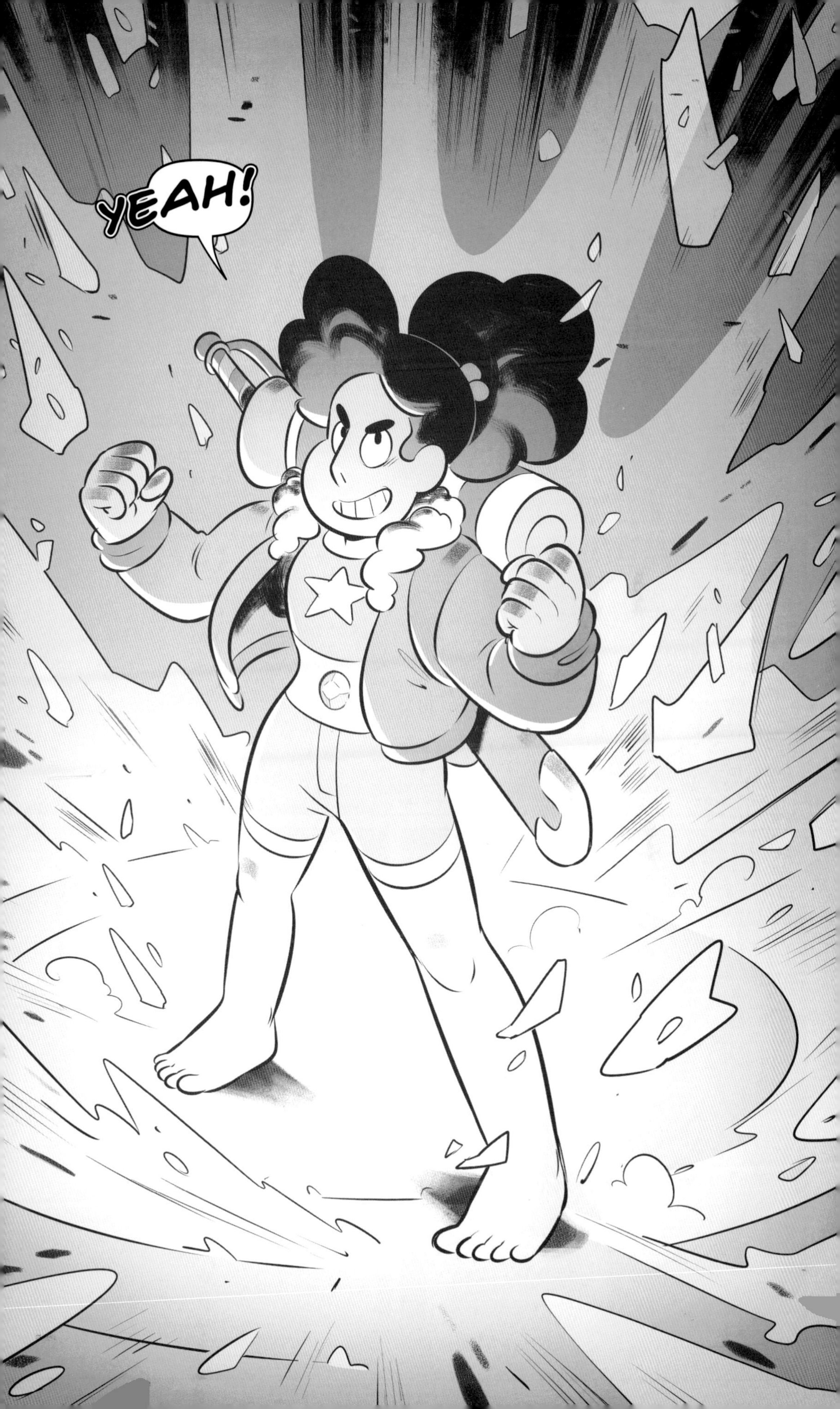
YEAH!

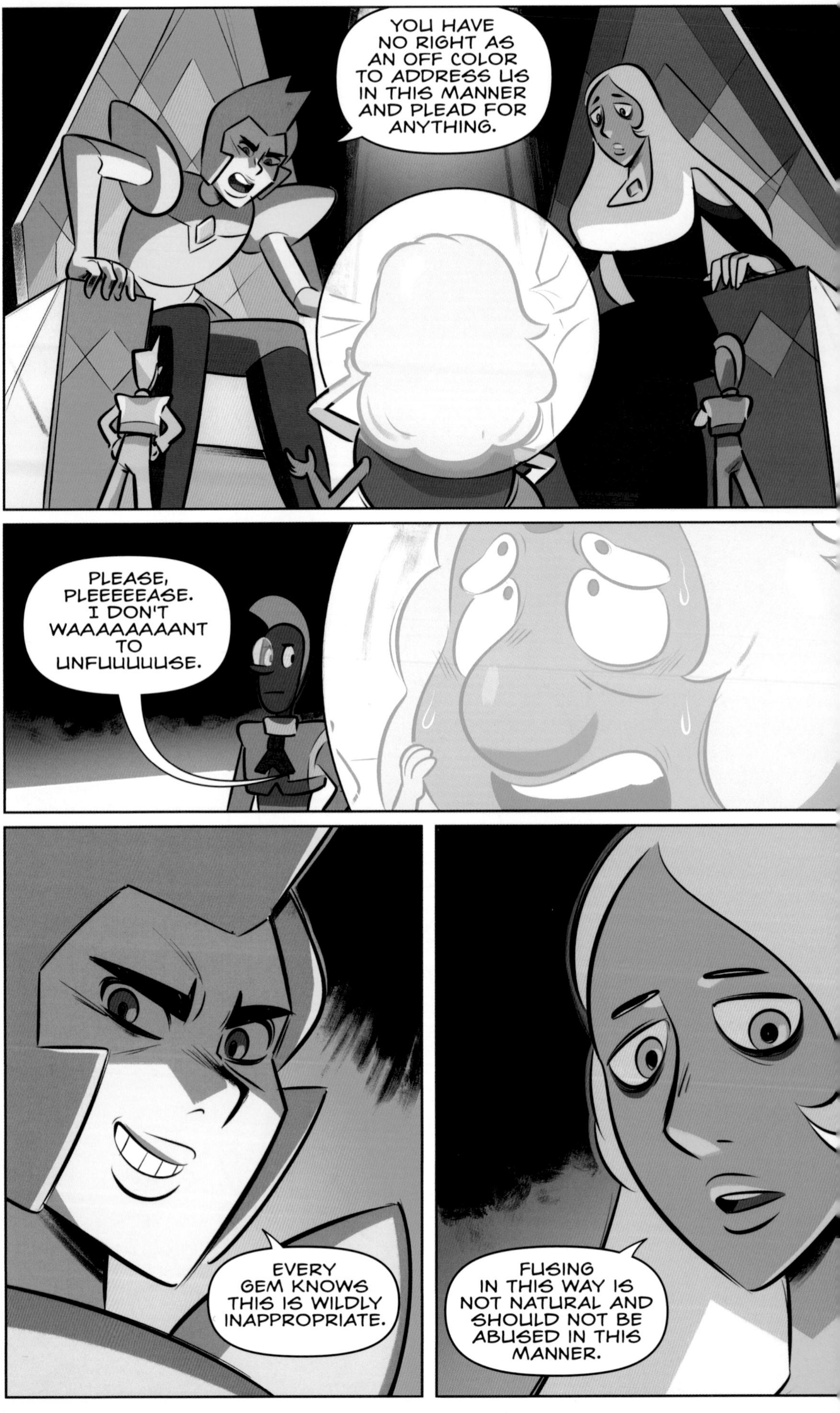
YOU HAVE NO RIGHT AS AN OFF COLOR TO ADDRESS US IN THIS MANNER AND PLEAD FOR ANYTHING.
PLEASE, PLEEEEEASE. I DON'T WAAAAAAAANT TO UNFUUUUUSE.
EVERY GEM KNOWS THIS IS WILDLY INAPPROPRIATE.
FUSING IN THIS WAY IS NOT NATURAL AND SHOULD NOT BE ABUSED IN THIS MANNER.

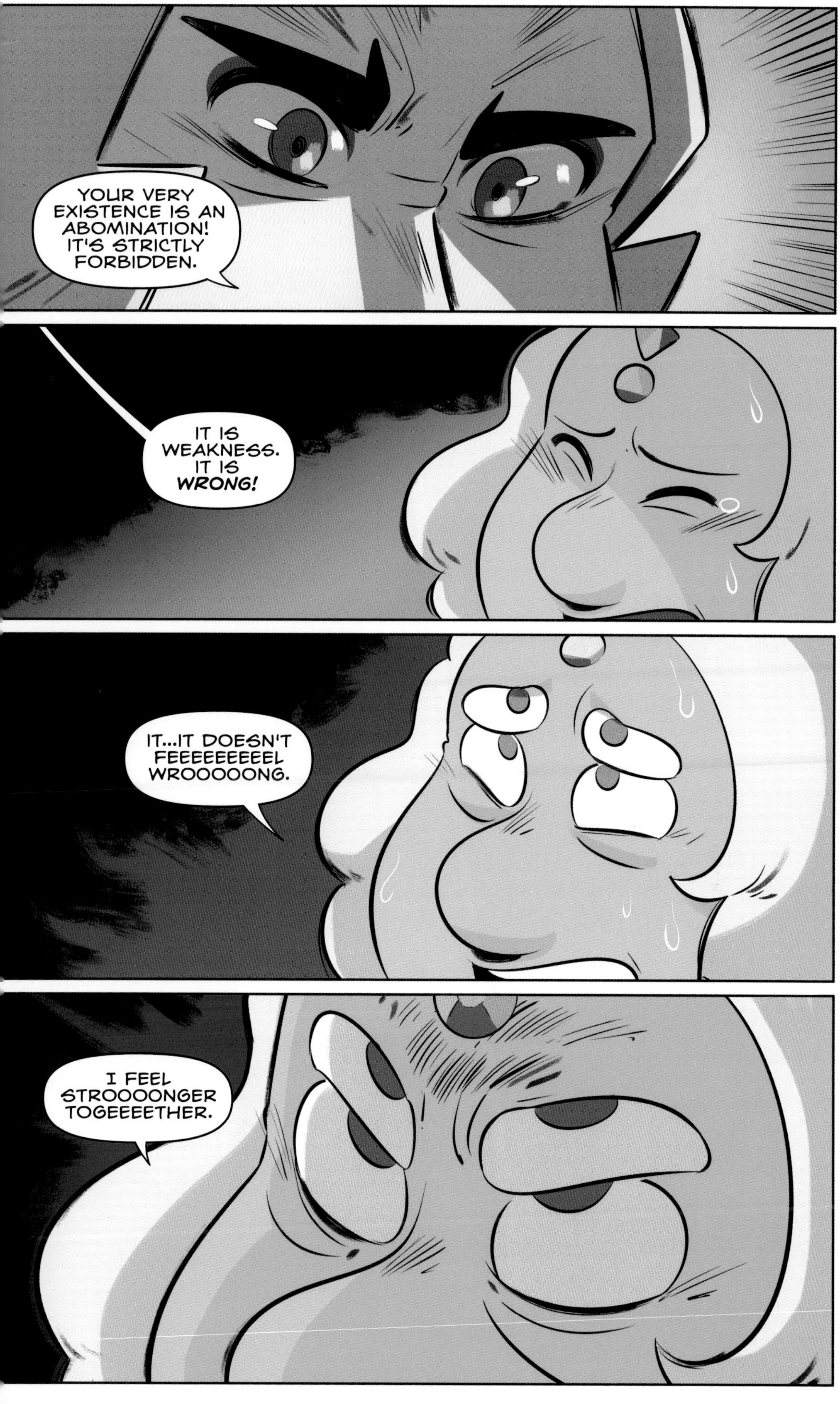
YOUR VERY EXISTENCE IS AN ABOMINATION! IT'S STRICTLY FORBIDDEN.
IT IS WEAKNESS. IT IS *WRONG!*
IT...IT DOESN'T FEEEEEEEEEL WROOOOONG.
I FEEL STROOOONGER TOGEEEETHER.

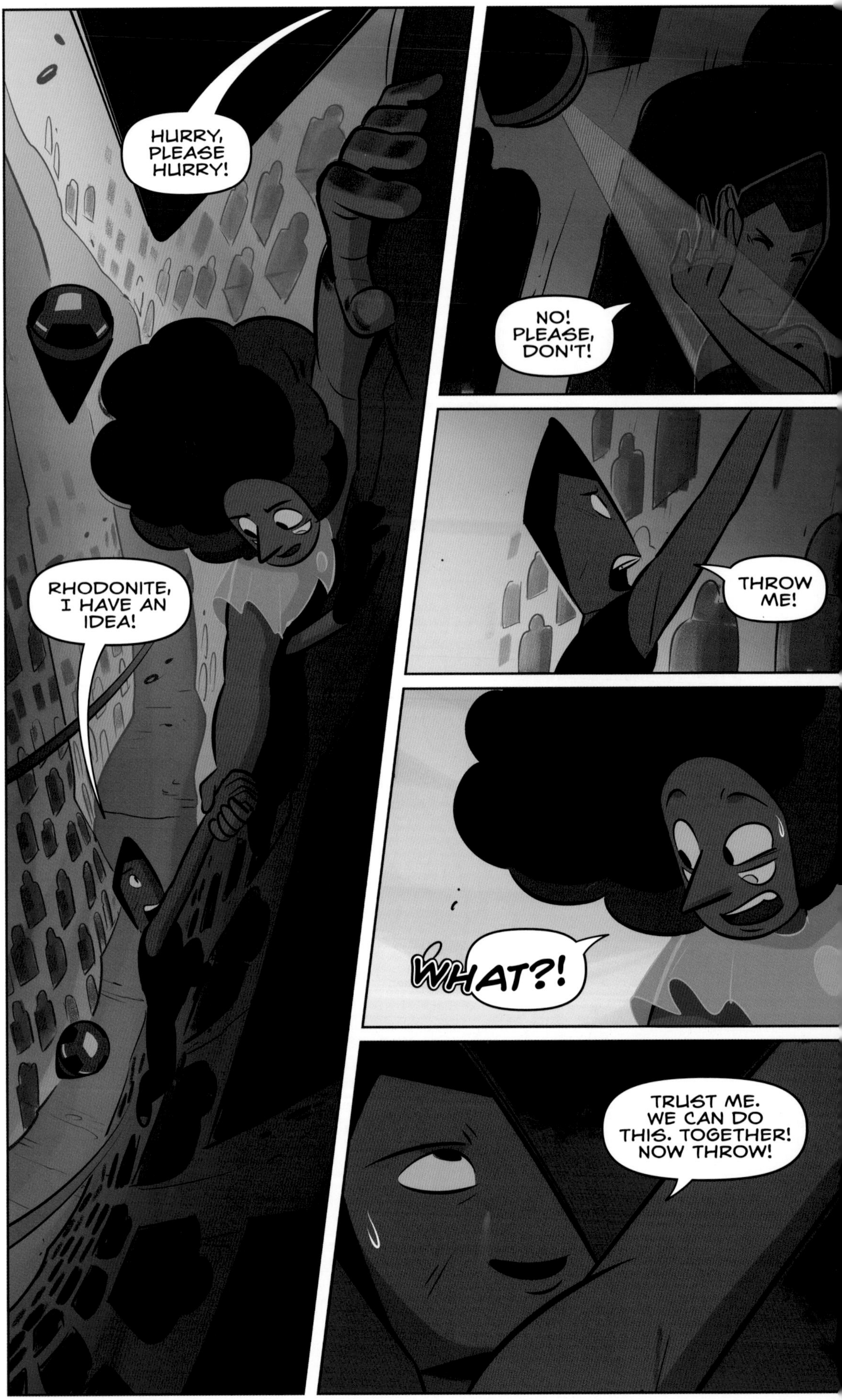
HURRY, PLEASE HURRY!
RHODONITE, I HAVE AN IDEA!
NO! PLEASE, DON'T!
THROW ME!
WHAT?!
TRUST ME. WE CAN DO THIS. TOGETHER! NOW THROW!

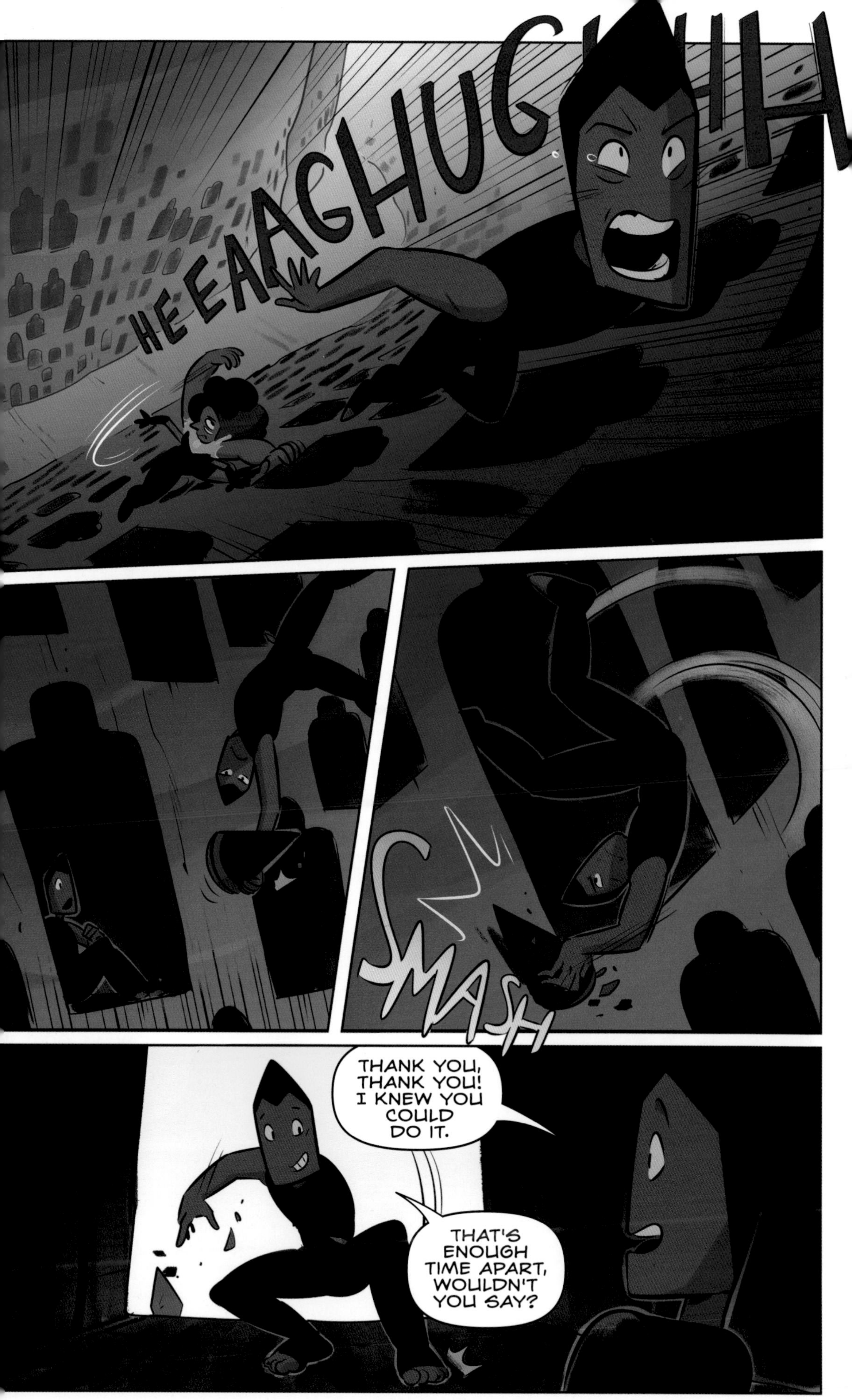
HEEAAGHUGHHHH
SMASH
THANK YOU, THANK YOU! I KNEW YOU COULD DO IT.
THAT'S ENOUGH TIME APART, WOULDN'T YOU SAY?

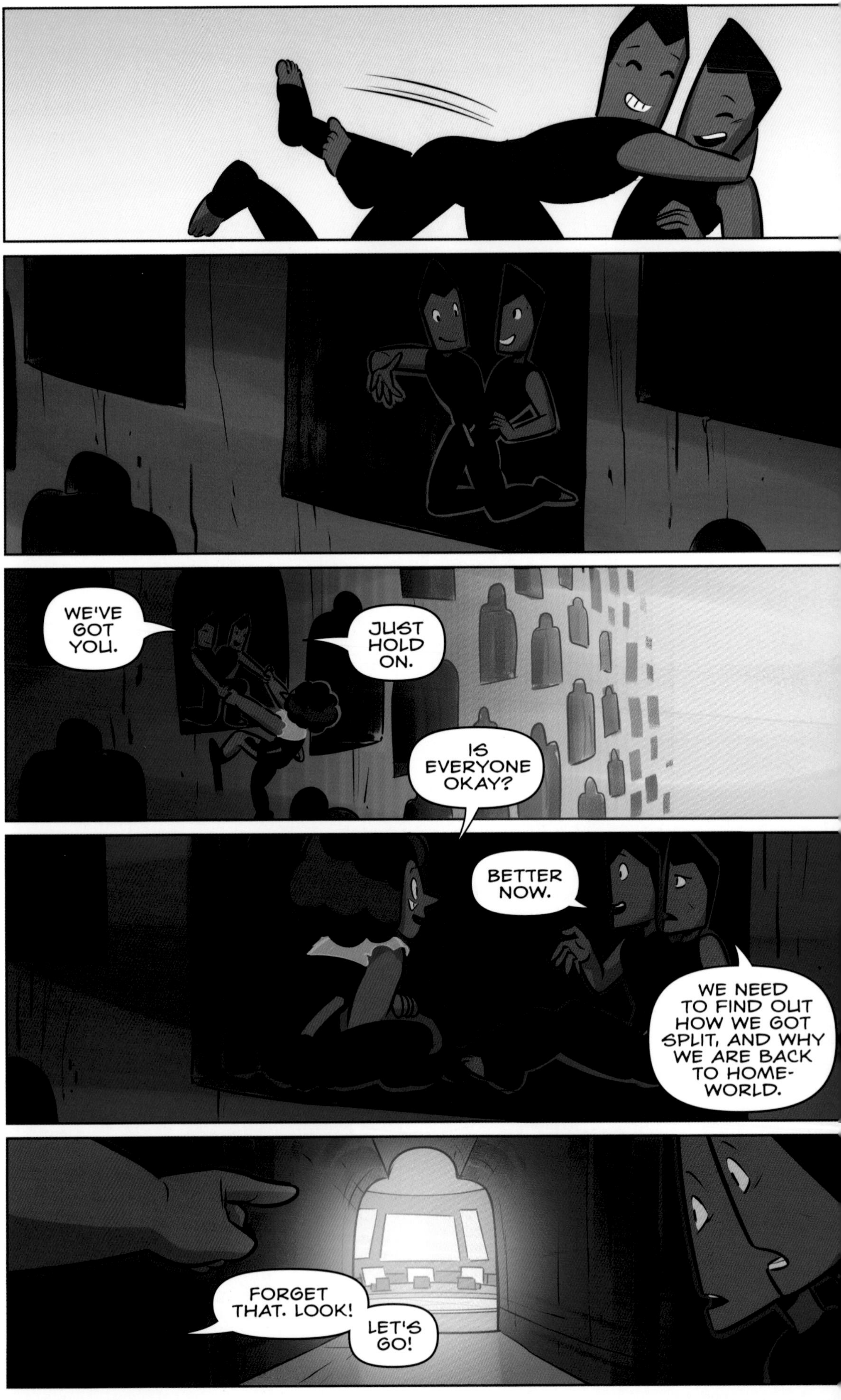
WE'VE GOT YOU.
JUST HOLD ON.
IS EVERYONE OKAY?
BETTER NOW.
WE NEED TO FIND OUT HOW WE GOT SPLIT, AND WHY WE ARE BACK TO HOME-WORLD.
FORGET THAT. LOOK!
LET'S GO!

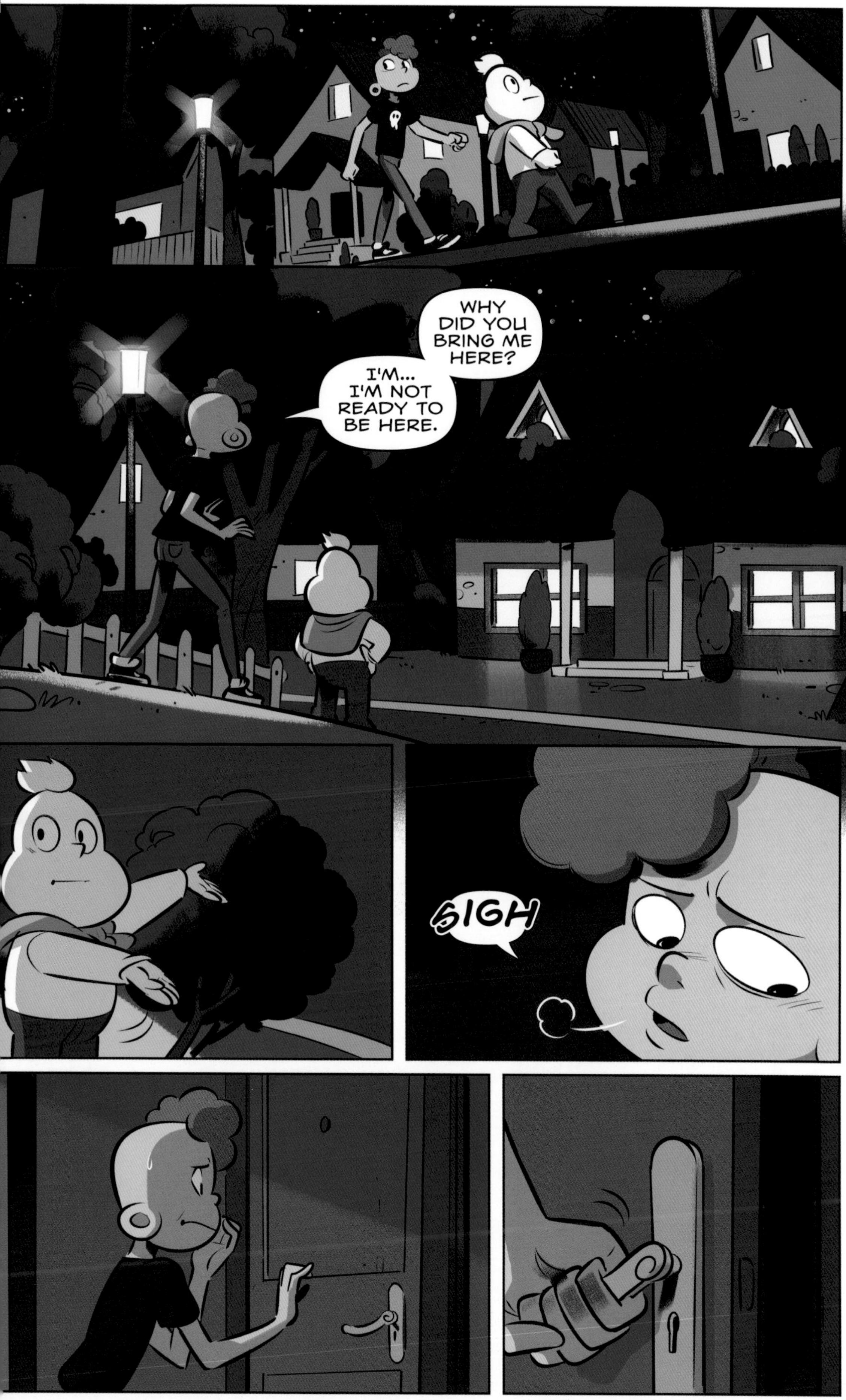
WHY DID YOU BRING ME HERE?
I'M... I'M NOT READY TO BE HERE.
SIGH

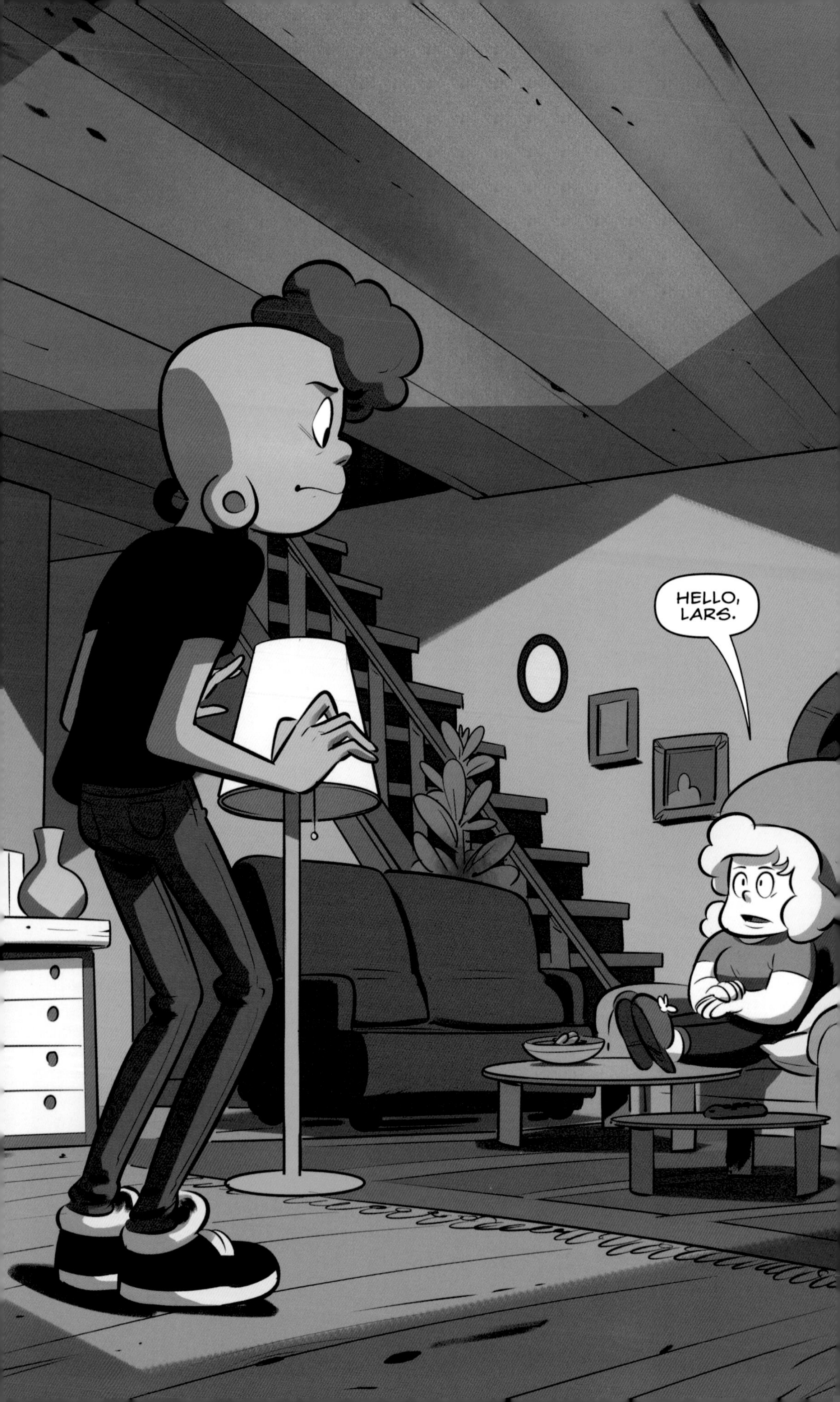
HELLO, LARS.

Issue Twenty-Seven Preorder Cover

FRANCESCA PERRONE

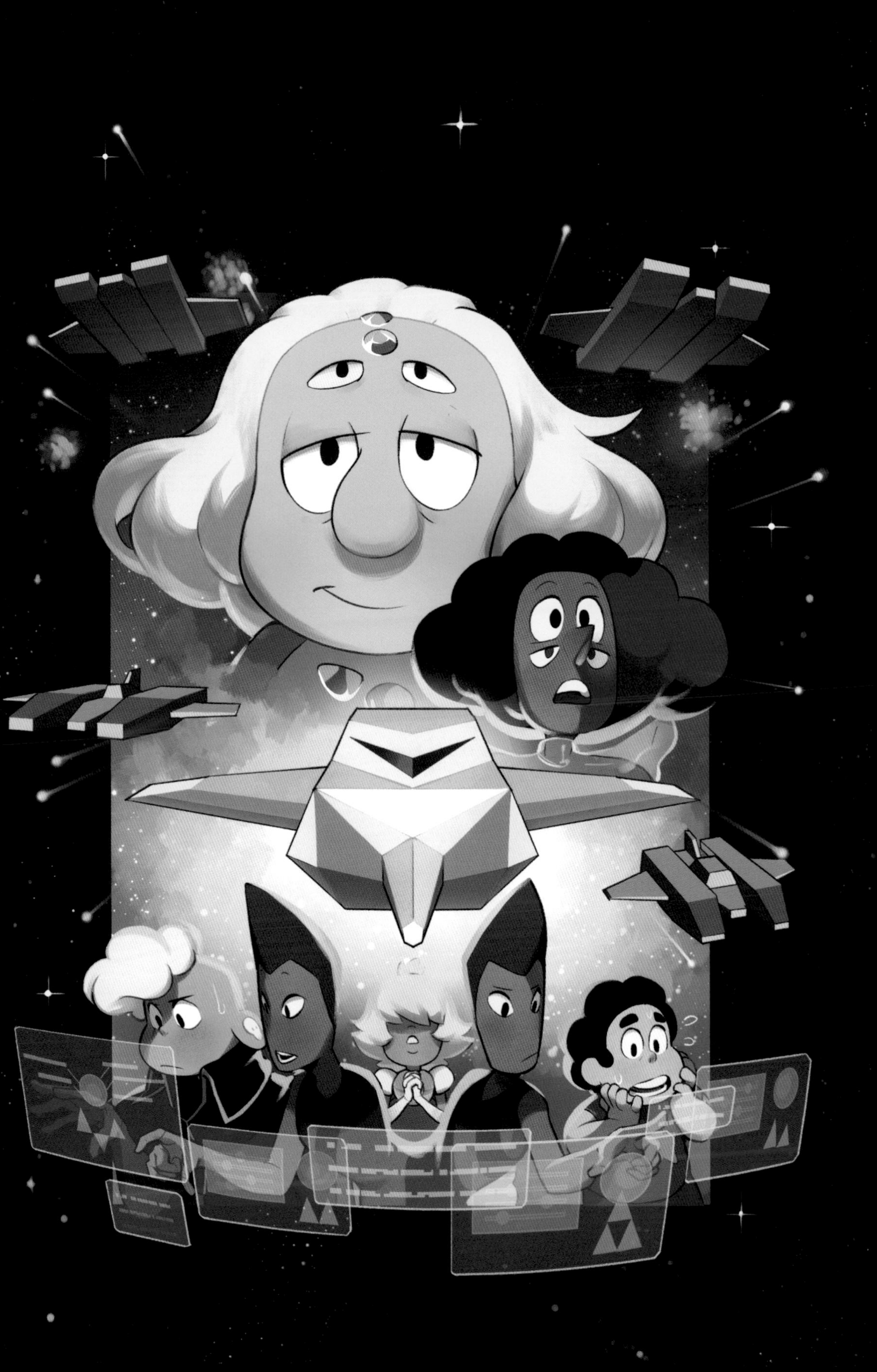

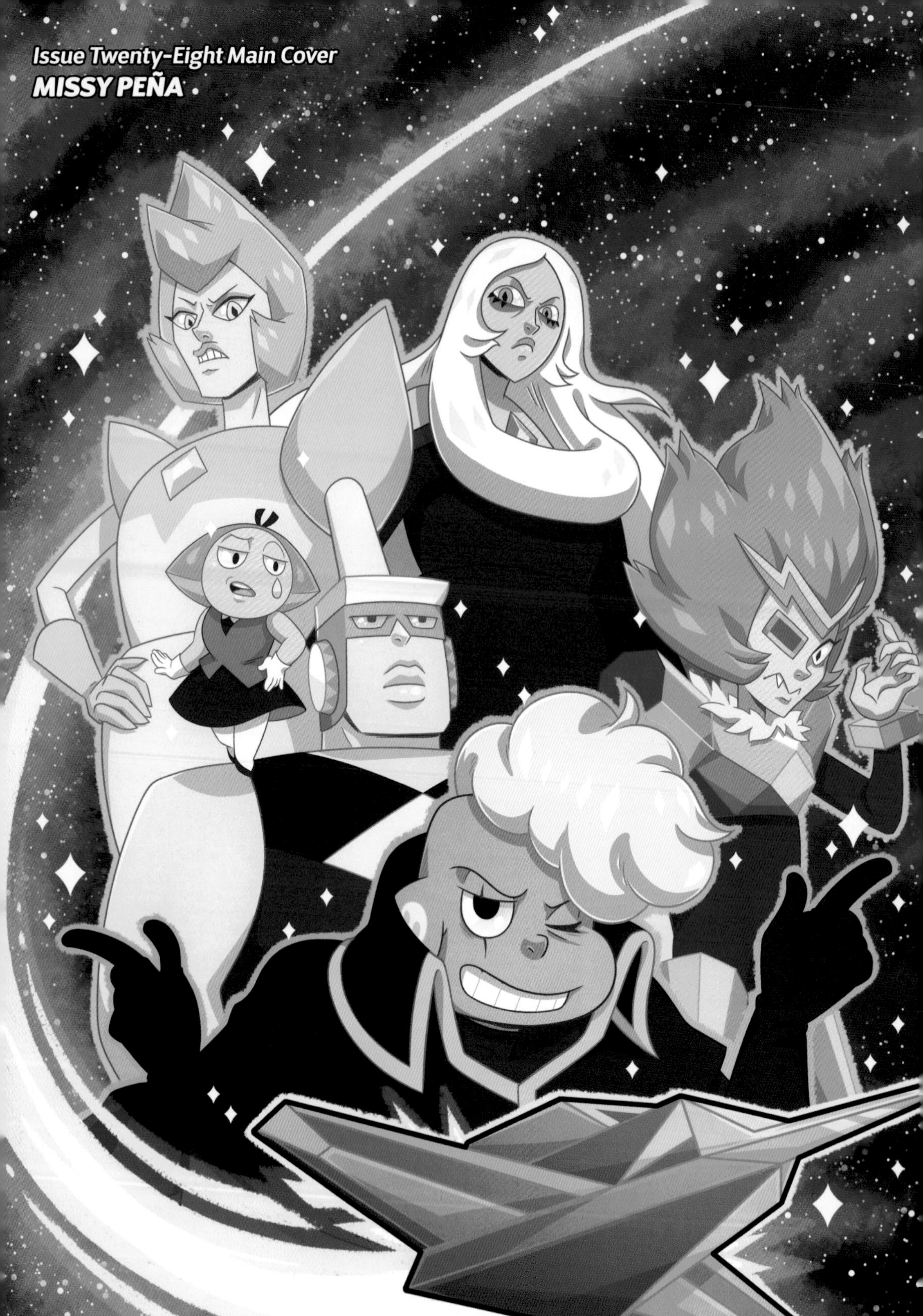
Issue Twenty-Eight Main Cover
MISSY PEÑA

CHAPTER TWENTY-EIGHT

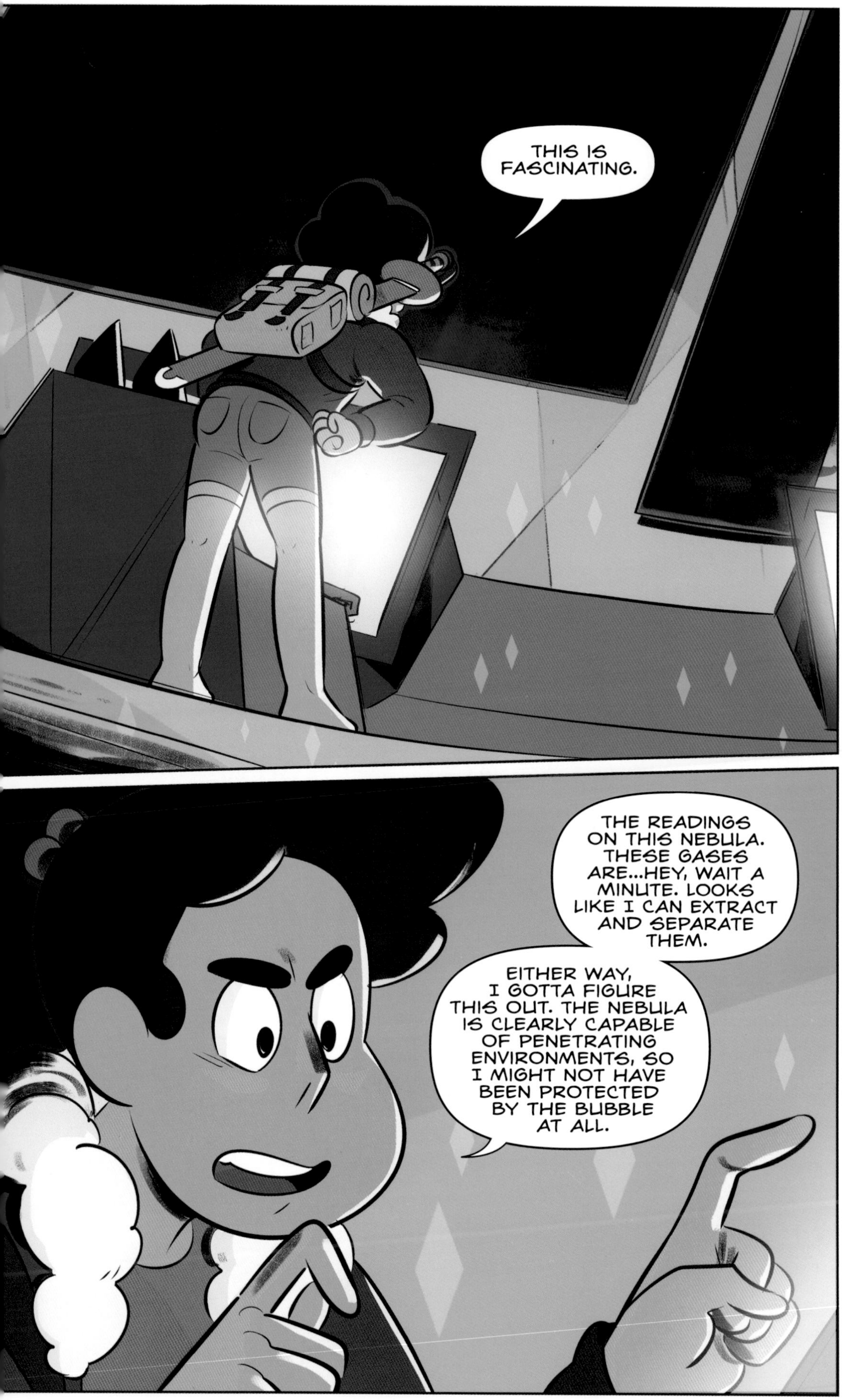
THIS IS FASCINATING.
THE READINGS ON THIS NEBULA. THESE GASES ARE...HEY, WAIT A MINUTE. LOOKS LIKE I CAN EXTRACT AND SEPARATE THEM.
EITHER WAY, I GOTTA FIGURE THIS OUT. THE NEBULA IS CLEARLY CAPABLE OF PENETRATING ENVIRONMENTS, SO I MIGHT NOT HAVE BEEN PROTECTED BY THE BUBBLE AT ALL.

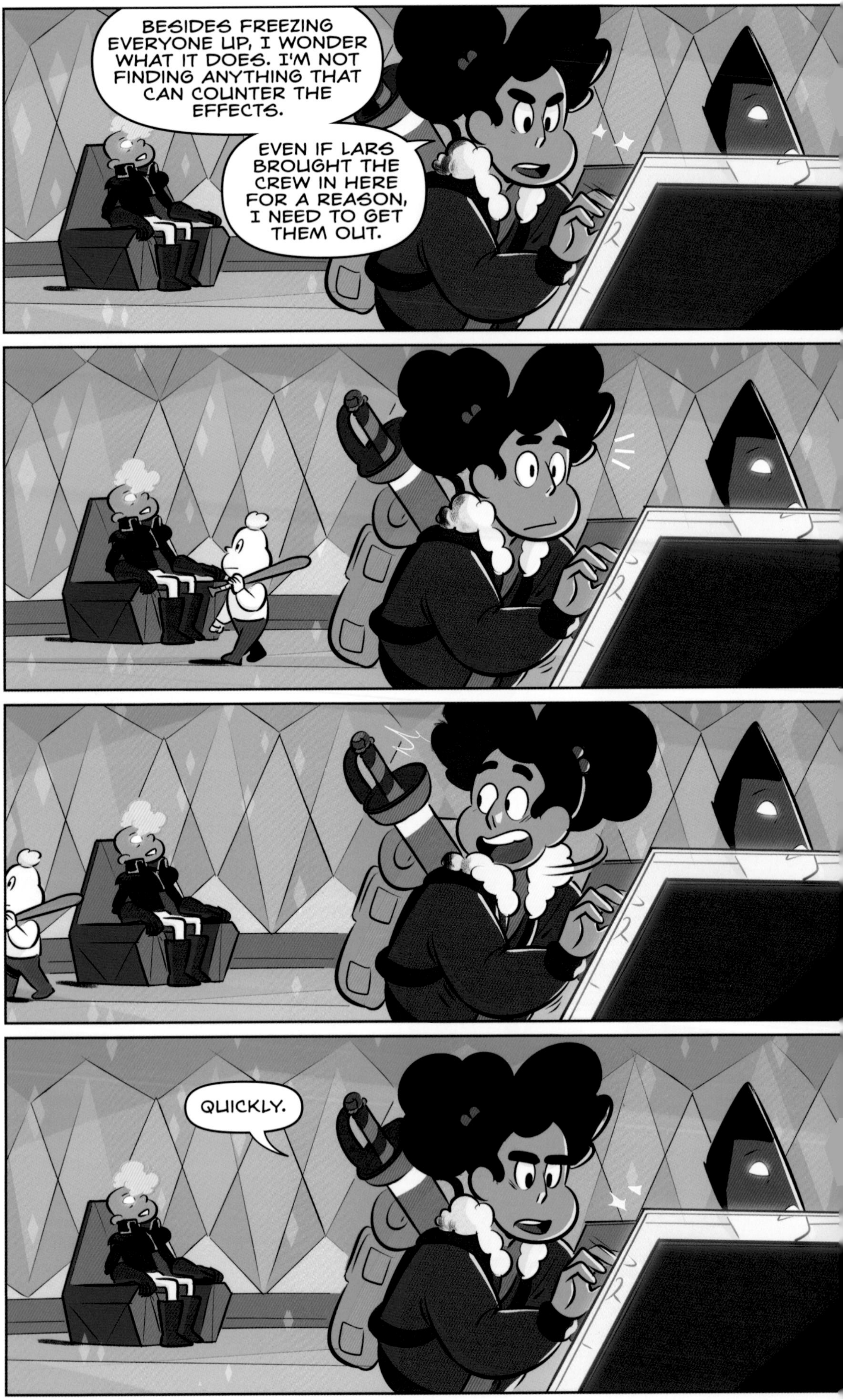
BESIDES FREEZING EVERYONE UP, I WONDER WHAT IT DOES. I'M NOT FINDING ANYTHING THAT CAN COUNTER THE EFFECTS.
EVEN IF LARS BROUGHT THE CREW IN HERE FOR A REASON, I NEED TO GET THEM OUT.
QUICKLY.

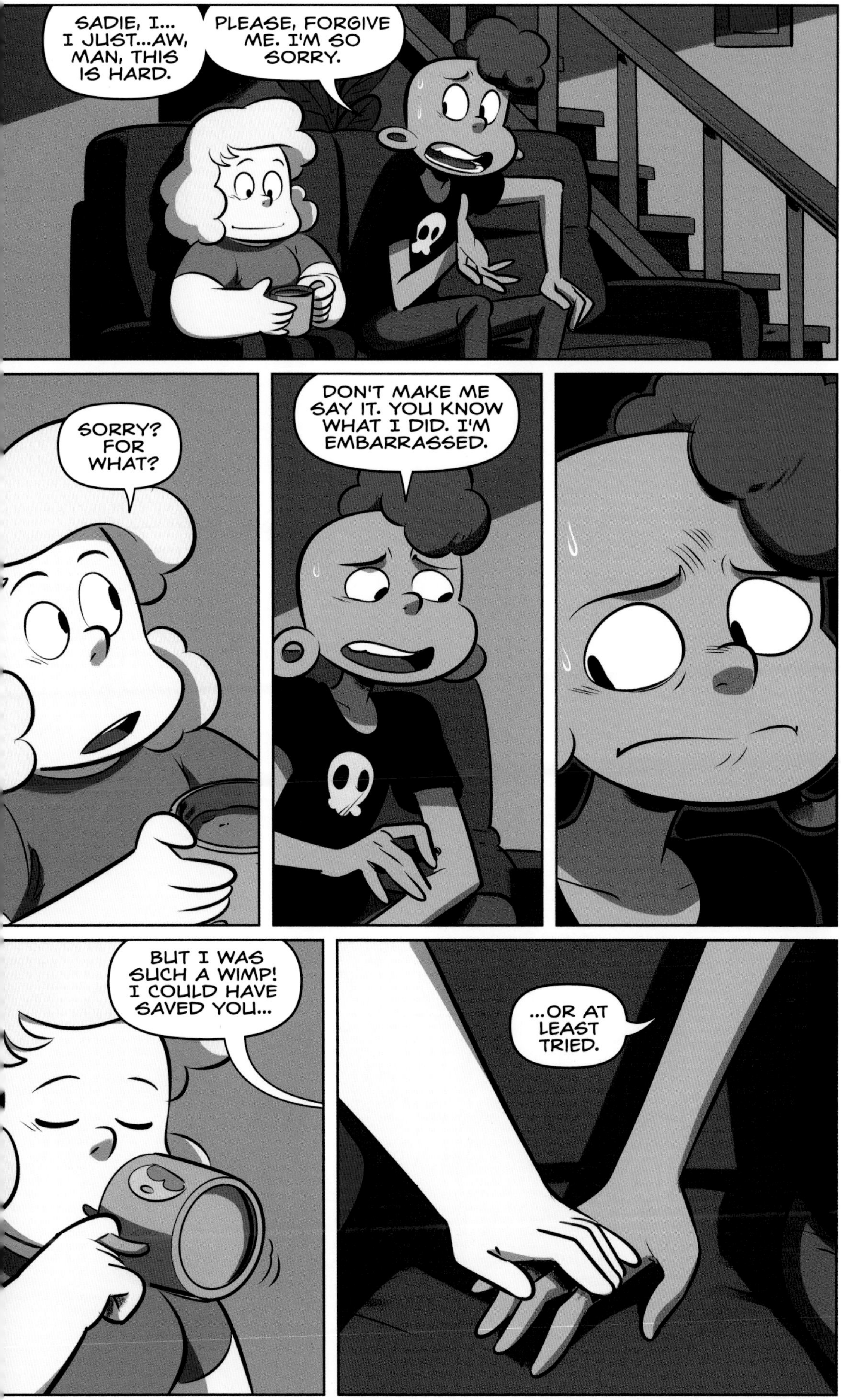

SADIE, I... I JUST...AW, MAN, THIS IS HARD.
PLEASE, FORGIVE ME. I'M SO SORRY.
SORRY? FOR WHAT?
DON'T MAKE ME SAY IT. YOU KNOW WHAT I DID. I'M EMBARRASSED.
BUT I WAS SUCH A WIMP! I COULD HAVE SAVED YOU...
...OR AT LEAST TRIED.

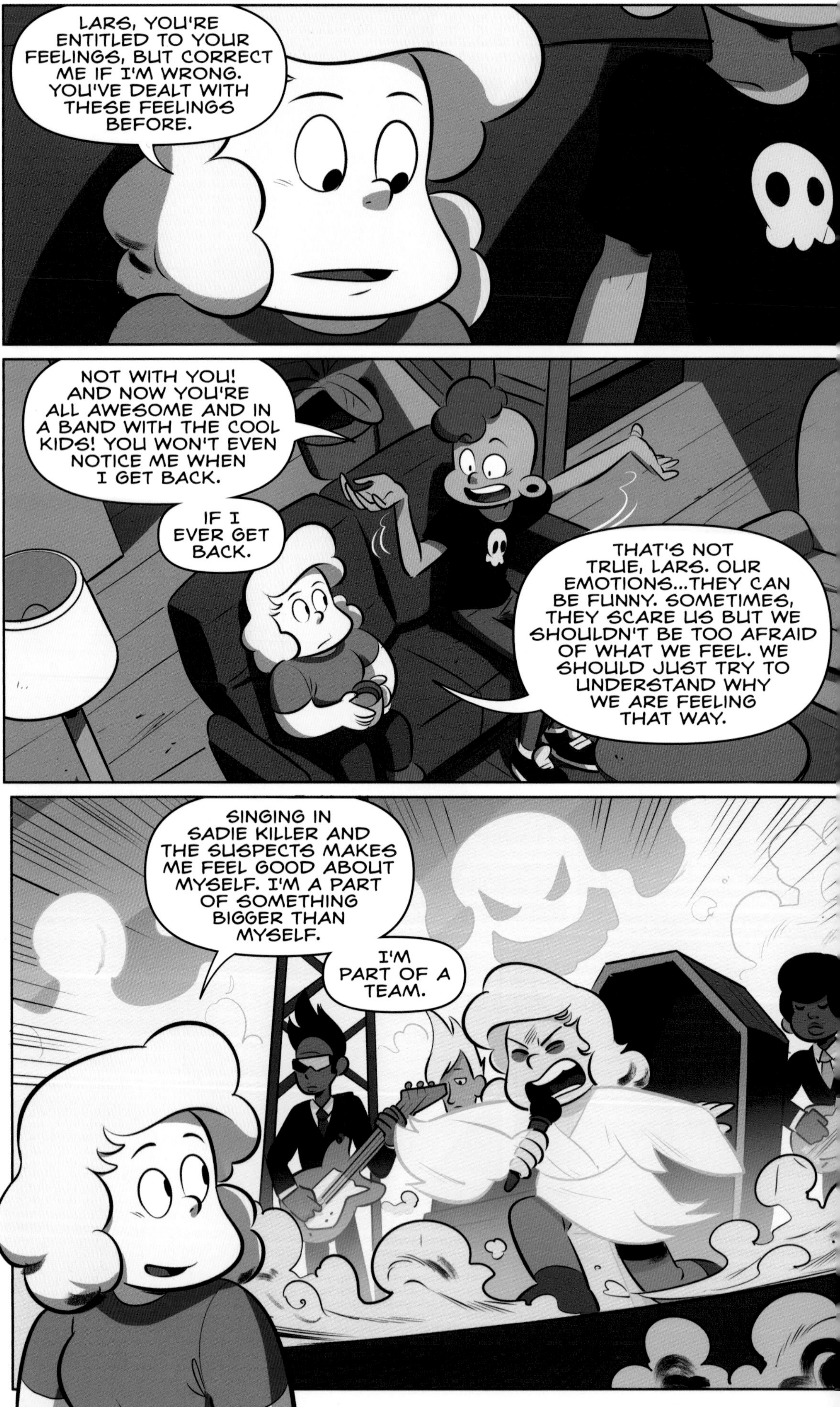
LARS, YOU'RE ENTITLED TO YOUR FEELINGS, BUT CORRECT ME IF I'M WRONG. YOU'VE DEALT WITH THESE FEELINGS BEFORE.
NOT WITH YOU! AND NOW YOU'RE ALL AWESOME AND IN A BAND WITH THE COOL KIDS! YOU WON'T EVEN NOTICE ME WHEN I GET BACK.
IF I EVER GET BACK.
THAT'S NOT TRUE, LARS. OUR EMOTIONS...THEY CAN BE FUNNY. SOMETIMES, THEY SCARE US BUT WE SHOULDN'T BE TOO AFRAID OF WHAT WE FEEL. WE SHOULD JUST TRY TO UNDERSTAND WHY WE ARE FEELING THAT WAY.
SINGING IN SADIE KILLER AND THE SUSPECTS MAKES ME FEEL GOOD ABOUT MYSELF. I'M A PART OF SOMETHING BIGGER THAN MYSELF.
I'M PART OF A TEAM.

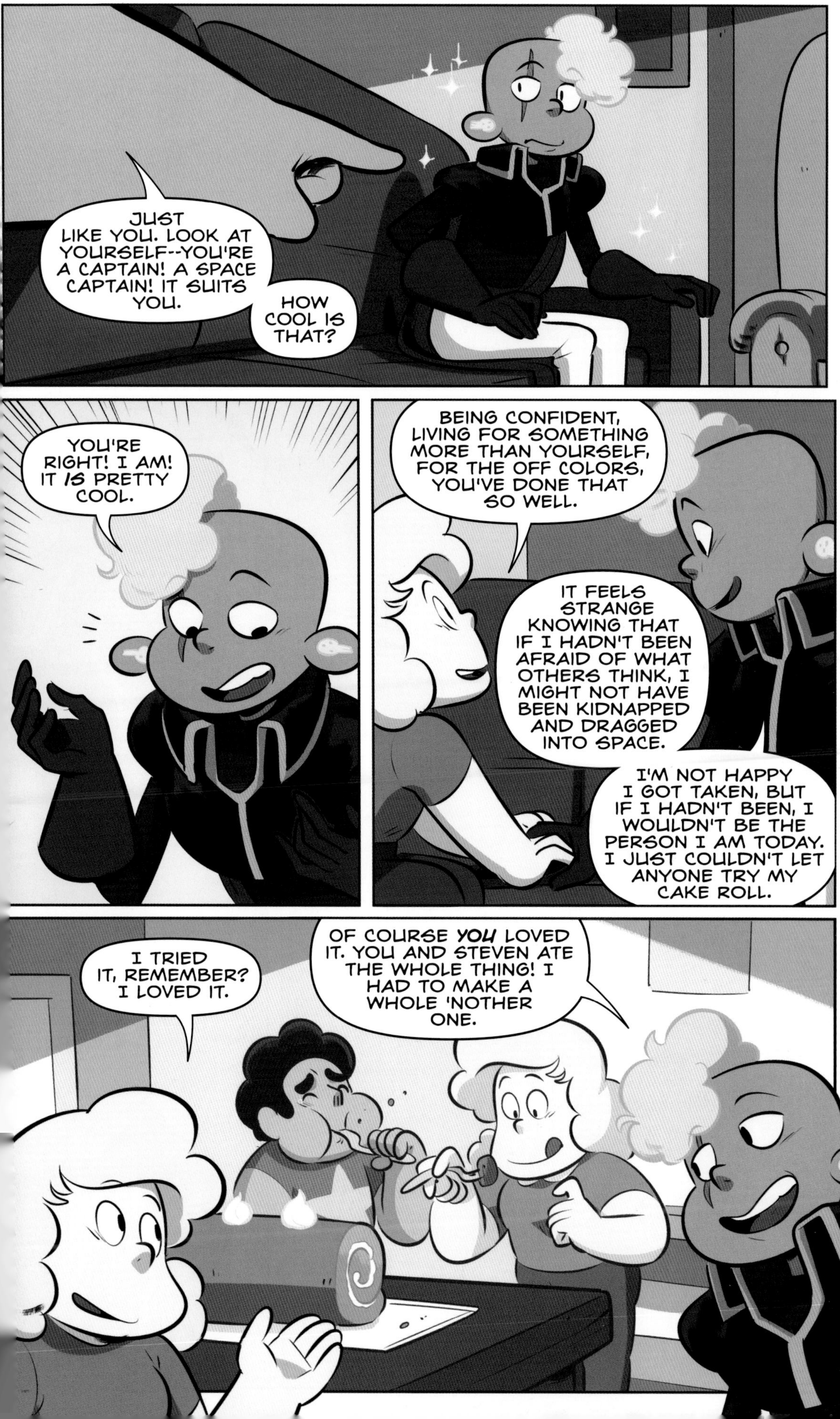
JUST LIKE YOU. LOOK AT YOURSELF--YOU'RE A CAPTAIN! A SPACE CAPTAIN! IT SUITS YOU.
HOW COOL IS THAT?
YOU'RE RIGHT! I AM! IT *IS* PRETTY COOL.
BEING CONFIDENT, LIVING FOR SOMETHING MORE THAN YOURSELF, FOR THE OFF COLORS, YOU'VE DONE THAT SO WELL.
IT FEELS STRANGE KNOWING THAT IF I HADN'T BEEN AFRAID OF WHAT OTHERS THINK, I MIGHT NOT HAVE BEEN KIDNAPPED AND DRAGGED INTO SPACE.
I'M NOT HAPPY I GOT TAKEN, BUT IF I HADN'T BEEN, I WOULDN'T BE THE PERSON I AM TODAY. I JUST COULDN'T LET ANYONE TRY MY CAKE ROLL.
I TRIED IT, REMEMBER? I LOVED IT.
OF COURSE *YOU* LOVED IT. YOU AND STEVEN ATE THE WHOLE THING! I HAD TO MAKE A WHOLE 'NOTHER ONE.

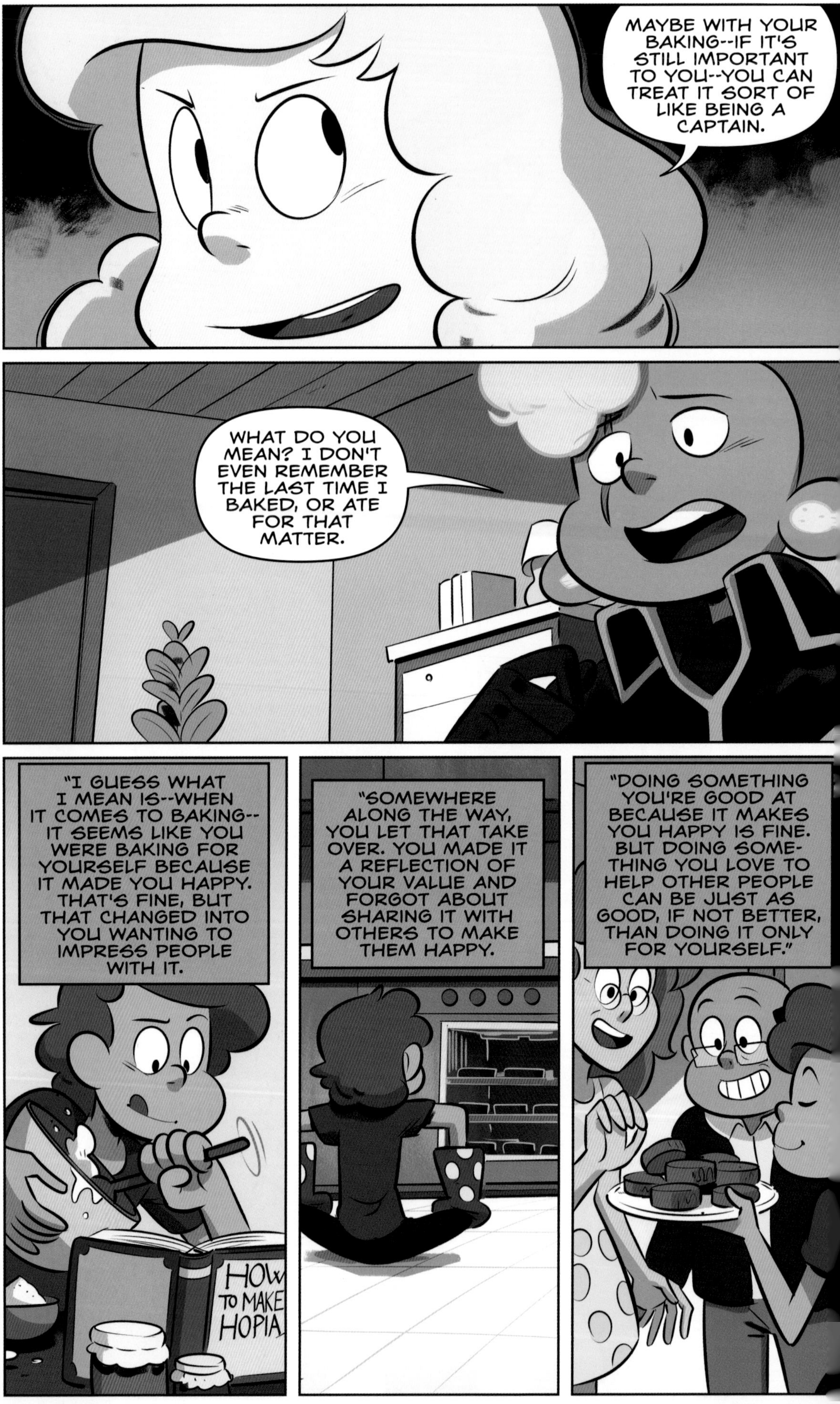
MAYBE WITH YOUR BAKING--IF IT'S STILL IMPORTANT TO YOU--YOU CAN TREAT IT SORT OF LIKE BEING A CAPTAIN.
WHAT DO YOU MEAN? I DON'T EVEN REMEMBER THE LAST TIME I BAKED, OR ATE FOR THAT MATTER.
"I GUESS WHAT I MEAN IS--WHEN IT COMES TO BAKING--IT SEEMS LIKE YOU WERE BAKING FOR YOURSELF BECAUSE IT MADE YOU HAPPY. THAT'S FINE, BUT THAT CHANGED INTO YOU WANTING TO IMPRESS PEOPLE WITH IT.
HOW TO MAKE HOPIA
"SOMEWHERE ALONG THE WAY, YOU LET THAT TAKE OVER. YOU MADE IT A REFLECTION OF YOUR VALUE AND FORGOT ABOUT SHARING IT WITH OTHERS TO MAKE THEM HAPPY.
"DOING SOMETHING YOU'RE GOOD AT BECAUSE IT MAKES YOU HAPPY IS FINE. BUT DOING SOMETHING YOU LOVE TO HELP OTHER PEOPLE CAN BE JUST AS GOOD, IF NOT BETTER, THAN DOING IT ONLY FOR YOURSELF."

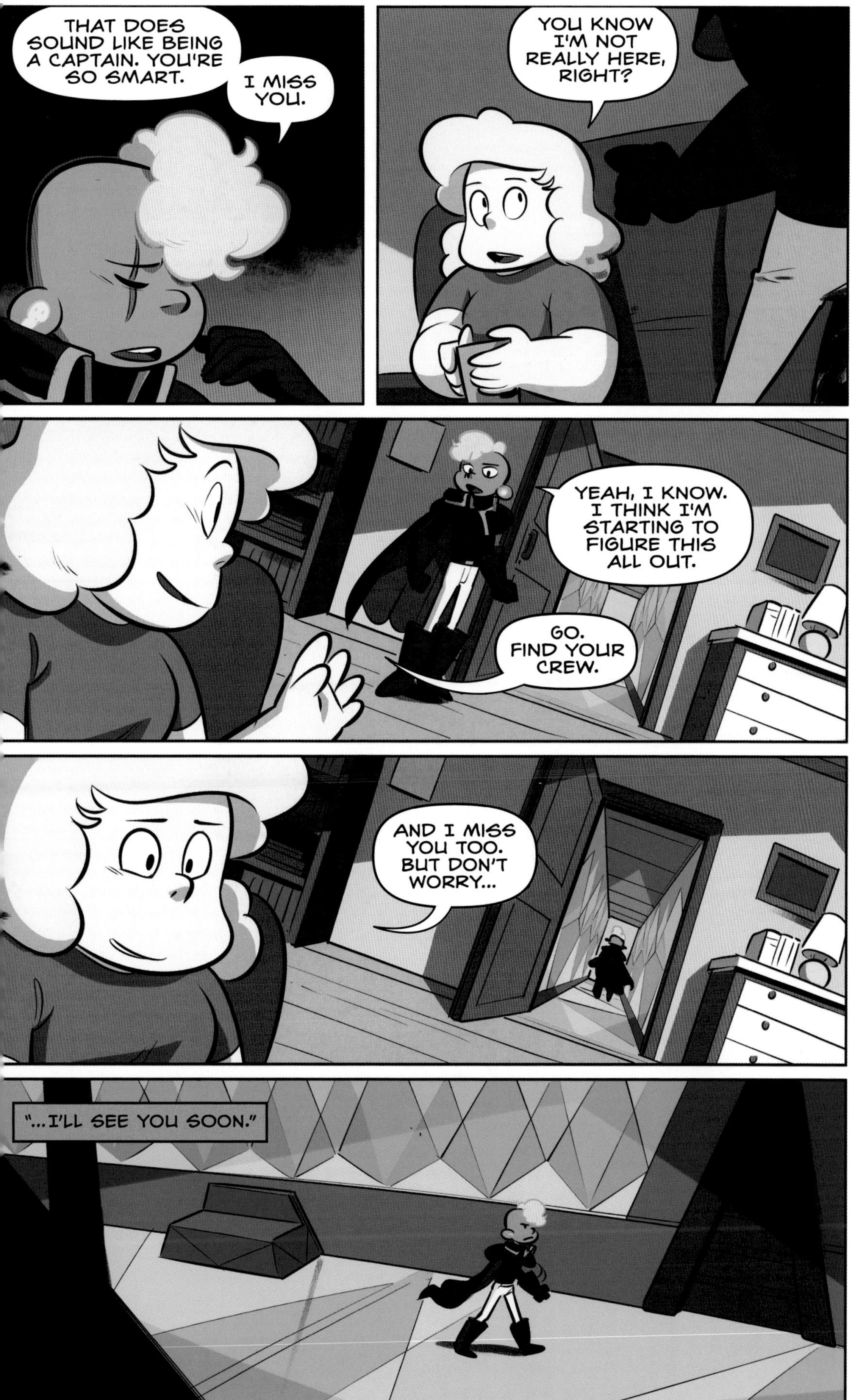
THAT DOES SOUND LIKE BEING A CAPTAIN. YOU'RE SO SMART.
I MISS YOU.
YOU KNOW I'M NOT REALLY HERE, RIGHT?
YEAH, I KNOW. I THINK I'M STARTING TO FIGURE THIS ALL OUT.
GO. FIND YOUR CREW.
AND I MISS YOU TOO. BUT DON'T WORRY...
"...I'LL SEE YOU SOON."

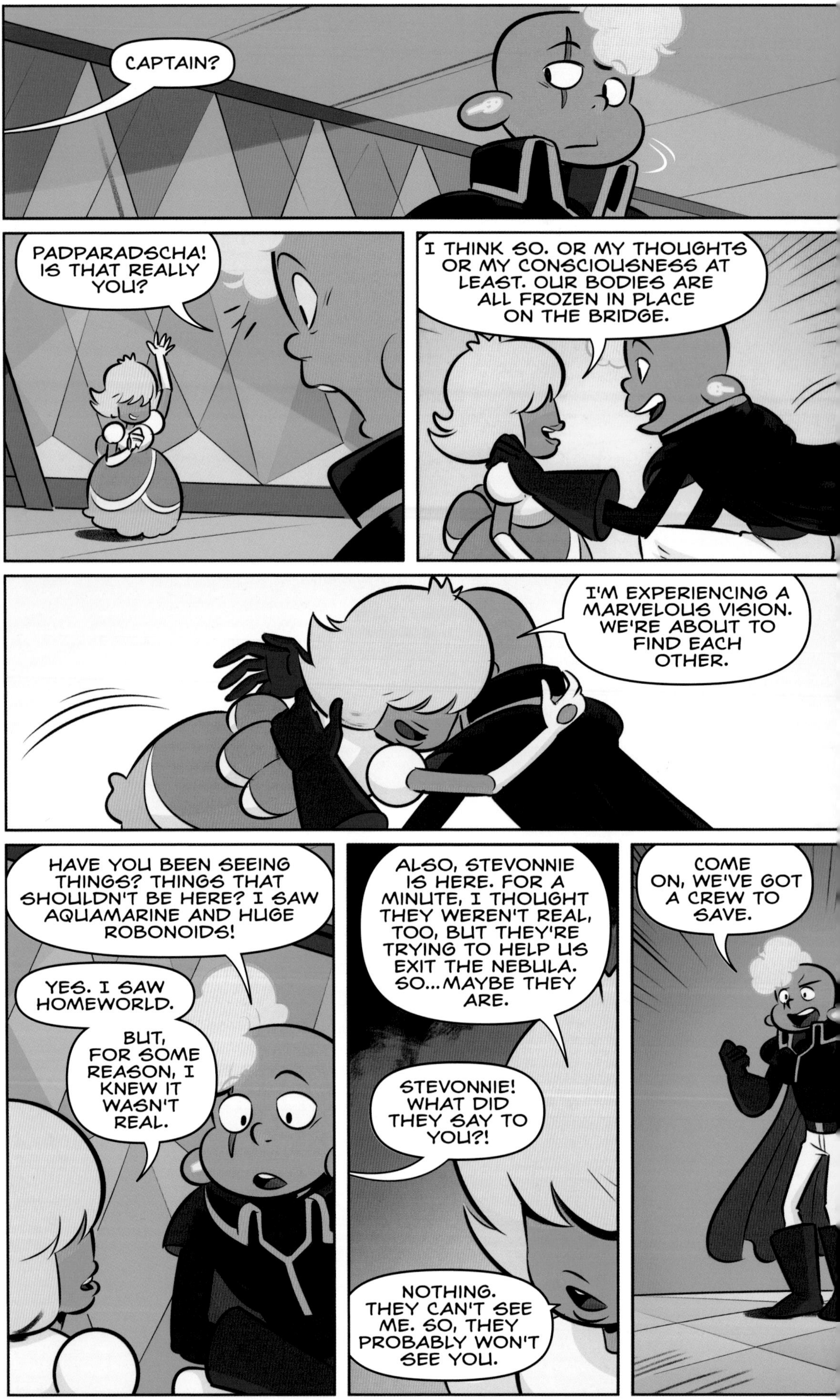
CAPTAIN?
PADPARADSCHA! IS THAT REALLY YOU?
I THINK SO. OR MY THOUGHTS OR MY CONSCIOUSNESS AT LEAST. OUR BODIES ARE ALL FROZEN IN PLACE ON THE BRIDGE.
I'M EXPERIENCING A MARVELOUS VISION. WE'RE ABOUT TO FIND EACH OTHER.
HAVE YOU BEEN SEEING THINGS? THINGS THAT SHOULDN'T BE HERE? I SAW AQUAMARINE AND HUGE ROBONOIDS!
YES. I SAW HOMEWORLD.
BUT, FOR SOME REASON, I KNEW IT WASN'T REAL.
ALSO, STEVONNIE IS HERE. FOR A MINUTE, I THOUGHT THEY WEREN'T REAL, TOO, BUT THEY'RE TRYING TO HELP US EXIT THE NEBULA. SO...MAYBE THEY ARE.
STEVONNIE! WHAT DID THEY SAY TO YOU?!
NOTHING. THEY CAN'T SEE ME. SO, THEY PROBABLY WON'T SEE YOU.
COME ON, WE'VE GOT A CREW TO SAVE.

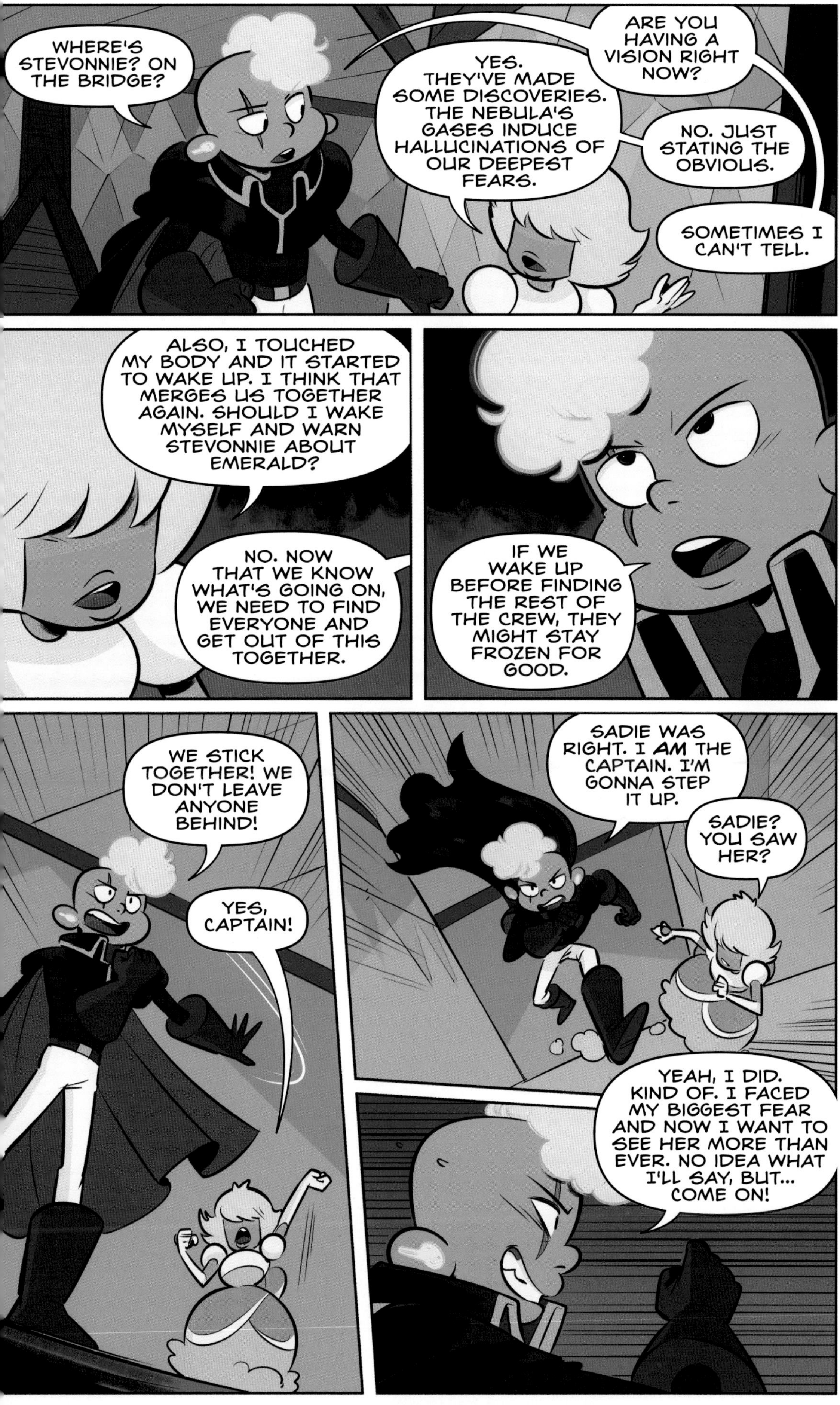

WHERE'S STEVONNIE? ON THE BRIDGE?
YES. THEY'VE MADE SOME DISCOVERIES. THE NEBULA'S GASES INDUCE HALLUCINATIONS OF OUR DEEPEST FEARS.
ARE YOU HAVING A VISION RIGHT NOW?
NO. JUST STATING THE OBVIOUS.
SOMETIMES I CAN'T TELL.
ALSO, I TOUCHED MY BODY AND IT STARTED TO WAKE UP. I THINK THAT MERGES US TOGETHER AGAIN. SHOULD I WAKE MYSELF AND WARN STEVONNIE ABOUT EMERALD?
NO. NOW THAT WE KNOW WHAT'S GOING ON, WE NEED TO FIND EVERYONE AND GET OUT OF THIS TOGETHER.
IF WE WAKE UP BEFORE FINDING THE REST OF THE CREW, THEY MIGHT STAY FROZEN FOR GOOD.
WE STICK TOGETHER! WE DON'T LEAVE ANYONE BEHIND!
YES, CAPTAIN!
SADIE WAS RIGHT. I AM THE CAPTAIN. I'M GONNA STEP IT UP.
SADIE? YOU SAW HER?
YEAH, I DID. KIND OF. I FACED MY BIGGEST FEAR AND NOW I WANT TO SEE HER MORE THAN EVER. NO IDEA WHAT I'LL SAY, BUT... COME ON!

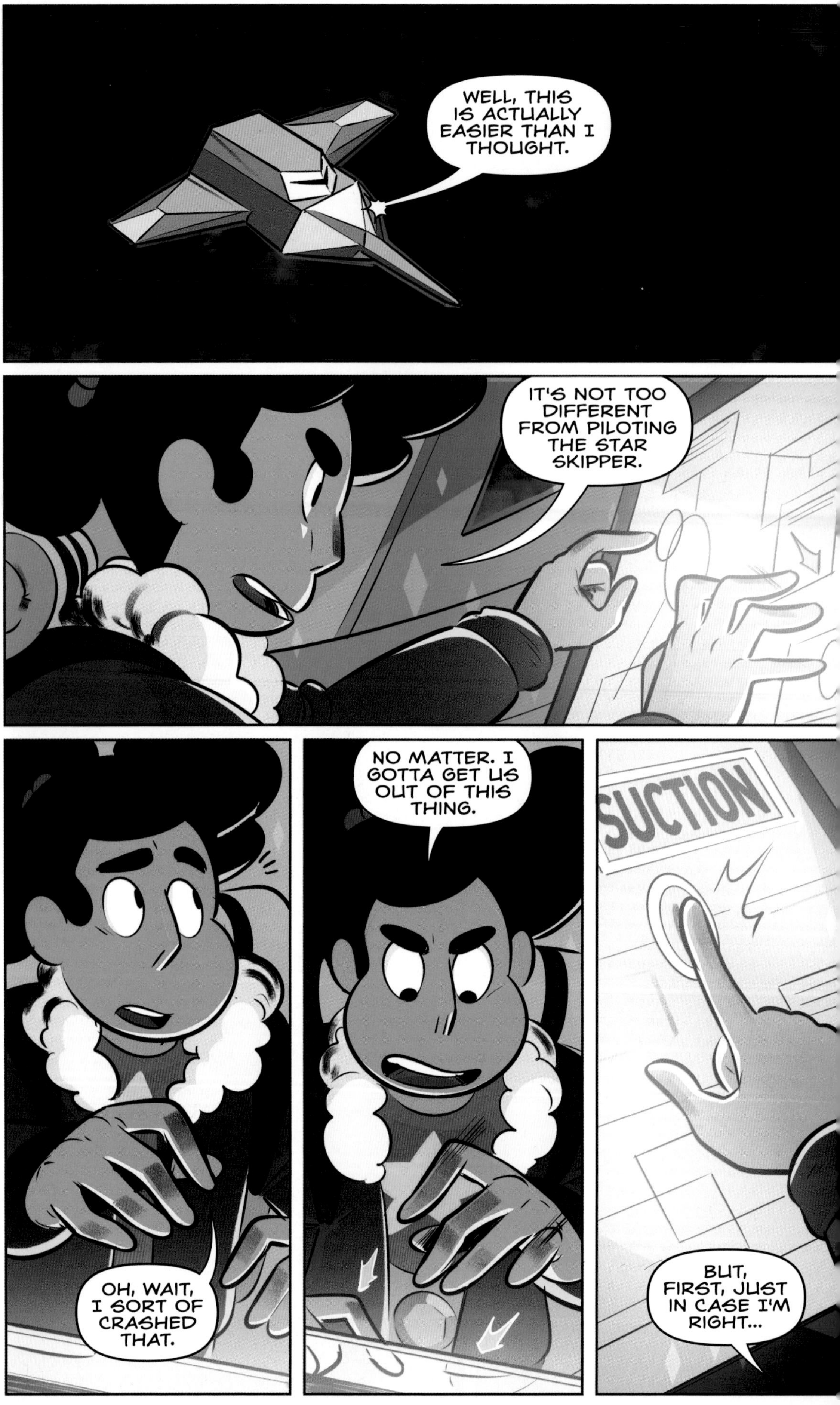
WELL, THIS IS ACTUALLY EASIER THAN I THOUGHT.
IT'S NOT TOO DIFFERENT FROM PILOTING THE STAR SKIPPER.
OH, WAIT, I SORT OF CRASHED THAT.
NO MATTER. I GOTTA GET US OUT OF THIS THING.
SUCTION
BUT, FIRST, JUST IN CASE I'M RIGHT...

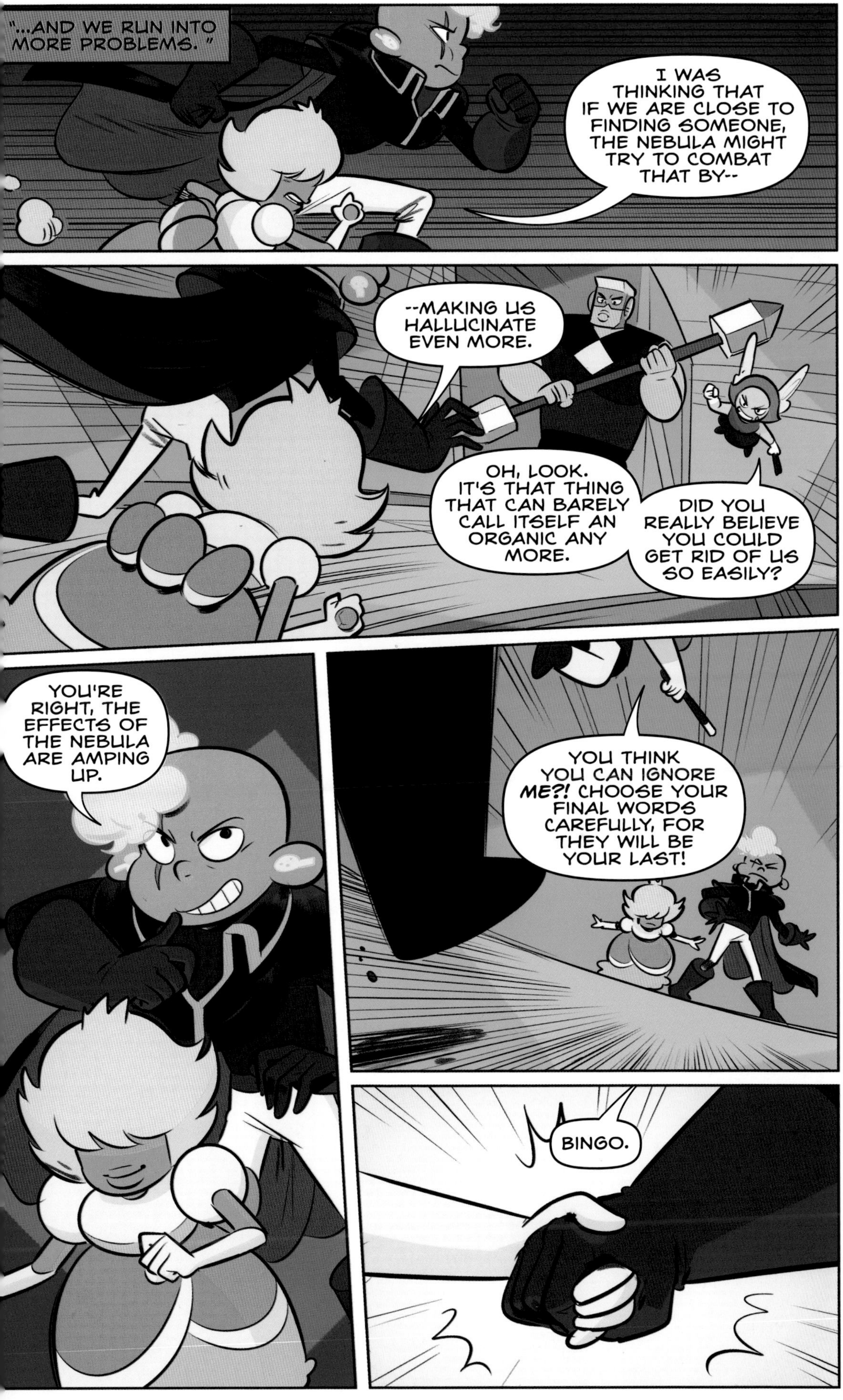
"...AND WE RUN INTO MORE PROBLEMS."
I WAS THINKING THAT IF WE ARE CLOSE TO FINDING SOMEONE, THE NEBULA MIGHT TRY TO COMBAT THAT BY--
--MAKING US HALLUCINATE EVEN MORE.
OH, LOOK. IT'S THAT THING THAT CAN BARELY CALL ITSELF AN ORGANIC ANY MORE.
DID YOU REALLY BELIEVE YOU COULD GET RID OF US SO EASILY?
YOU'RE RIGHT, THE EFFECTS OF THE NEBULA ARE AMPING UP.
YOU THINK YOU CAN IGNORE *ME?!* CHOOSE YOUR FINAL WORDS CAREFULLY, FOR THEY WILL BE YOUR LAST!
BINGO.

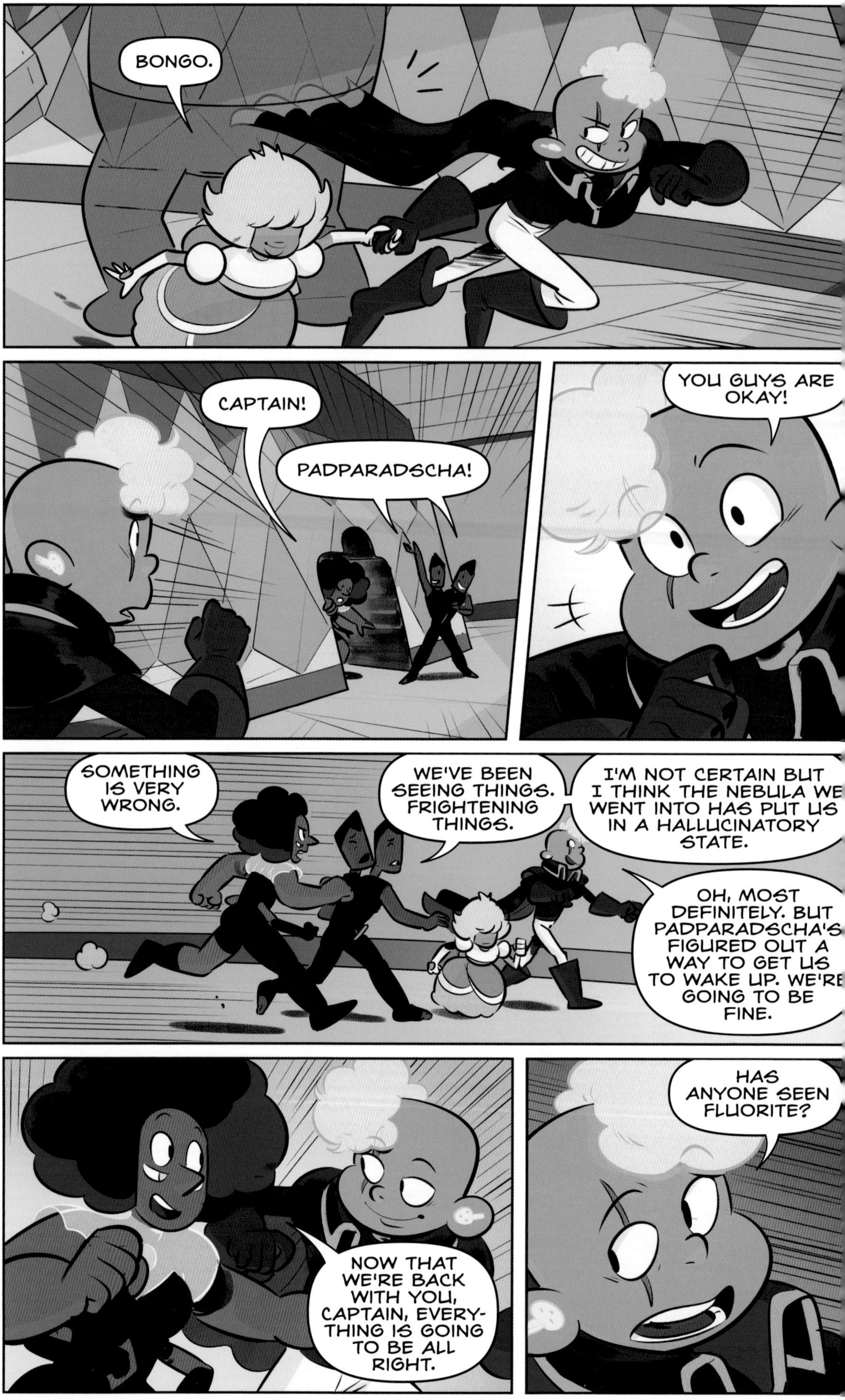
BONGO.
CAPTAIN!
PADPARADSCHA!
YOU GUYS ARE OKAY!
SOMETHING IS VERY WRONG.
WE'VE BEEN SEEING THINGS. FRIGHTENING THINGS.
I'M NOT CERTAIN BUT I THINK THE NEBULA WE WENT INTO HAS PUT US IN A HALLUCINATORY STATE.
OH, MOST DEFINITELY. BUT PADPARADSCHA'S FIGURED OUT A WAY TO GET US TO WAKE UP. WE'RE GOING TO BE FINE.
NOW THAT WE'RE BACK WITH YOU, CAPTAIN, EVERYTHING IS GOING TO BE ALL RIGHT.
HAS ANYONE SEEN FLUORITE?

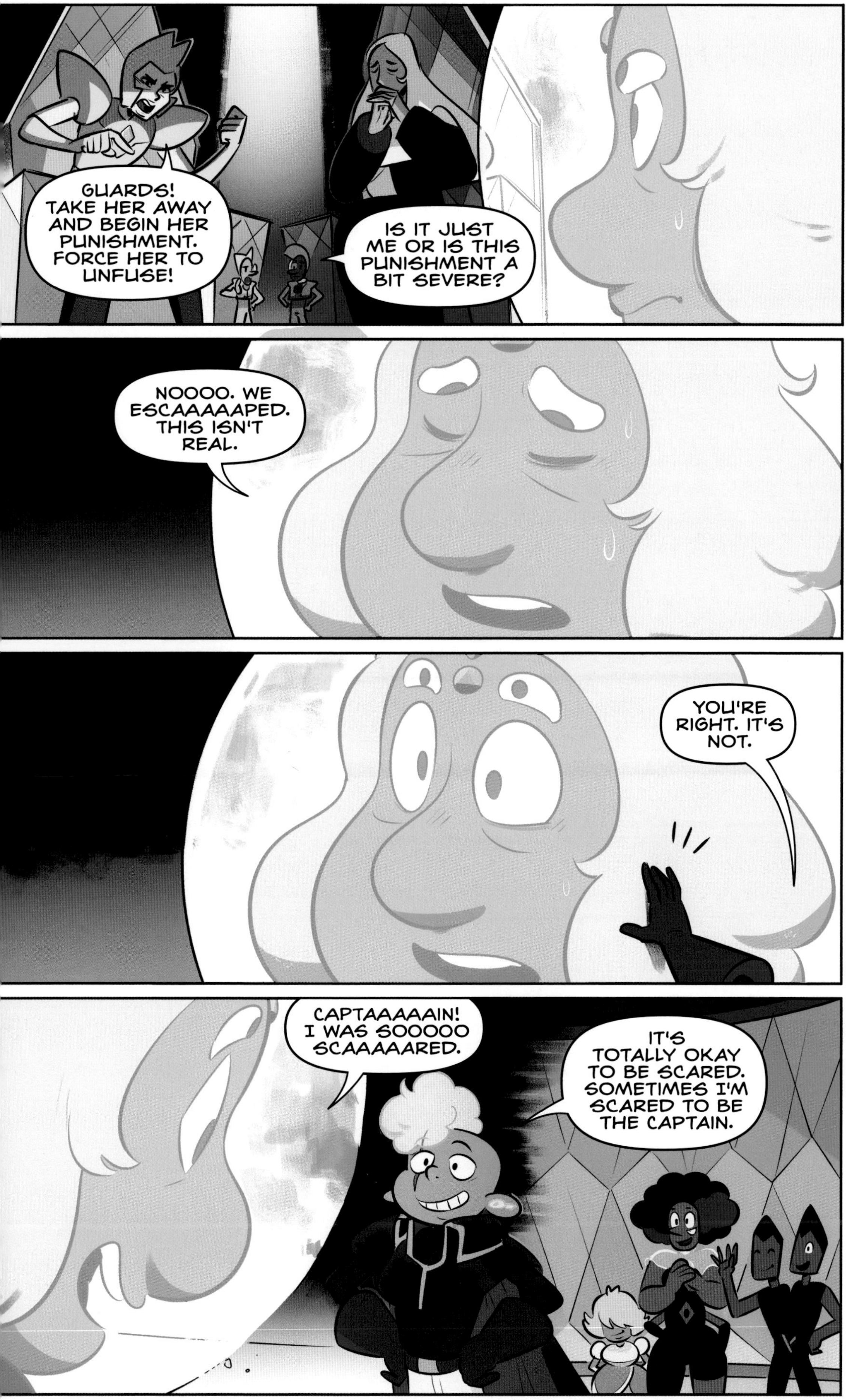
GUARDS! TAKE HER AWAY AND BEGIN HER PUNISHMENT. FORCE HER TO UNFUSE!
IS IT JUST ME OR IS THIS PUNISHMENT A BIT SEVERE?
NOOOO. WE ESCAAAAAPED. THIS ISN'T REAL.
YOU'RE RIGHT. IT'S NOT.
CAPTAAAAAAIN! I WAS SOOOOO SCAAAAARED.
IT'S TOTALLY OKAY TO BE SCARED. SOMETIMES I'M SCARED TO BE THE CAPTAIN.

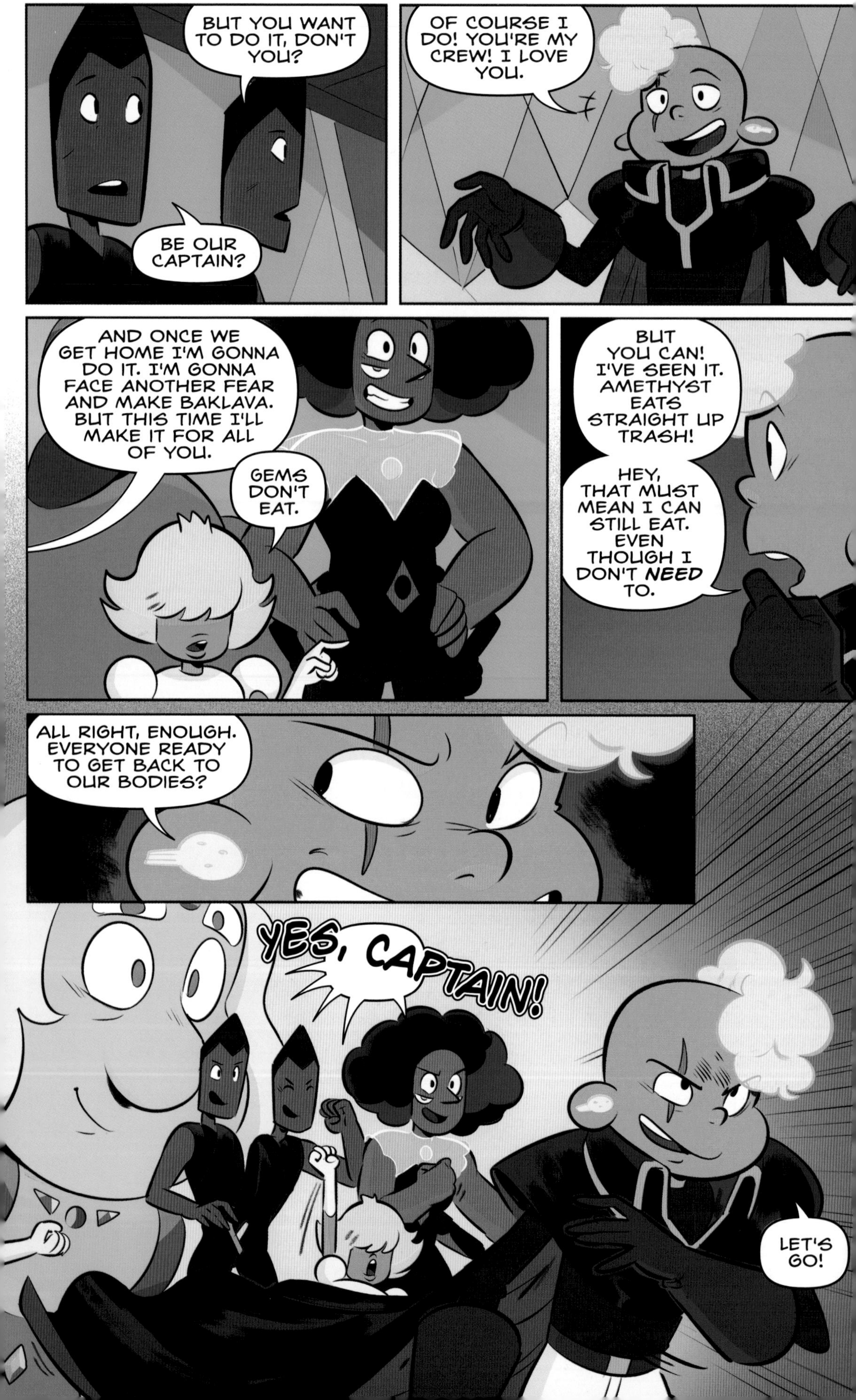
BUT YOU WANT TO DO IT, DON'T YOU?
BE OUR CAPTAIN?
OF COURSE I DO! YOU'RE MY CREW! I LOVE YOU.
AND ONCE WE GET HOME I'M GONNA DO IT. I'M GONNA FACE ANOTHER FEAR AND MAKE BAKLAVA. BUT THIS TIME I'LL MAKE IT FOR ALL OF YOU.
GEMS DON'T EAT.
BUT YOU CAN! I'VE SEEN IT. AMETHYST EATS STRAIGHT UP TRASH!
HEY, THAT MUST MEAN I CAN STILL EAT. EVEN THOUGH I DON'T *NEED* TO.
ALL RIGHT, ENOUGH. EVERYONE READY TO GET BACK TO OUR BODIES?
YES, CAPTAIN!
LET'S GO!

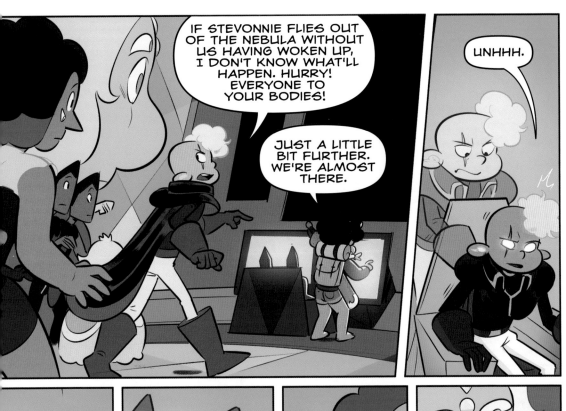

IF STEVONNIE FLIES OUT OF THE NEBULA WITHOUT US HAVING WOKEN UP, I DON'T KNOW WHAT'LL HAPPEN. HURRY! EVERYONE TO YOUR BODIES!

JUST A LITTLE BIT FURTHER. WE'RE ALMOST THERE.

UNHHH.

STEVONNIE!

WELCOME BACK!

IT'S GOOD TO BE BACK.

CAPTAIN, WE AREN'T THE ONLY ONES WHO ARE BACK.

OH NO. OUR SHIELDS AREN'T RESPONDING!

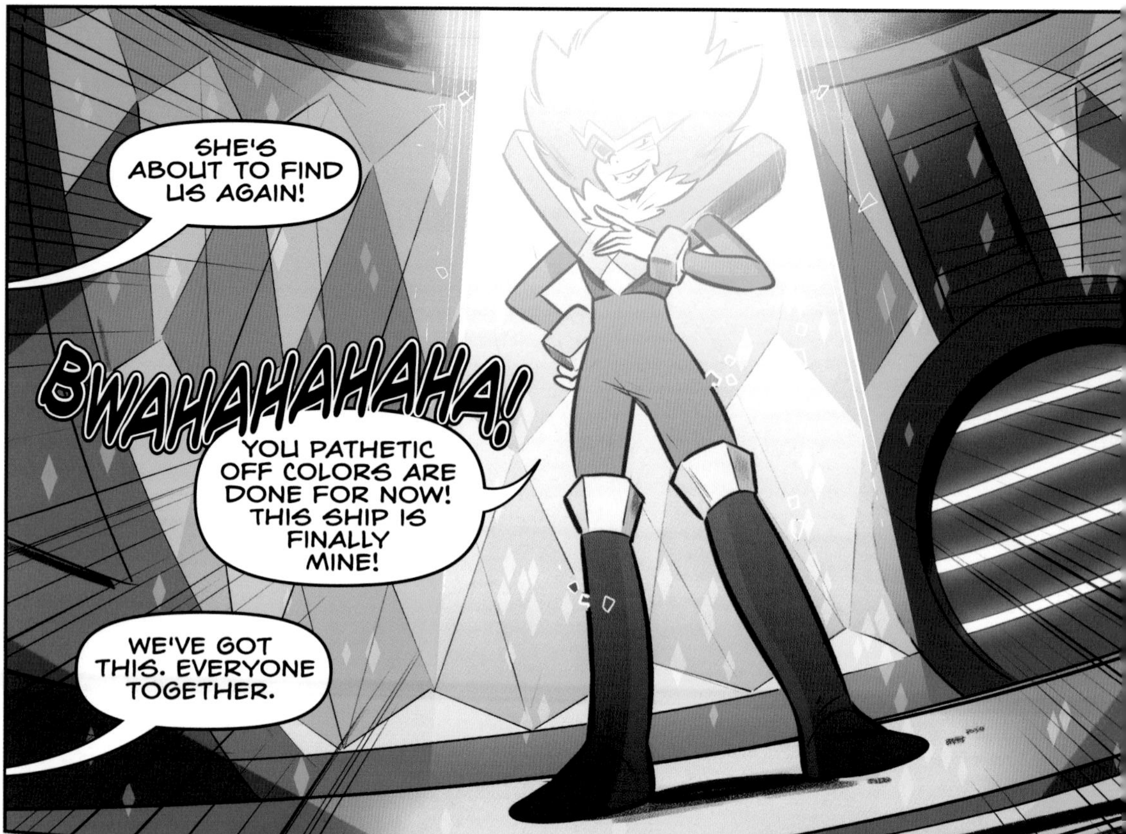
SHE'S ABOUT TO FIND US AGAIN!
BWAHAHAHAHAHA!
YOU PATHETIC OFF COLORS ARE DONE FOR NOW! THIS SHIP IS FINALLY MINE!
WE'VE GOT THIS. EVERYONE TOGETHER.

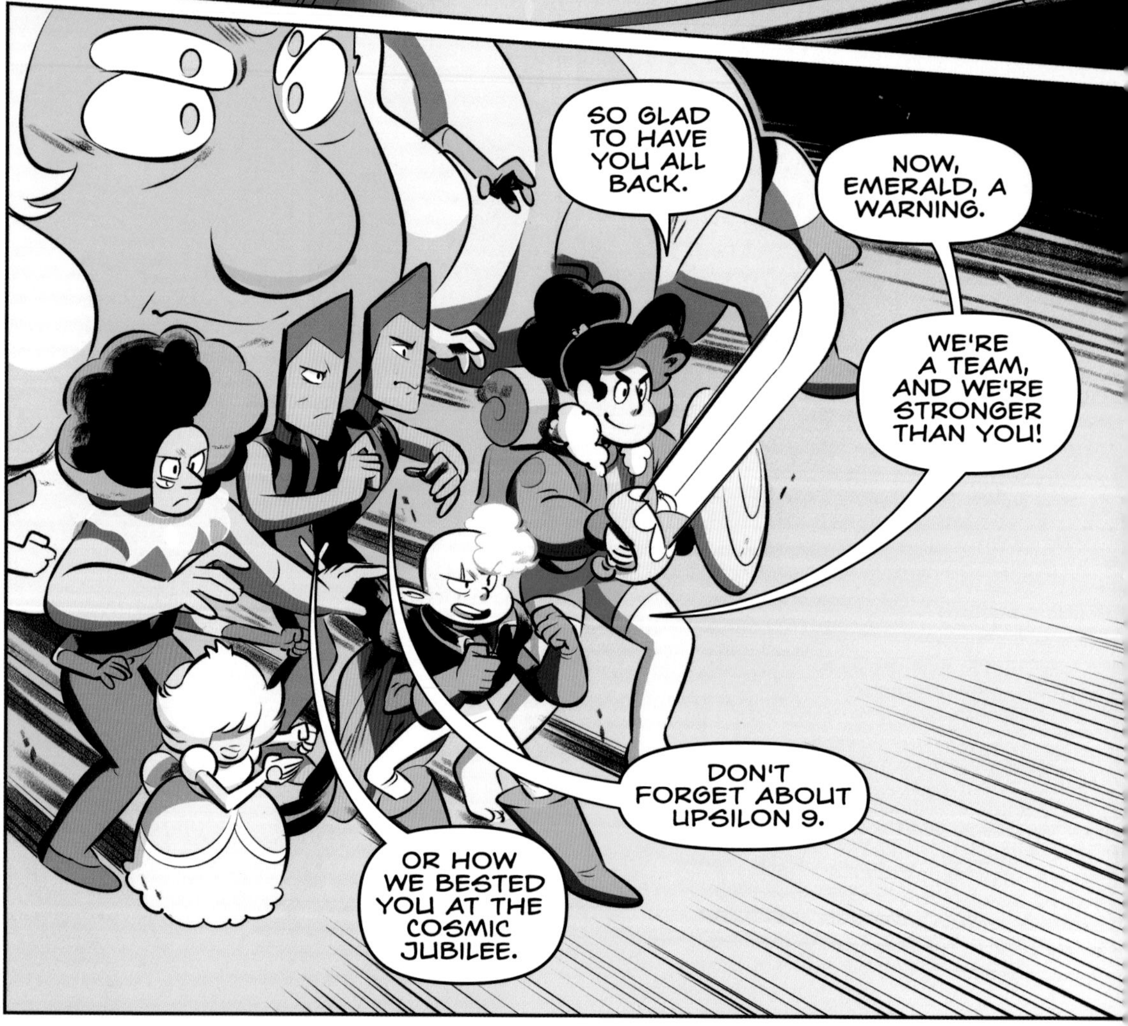
SO GLAD TO HAVE YOU ALL BACK.
NOW, EMERALD, A WARNING.
WE'RE A TEAM, AND WE'RE STRONGER THAN YOU!
DON'T FORGET ABOUT UPSILON 9.
OR HOW WE BESTED YOU AT THE COSMIC JUBILEE.

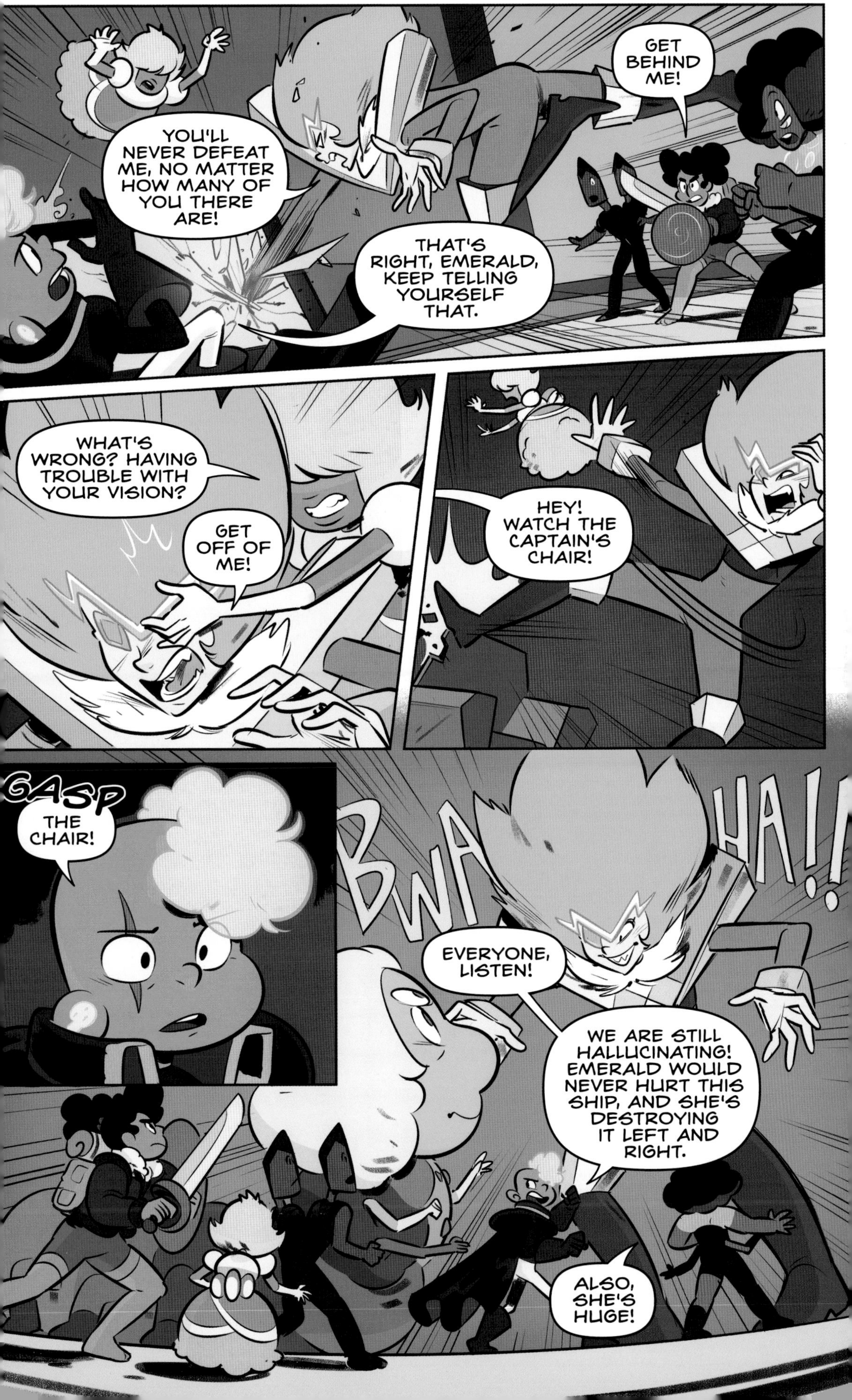
GET BEHIND ME!
YOU'LL NEVER DEFEAT ME, NO MATTER HOW MANY OF YOU THERE ARE!
THAT'S RIGHT, EMERALD, KEEP TELLING YOURSELF THAT.
WHAT'S WRONG? HAVING TROUBLE WITH YOUR VISION?
GET OFF OF ME!
HEY! WATCH THE CAPTAIN'S CHAIR!
GASP
THE CHAIR!
BWAHA!!
EVERYONE, LISTEN!
WE ARE STILL HALLUCINATING! EMERALD WOULD NEVER HURT THIS SHIP, AND SHE'S DESTROYING IT LEFT AND RIGHT.
ALSO, SHE'S HUGE!

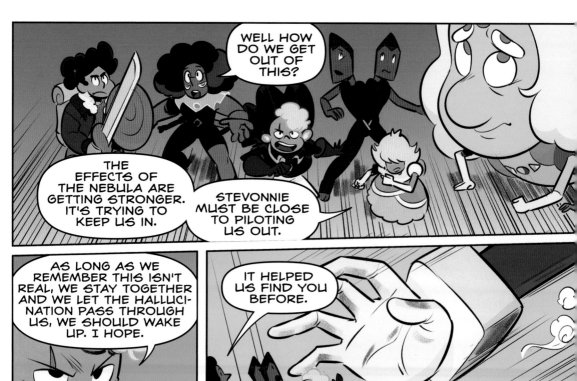

WELL HOW DO WE GET OUT OF THIS?

THE EFFECTS OF THE NEBULA ARE GETTING STRONGER. IT'S TRYING TO KEEP US IN.

STEVONNIE MUST BE CLOSE TO PILOTING US OUT.

AS LONG AS WE REMEMBER THIS ISN'T REAL, WE STAY TOGETHER AND WE LET THE HALLUCINATION PASS THROUGH US, WE SHOULD WAKE UP. I HOPE.

IT HELPED US FIND YOU BEFORE.

IT'S WORTH A SHOT.

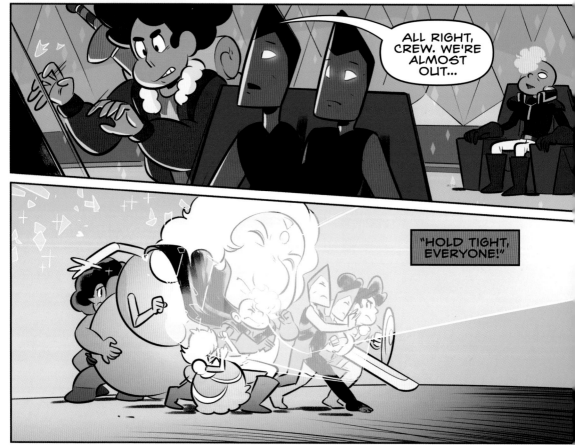

ALL RIGHT, CREW. WE'RE ALMOST OUT...

"HOLD TIGHT, EVERYONE!"

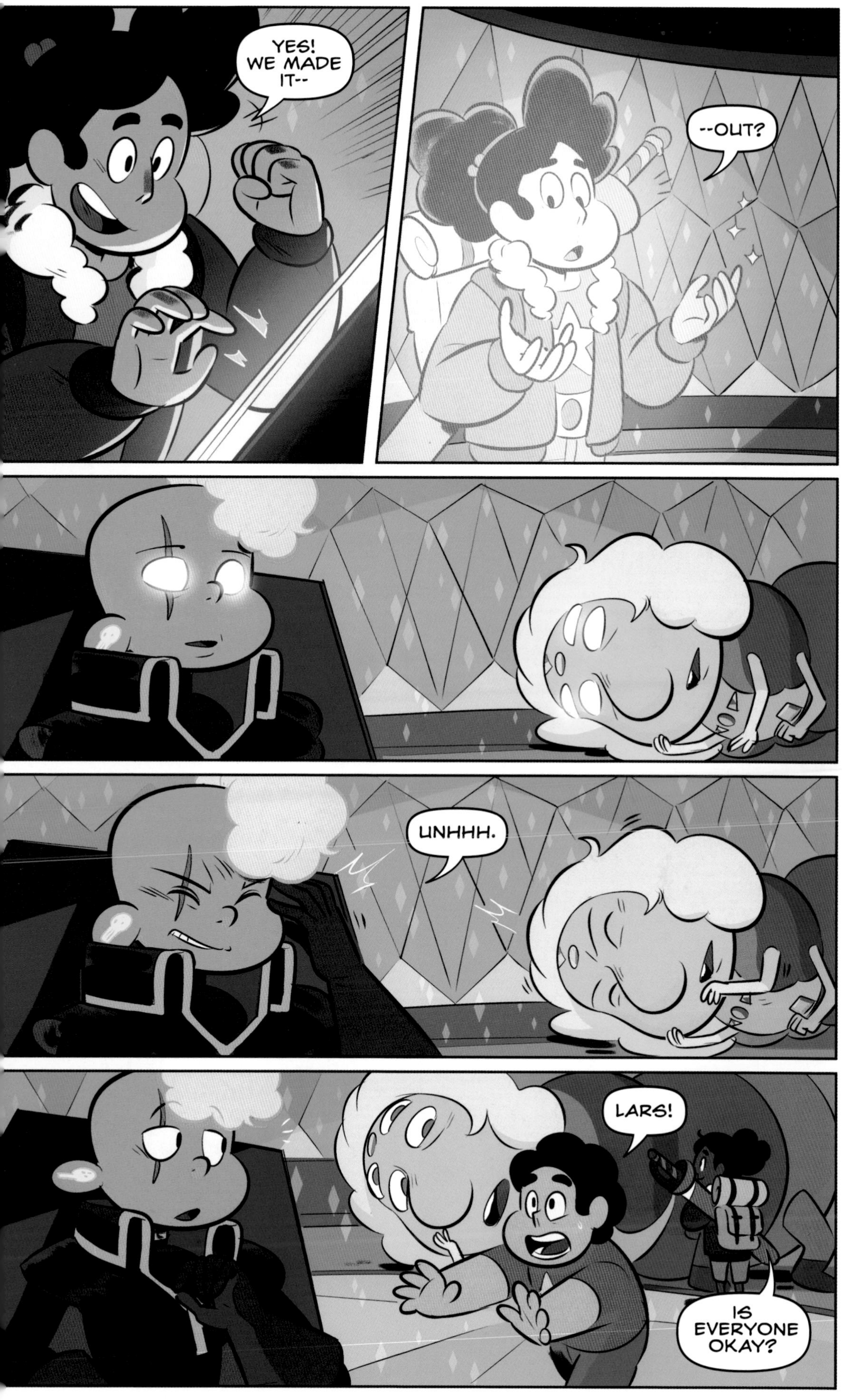
YES! WE MADE IT--
--OUT?
UNHHH.
LARS!
IS EVERYONE OKAY?

STEVEN! IT'S A GOOD THING YOU AND CONNIE DECIDED TO VISIT.

I'M GLAD EVERYONE'S ALL RIGHT. WE'RE OUT OF THE NEBULA NOW.

BUT WHAT ABOUT EMERALD! SHE CAN STILL FIND US!

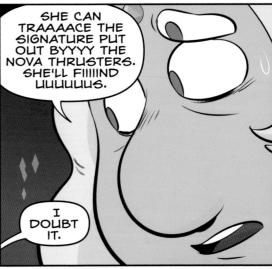

SHE CAN TRAAAACE THE SIGNATURE PUT OUT BYYYY THE NOVA THRUSTERS. SHE'LL FIIIIND UUUUUUS.

I DOUBT IT.

SEE, WHILE WE WERE ALL IN THE NEBULA, STEVONNIE WAS ABLE TO PLOT A COURSE STRAIGHT THROUGH IT WHILE ALSO TRACING EMERALD'S COURSE.

IT SEEMS THAT SHE'S HAVING TO GO ALL THE WAY AROUND IT, WHICH COULD TAKE QUITE SOME TIME. THE NEBULA IS PRETTY BIG.

AND WHILE SHE'S DOING THAT, YOU GUYS ARE OUT THE OTHER SIDE, ALL FUELED UP AND READY TO GO!

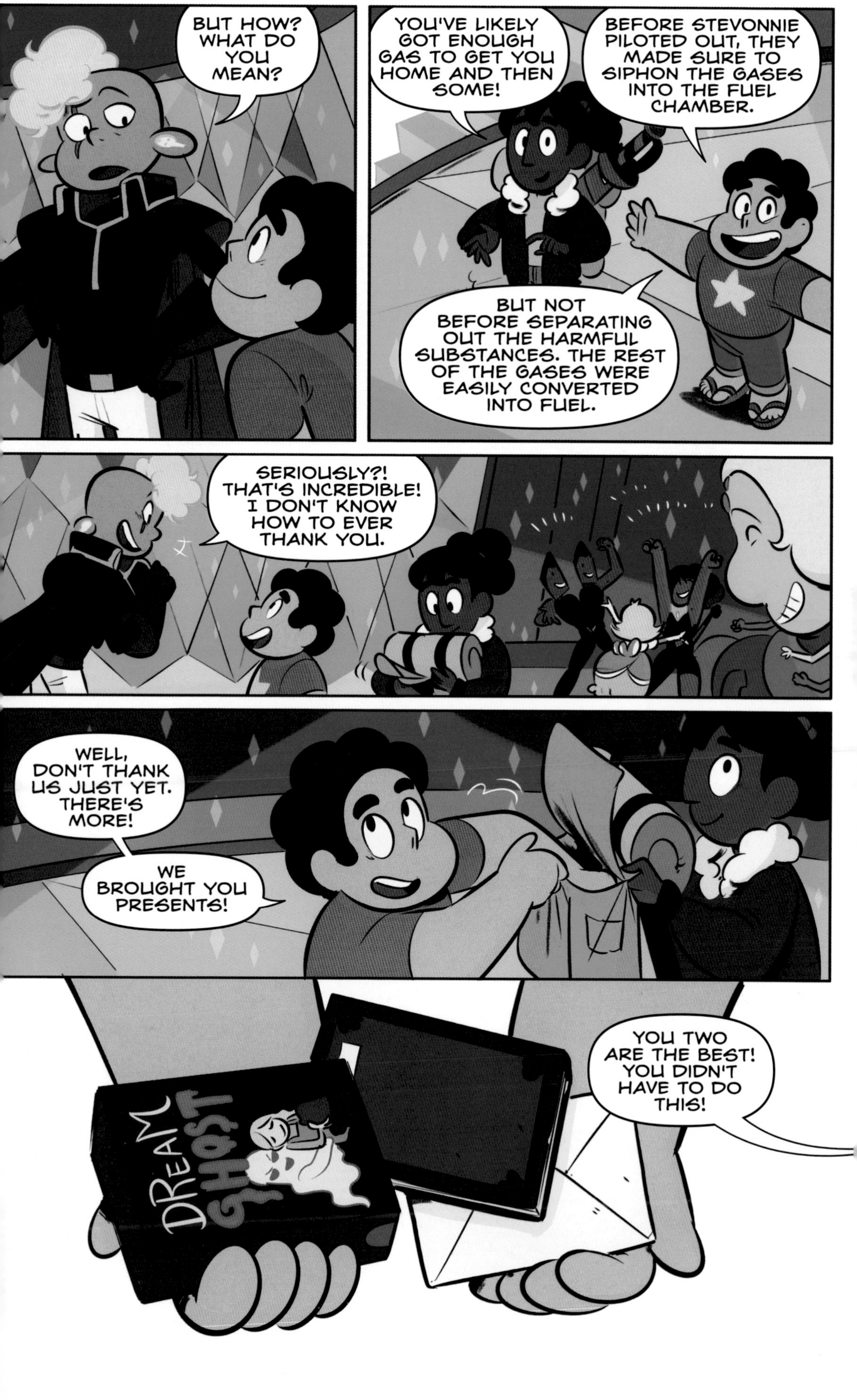
BUT HOW? WHAT DO YOU MEAN?
YOU'VE LIKELY GOT ENOUGH GAS TO GET YOU HOME AND THEN SOME!
BEFORE STEVONNIE PILOTED OUT, THEY MADE SURE TO SIPHON THE GASES INTO THE FUEL CHAMBER.
BUT NOT BEFORE SEPARATING OUT THE HARMFUL SUBSTANCES. THE REST OF THE GASES WERE EASILY CONVERTED INTO FUEL.
SERIOUSLY?! THAT'S INCREDIBLE! I DON'T KNOW HOW TO EVER THANK YOU.
WELL, DON'T THANK US JUST YET. THERE'S MORE!
WE BROUGHT YOU PRESENTS!
DREAM GHOST
YOU TWO ARE THE BEST! YOU DIDN'T HAVE TO DO THIS!

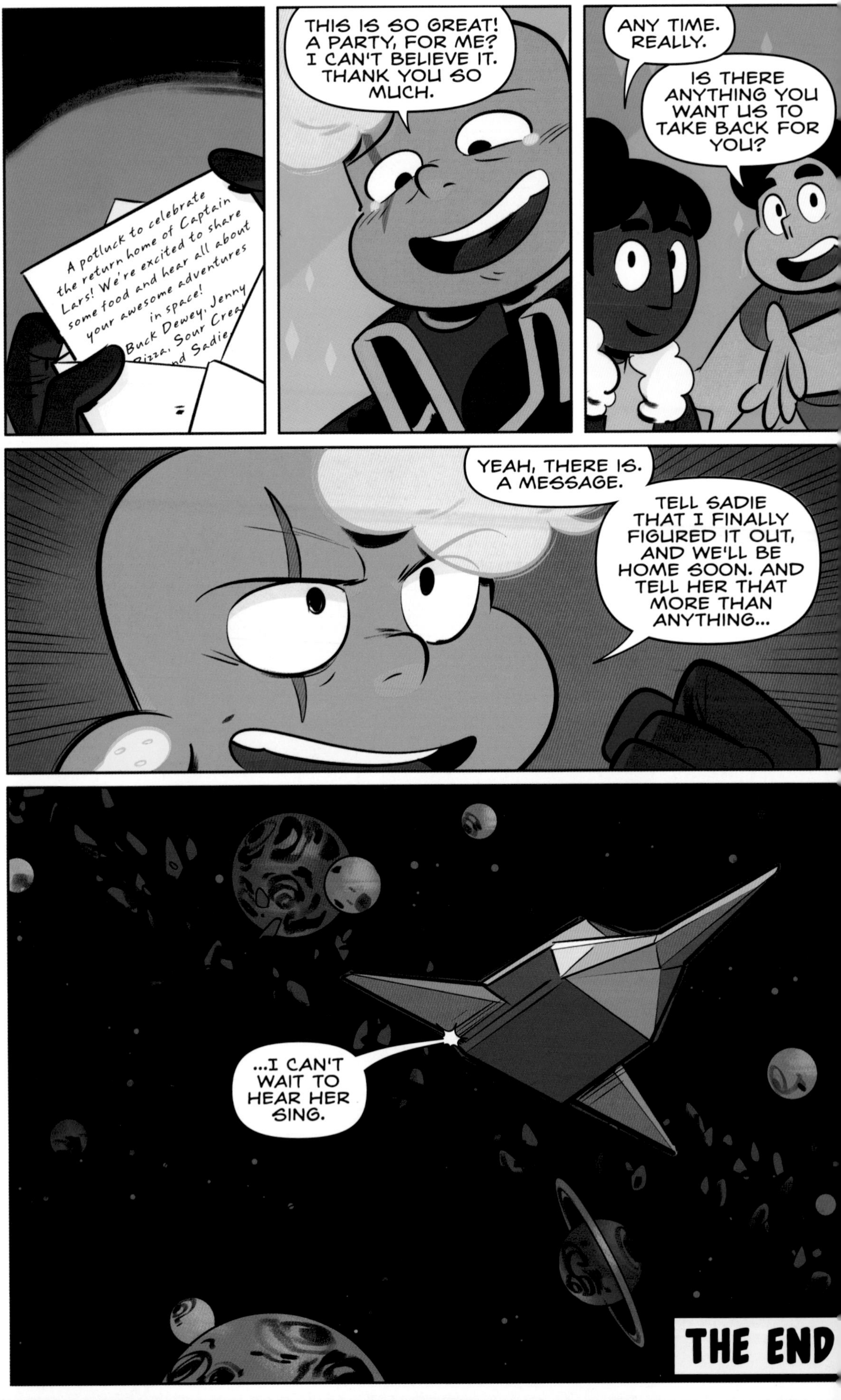
A potluck to celebrate the return home of Captain Lars! We're excited to share some food and hear all about your awesome adventures in space!
Buck Dewey, Jenny
THIS IS SO GREAT! A PARTY, FOR ME? I CAN'T BELIEVE IT. THANK YOU SO MUCH.
ANY TIME. REALLY.
IS THERE ANYTHING YOU WANT US TO TAKE BACK FOR YOU?
YEAH, THERE IS. A MESSAGE.
TELL SADIE THAT I FINALLY FIGURED IT OUT, AND WE'LL BE HOME SOON. AND TELL HER THAT MORE THAN ANYTHING...
...I CAN'T WAIT TO HEAR HER SING.
THE END

Issue Twenty-Eight Preorder Cover

FRANCESCA PERRONE

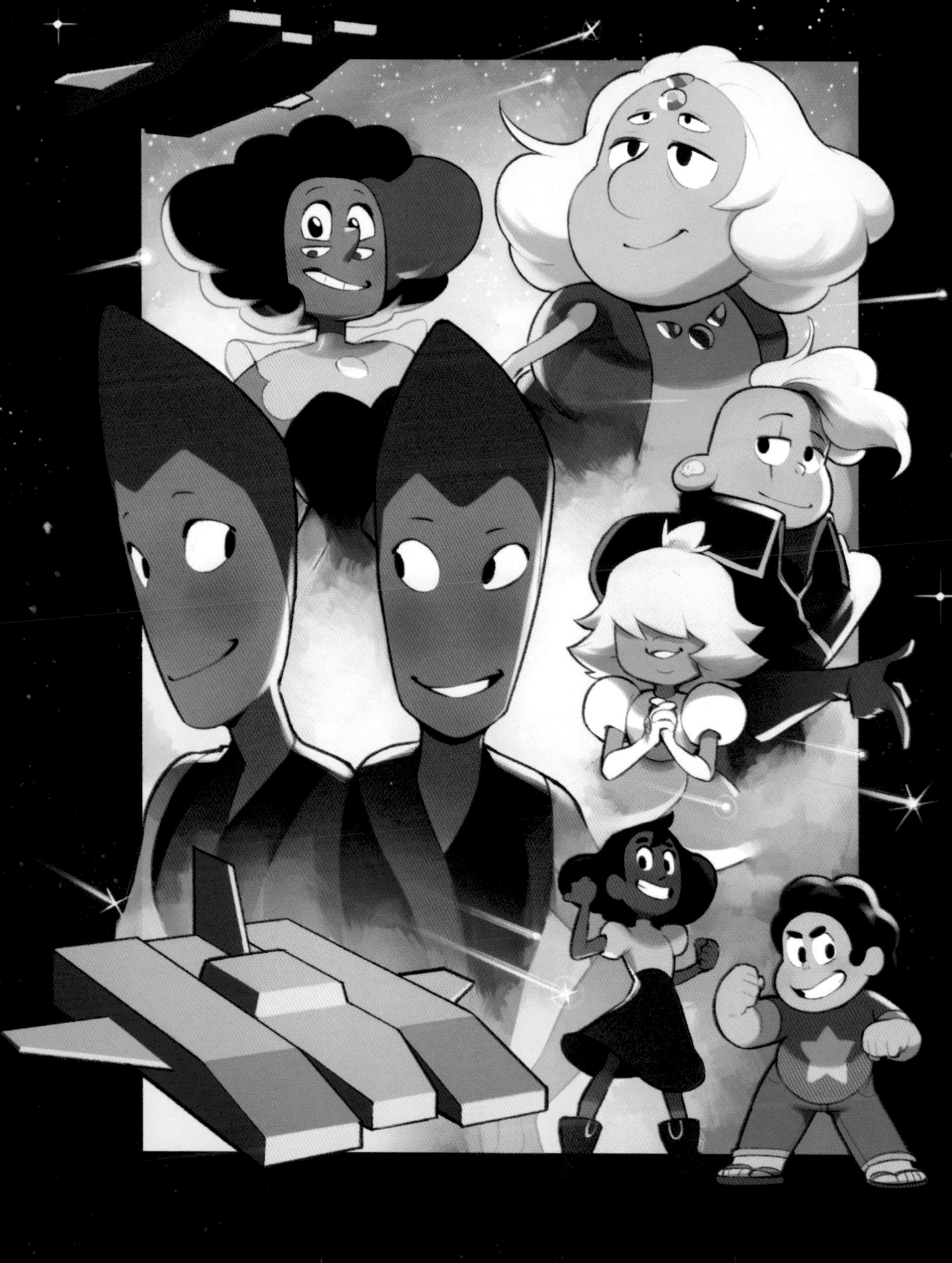

COVER GALLERY

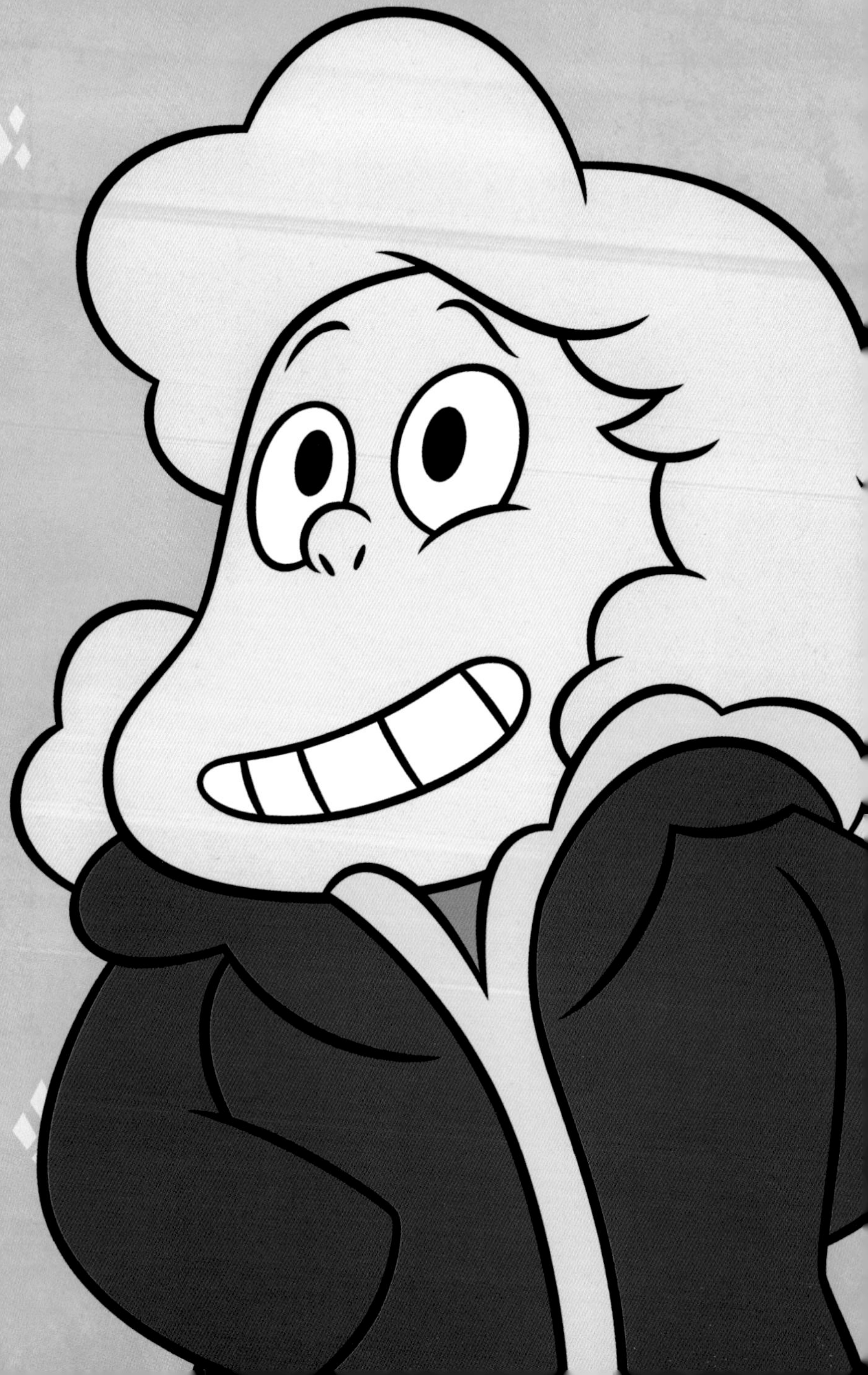

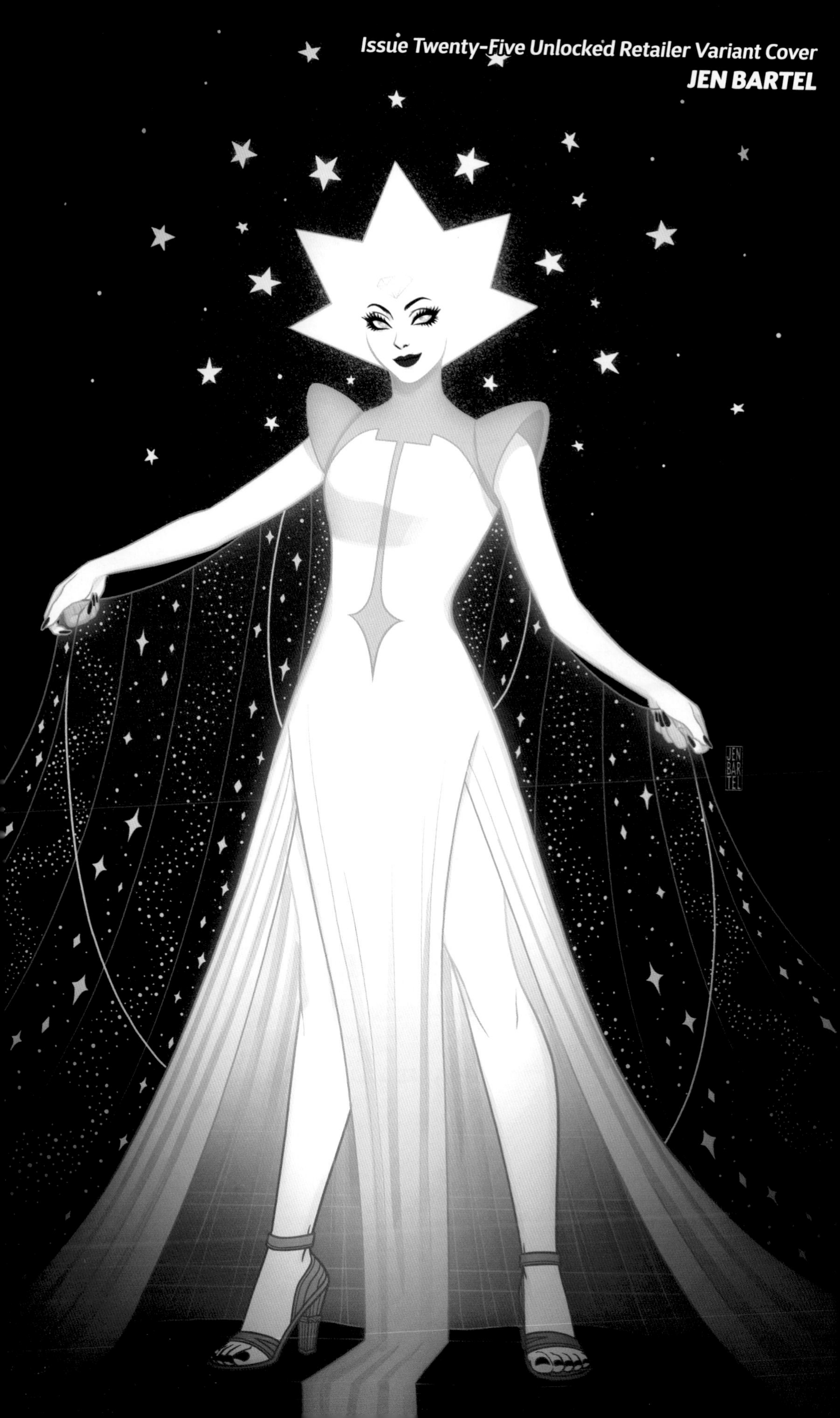
JEN
BAR
TEL

Issue Twenty-Five Unlocked Retailer Variant Cover
JEN BARTEL

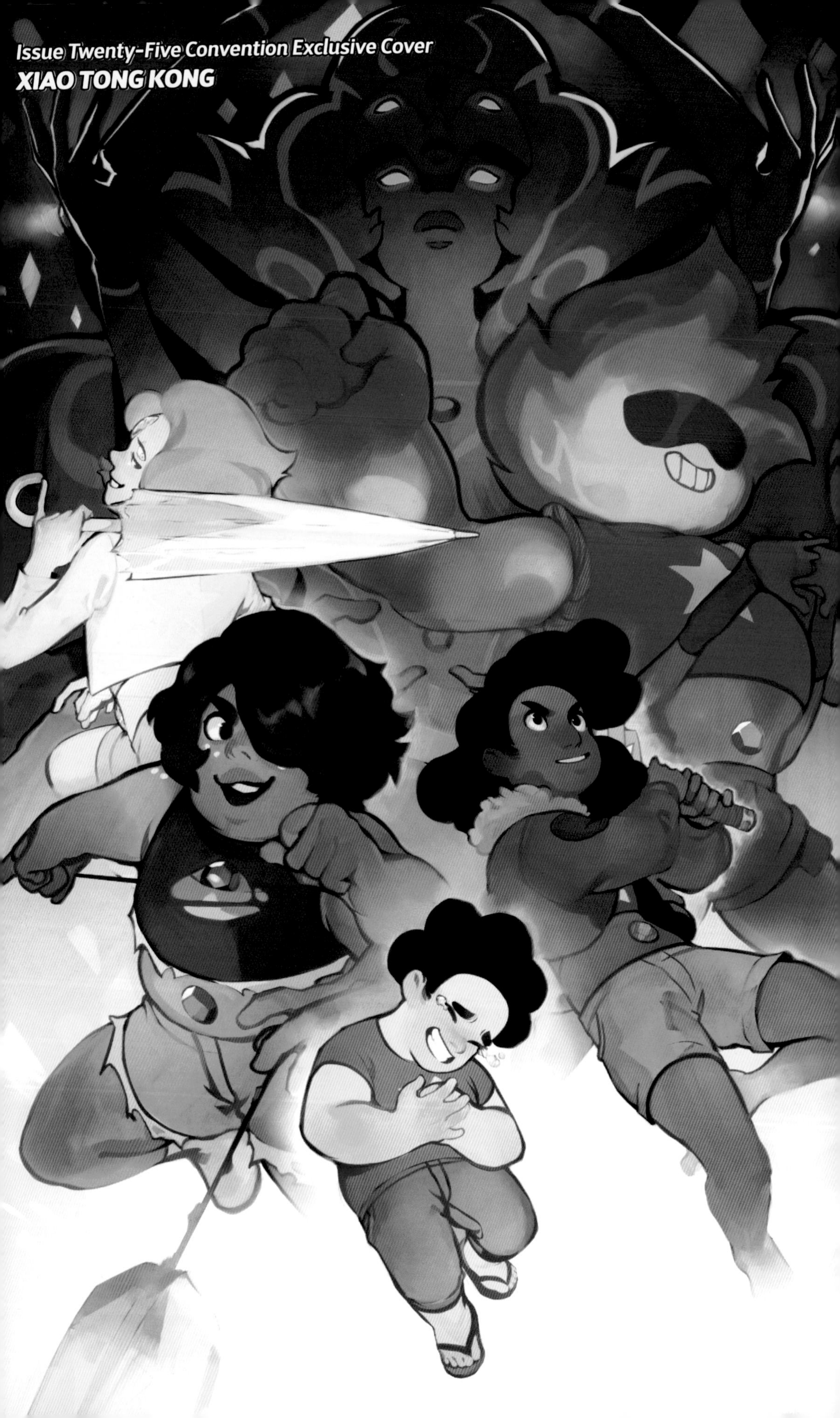

Issue Twenty-Five Convention Exclusive Cover
XIAO TONG KONG

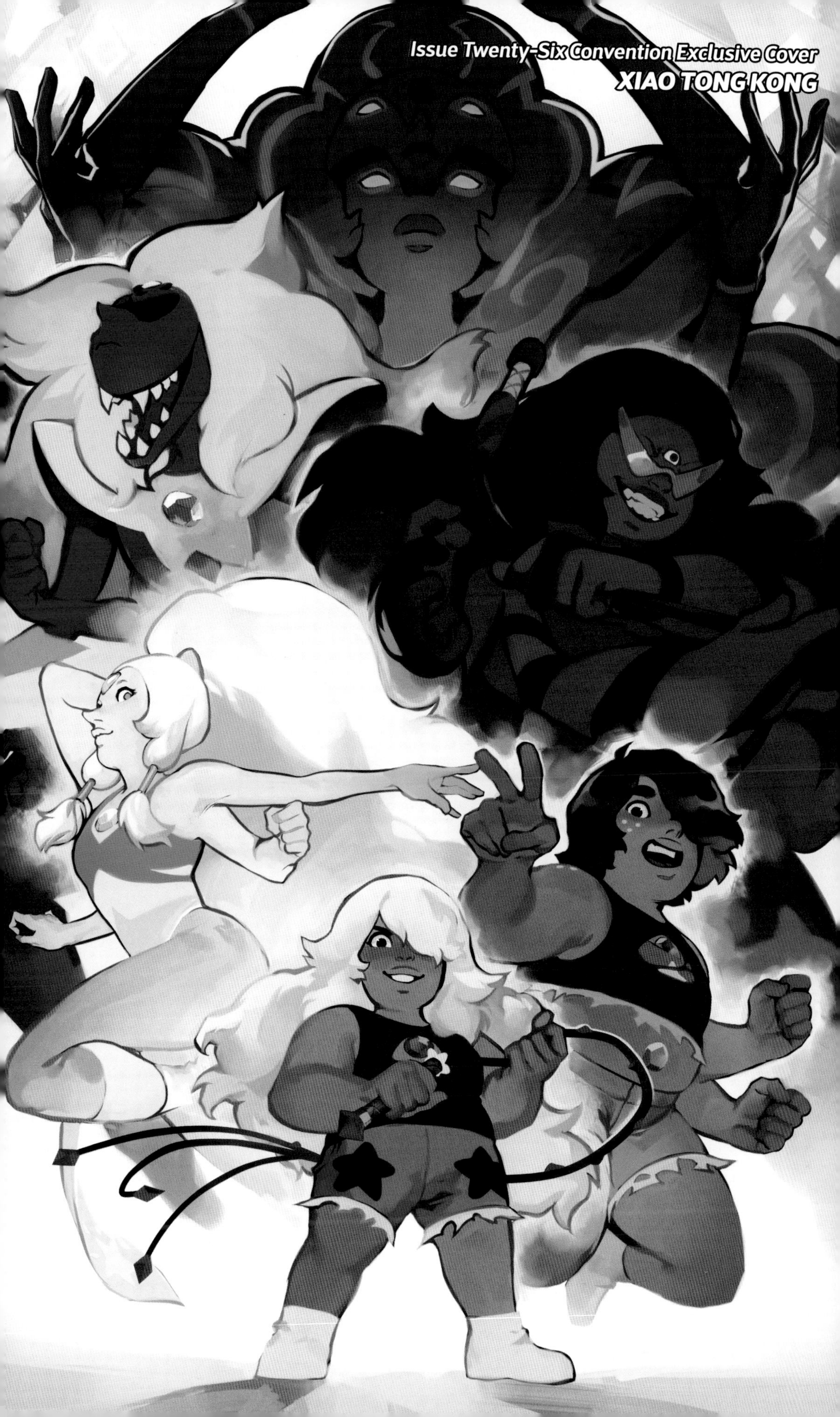

Issue Twenty-Six Convention Exclusive Cover
XIAO TONG KONG

Issue Twenty-Seven Convention Exclusive Cover
XIAO TONG KONG

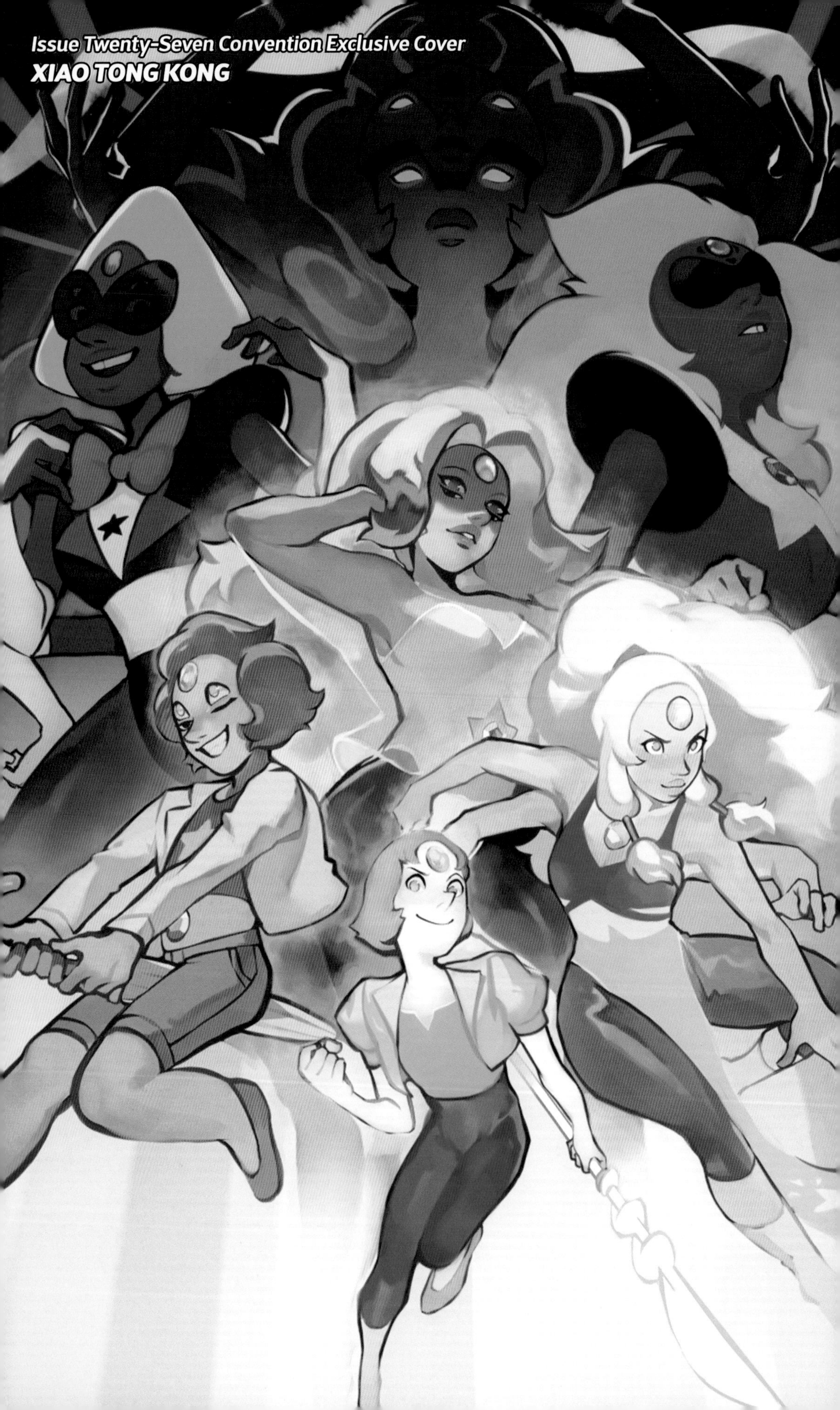

Issue Twenty-Eight Convention Exclusive Cover

XIAO TONG KONG

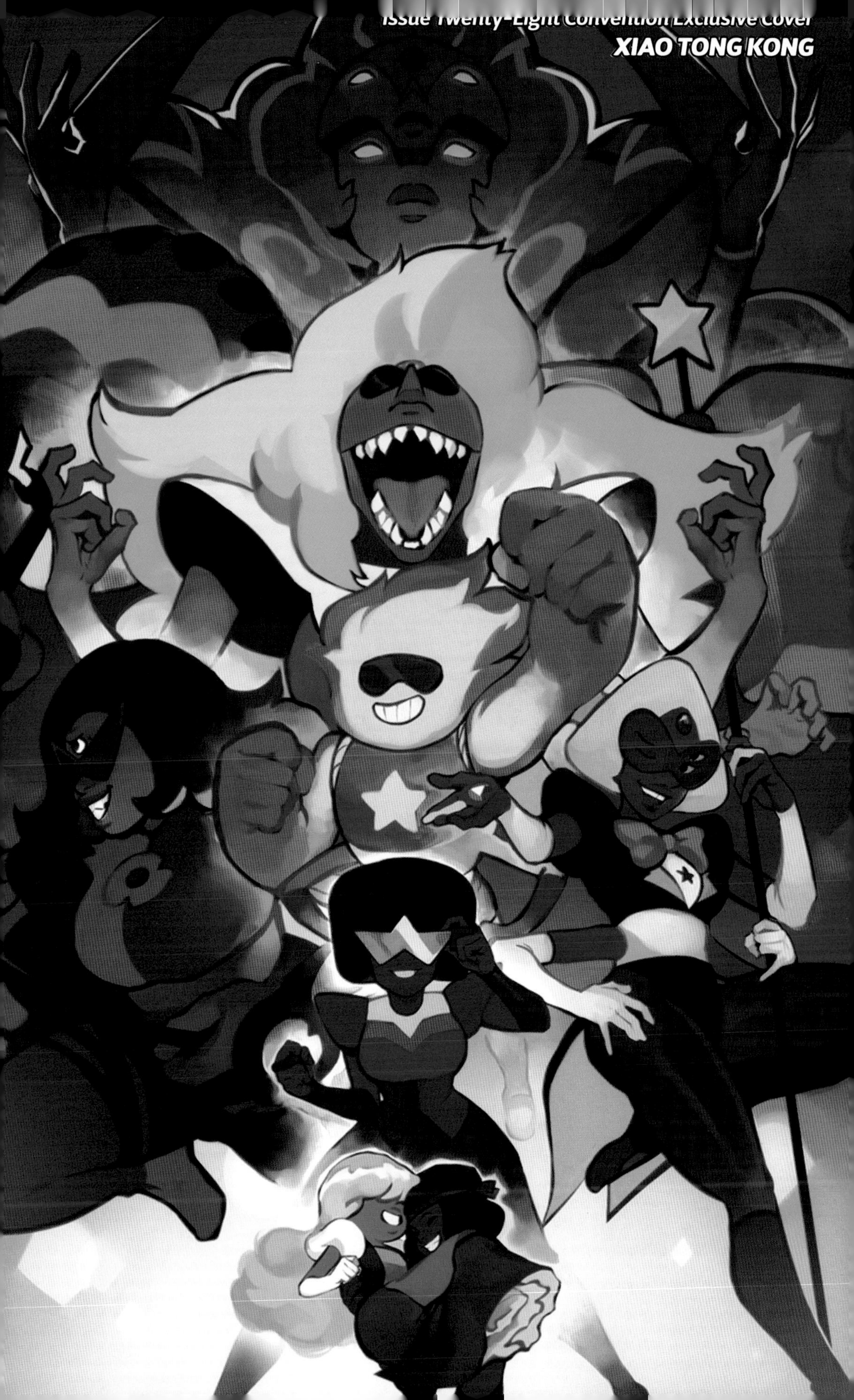

DISCOVER
EXPLOSIVE NEW WORLDS

ADVENTURE TIME

sam sykes · selina espiritu · sarah stern
Brave Chef Brianna

KELLY THOMPSON BRIANNE DROUHARD M. VICTORIA ROBADO
MEGA PRINCESS

THE NOT-SO SECRET SOCIETY
DALEY · CRAFTS · CLARK · BRUNI
KEEP OUT
CAUTION

OVER THE GARDEN WALL

STEVEN UNIVERSE
VOLUME ONE

Adventure Time
Pendleton Ward and Others
Volume 1
ISBN: 978-1-60886-280-1 | $14.99 US
Volume 2
ISBN: 978-1-60886-323-5 | $14.99 US
Adventure Time: Islands
ISBN: 978-1-60886-972-5 | $9.99 US

The Amazing World of Gumball
Ben Bocquelet and Others
Volume 1
ISBN: 978-1-60886-488-1 | $14.99 US
Volume 2
ISBN: 978-1-60886-793-6 | $14.99 US

Brave Chef Brianna
Sam Sykes, Selina Espiritu
ISBN: 978-1-68415-050-2 | $14.99 US

Mega Princess
Kelly Thompson, Brianne Drouhard
ISBN: 978-1-68415-007-6 | $14.99 US

The Not-So Secret Society
Matthew Daley, Arlene Daley, Wook Jin Clark
ISBN: 978-1-60886-997-8 | $9.99 US

Over the Garden Wall
Patrick McHale, Jim Campbell and Others
Volume 1
ISBN: 978-1-60886-940-4 | $14.99 US
Volume 2
ISBN: 978-1-68415-006-9 | $14.99 US

Steven Universe
Rebecca Sugar and Others
Volume 1
ISBN: 978-1-60886-706-6 | $14.99 US
Volume 2
ISBN: 978-1-60886-796-7 | $14.99 US

Steven Universe & The Crystal Gems
ISBN: 978-1-60886-921-3 | $14.99 US

Steven Universe: Too Cool for School
ISBN: 978-1-60886-771-4 | $14.99 US

kaboom!™

AVAILABLE AT YOUR LOCAL COMICS SHOP AND BOOKSTORE
To find a comics shop in your area, visit www.comicshoplocator.com
WWW.**BOOM-STUDIOS**.COM